PENGUIN BOOKS

THE PENGUIN
KRISHNAMURTI READER

Krishnamurti was born in south India of Brahmin parents. In
1911, at the age of fifteen, he was brought to England by Mrs
Annie Besant. He was educated privately over here and was
groomed for the rôle of World Teacher, but in 1929 he dis-
banded the organization which had proclaimed him and of
which he was the head, and declared that he did not want
disciples. Since then he has travelled ceaselessly all over the
world giving public talks and private interviews. The essence
of his teaching is that only through a complete change of heart
in the individual can there come about a change in society and
so peace to the world. He believes that this radical change can
take place in every individual, not gradually but instan-
taneously. He helps us to see ourselves as we really are, for it is
in seeing with absolute clarity that the inward revolution takes
place.

The Second Penguin Krishnamurti Reader, The Impossible Question
and *Beginnings of Learning* have also been published in
Penguins.

THE PENGUIN
KRISHNAMURTI
READER

Compiled by
MARY LUTYENS

PENGUIN BOOKS

Penguin Books Ltd, Harmondsworth, Middlesex, England
Viking Penguin Inc., 40 West 23rd Street, New York, New York 10010, U.S.A.
Penguin Books Australia Ltd, Ringwood, Victoria, Australia
Penguin Books Canada Ltd, 2801 John Street, Markham, Ontario, Canada L3R 1B4
Penguin Books (N.Z.) Ltd, 182–190 Wairau Road, Auckland 10, New Zealand

—

This selection is made from *The First and Last Freedom*,
Life Ahead and *This Matter of Culture*,
published in Great Britain by Victor Gollancz
1954, 1963 and 1964
Published in Penguin Books 1970
Reprinted 1970, 1971, 1973, 1974, 1976, 1978, 1979, 1982, 1984

—

—

Printed and bound in Great Britain by
Cox & Wyman Ltd, Reading
Set in Intertype Georgian

Contents

PART ONE

The Problems of Living

I

WHAT ARE WE SEEKING?

WHAT is it that most of us are seeking? What is it that each one of us wants? Surely it is important to find out. Probably most of us are seeking some kind of happiness, some kind of peace; in a world that is ridden with turmoil, wars, contention, strife, we want a refuge where there can be some peace. I think that is what most of us want. So we pursue, go from one leader to another, from one religious organization to another, from one teacher to another.

Now, is it that we are seeking happiness or is it that we are seeking gratification of some kind from which we hope to derive happiness? There is a difference between happiness and gratification. Can you *seek* happiness? Perhaps you can find gratification but surely you cannot *find* happiness. Happiness is derivative; it is a by-product of something else. So, before we give our minds and hearts to something which demands a great deal of earnestness, attention, thought, care, we must find out, must we not?, what it is that we are seeking; whether it is happiness, or gratification. I am afraid most of us are seeking gratification. We want to be gratified, we want to find a sense of fullness at the end of our search.

After all, if one is seeking peace one can find it very easily. One can devote oneself blindly to some kind of cause, to an idea, and take shelter there. Surely that does not solve the problem. Mere isolation in an enclosing idea is not a release from conflict. So we must find, must we not?, what it is, inwardly, as well as outwardly, that each one of us wants. If we are clear on that matter, then we don't have to go anywhere, to any teacher, to any church, to any organization. But our difficulty is, to be clear in ourselves regarding our intention. Can we be clear? And does that clarity come through searching, through trying to find out what others say, from the highest teacher to the ordinary preacher in a

9

church round the corner? Have you got to go to somebody to find out? Yet that is what we are doing, is it not? We read innumerable books, we attend many meetings and discuss, we join various organizations – trying thereby to find a remedy to the conflict, to the miseries in our lives. Or, if we don't do all that, we think we have found; that is, we say that a particular organization, a particular teacher, a particular book satisfies us; we have found everything we want in that; and we remain in that, crystallized and enclosed.

Do we not seek, through all this confusion, something permanent, something lasting, something which we call real? – God, truth, what you like – the name doesn't matter, the word is not the thing, surely. So don't let us be caught in words. Leave that to the professional lecturers. There is a search for something permanent, is there not?, in most of us – something we can cling to, something which will give us assurance, a hope, a lasting enthusiasm, a lasting certainty, because in ourselves we are so uncertain. We do not know ourselves. We know a lot about facts, what the books have said; but we do not know for ourselves, we do not have a direct experience.

And what is it that we call permanent? What is it that we are seeking, which will, or which we hope will give us permanency? Are we not seeking lasting happiness, lasting gratification, lasting certainty? We want something that will endure everlastingly, which will gratify us. If we strip ourselves of all the words and phrases, and actually look at it, this is what we want. We want permanent pleasure, permanent gratification – which we call truth, God or what you will.

Very well, we want pleasure. Perhaps that may be putting it very crudely, but that is actually what we want – knowledge that will give us pleasure, experience that will give us pleasure, a gratification that will not wither away by tomorrow. And we have experimented with various gratifications, and they have all faded away; and we hope now to find permanent gratification in reality, in God. Surely, that is what we are all seeking – the clever ones and the stupid ones, the theorist and the factual person who is striving after something. And is there permanent gratification? Is there something which will endure?

Now, if you seek permanent gratification, surely you must understand, must you not?, the thing you are seeking. When you say, 'I am seeking permanent happiness' – God, or truth, or what you like – must you not also understand the thing that is searching, the searcher, the seeker? Because there may be no such thing as permanent security, permanent happiness. Truth may be something entirely different; and I think it *is* utterly different from what you can see, conceive, formulate. Therefore, before we seek something permanent, is it not obviously necessary to understand the seeker? Is the seeker different from the thing he seeks? When you say, 'I am seeking happiness', is the seeker different from the object of his search? Is the thinker different from the thought? Are they not a joint phenomenon, rather than separate processes? Therefore it is essential, is it not?, to understand the seeker, before you try to find out what it is he is seeking.

So we have to come to the point when we ask ourselves, really earnestly and profoundly, if peace, happiness, reality, God, or what you will, can be given to us by someone else. Can this incessant search, this longing, give us that extraordinary sense of reality, that creative being, which comes when we really understand ourselves? Does self-knowledge come through search, through following someone else, through belonging to any particular organization, through reading books, and so on? After all, that is the main issue, is it not?, that so long as I do not understand myself, I have no basis for thought, and all my search will be in vain. I can escape into illusions, I can run away from contention, strife, struggle; I can worship another; I can look for my salvation through somebody else. But so long as I am ignorant of myself, so long as I am unaware of the total process of myself, I have no basis for thought, for affection, for action.

But that is the last thing we want: to know ourselves. Yet that is the only foundation on which we can build. Before we can build, before we can transform, before we can condemn or destroy, we must know that which we are. If we are petty, jealous, vain, greedy – *that* is what we create about us, *that* is the society in which we live.

It seems to me that before we set out on a joureny to find reality, to find God, before we can act, before we can have any relationship with another, which is society, it is essential that we begin to understand ourselves first. I consider the earnest person to be one who is completely concerned with this, *first*, and not with how to arrive at a particular goal, because, if you and I do not understand ourselves, how can we, in action, bring about a transformation in society, in relationship, in anything that we do? And it does not mean, obviously, that self-knowledge is opposed to, or isolated from, relationship. It does not mean, obviously, emphasis on the individual, the me, as opposed to the mass, as opposed to another.

Now without knowing yourself, without knowing your own way of thinking and why you think certain things, without knowing the background of your conditioning and why you have certain beliefs about art and religion, about your country and your neighbour and about yourself, how can you think truly about anything? Without knowing your background, without knowing the substance of your thought and whence it comes – surely your search is utterly futile, your action has no meaning?

Before we can find out what the end-purpose of life is, what it all means – wars, national antagonisms, conflicts, the whole mess – we must begin with ourselves, must we not? It sounds so simple, but it is *extremely* difficult. To follow oneself, to see how one's thought operates, one has to be extraordinarily alert, so that as one begins to be more and more alert to the intricacies of one's own thinking and responses and feelings, one begins to have a greater awareness, not only of oneself but of another with whom one is in relationship. To know oneself is to study oneself in action, which is relationship. The difficulty is that we are so impatient; we want to get on, we want to reach an end, and so we have neither the time nor the occasion to give ourselves the opportunity to study, to observe. Alternatively we have committed ourselves to various activities – to earning a livelihood, to rearing children – or have taken on certain responsibilities of various organizations; we have so committed ourselves in different ways that we have hardly any time for self-reflection, to observe, to study. So really the responsibility of the reaction depends on oneself, not on another. The pursuit, all the world over, of *gurus* and their systems, reading the latest books on this and that, and so on, seems to me so utterly empty, so utterly futile, for you may wander all over the earth but you have to come back to yourself. And, as most of us are totally unaware of ourselves, it is extremely difficult to begin to see clearly the process of our thinking and feeling and acting.

The more you know yourself, the more clarity there is. Self-knowledge has no end – you don't come to an achievement, you don't come to a conclusion. It is an endless river. As one studies it, as one goes into it more and more, one finds peace. Only when the mind is tranquil – through self-knowledge and not through imposed self-discipline – only then, in that tranquility, in that silence, can reality come into being. It is only then that there can be bliss, that there can be creative action. And it seems to me that without this understanding, without this experience, merely to read books, to attend talks, to do propaganda, is so infantile – just an activity without much meaning; whereas if one is able to understand oneself, and thereby bring about that creative happiness, that experiencing of something that is not of the mind, then perhaps there can be a transformation in the immediate relationship about us and so in the world in which we live.

II

THE INDIVIDUAL AND SOCIETY

THE problem that confronts most of us is whether the individual is merely the instrument of society or the end of society. Are you and I as individuals to be used, directed, educated, controlled, shaped to a certain pattern by society and government; or does society, the State, exist for the individual? Is the individual the end of society; or is he merely a puppet to be taught, exploited, butchered as an instrument of war? That is the problem that is confronting most of us. That is the problem of the world; whether the individual is a mere instrument of society, a plaything of influences to be moulded; or whether society exists for the individual.

How are you going to find this out? It is a vital problem, isn't it? If the individual is merely an instrument of society, then society is much more important than the individual. If that is true, then we must give up individuality and work for society; our whole educational system must be entirely revolutionized and the individual turned into an instrument to be used and destroyed. But if society exists for the individual, then the function of society is not to make him conform to any pattern but to give him the feel, the urge of freedom. So we have to find out which is false.

How would you inquire into this problem? It is not dependent on any ideology, either of the left or of the right; and if it *is* dependent on an ideology, then it is merely a matter of opinion. Ideas always breed enmity, confusion, conflict. If you depend on books of the left or of the right or on sacred books, then you depend on mere opinion, whether of Buddha, of Christ, of capitalism, communism or what you will. They are ideas, not truth. A fact can never be denied. Opinion *about* facts can be denied. If we can discover what the truth of the matter is, we shall be able to act independently of opinion. Is it not, therefore, necessary to discard what others have said? The opinion of the leftist or other leaders is the outcome of their conditioning, so if you depend for your discovery on what is found in books, you are merely bound by opinion. It is not a matter of knowledge.

How is one to discover the truth of this? On that we will act. To find the truth of this, there must be freedom from all propaganda, which means you are capable of looking at the problem independently of opinion. The whole task of education is to awaken the individual. To see the truth of this, you will have to be very clear, which means you cannot depend on a leader. When you choose a leader you do so out of confusion, and so your leaders are also confused, and that is what is happening in the world. Therefore you cannot look to your leader for guidance or help.

A mind that wishes to understand a problem must not only understand the problem completely, wholly, but must be able to follow it swiftly, because the problem is never static. The problem is always new, whether it is a problem of starvation, a psychological problem, or any problem. Any crisis is always new; therefore, to understand it, a mind must always be fresh, clear, swift in its pursuit. I think most of us realize the urgency of an inward revolution, which alone can bring about a radical transformation of the outer, of society. This is the problem with which I myself and all seriously-intentioned people are occupied – how to bring about a fundamental, a radical transformation in society; and this transformation of the outer cannot take place without inner revolution. Since society is always static, any action, any reform, which is accomplished without this inward revolution becomes equally static; so there is no hope without this constant inward revolution, because, without it, outer action becomes repetitive, habitual. The action of relationship between you and another, between you and me, is society; and that society becomes static, it has no life-giving quality, so long as there is not this constant inward revolution, a creative, psychological transformation; and it is because there is not this constant inward revolution that

society is always becoming static, crystallized, and has therefore constantly to be broken up.

What is the relationship between yourself and the misery,
the confusion, in and around you? Surely this confusion, this
misery, did not come into being by itself. You and I have
created it, not a capitalist nor a communist nor a fascist
society, but you and I have created it in our relationship with
each other. What you are within has been projected without,
on to the world; what you are, what you think and what you
feel, what you do in your everyday existence, is projected
outwardly, and that constitutes the world. If we are miserable, confused, chaotic within, by projection that becomes
the world, that becomes society, because the relationship
between yourself and myself, between myself and another
is society – and if our relationship is confused, egocentric,
narrow, limited, national, we project that and bring chaos
into the world.

What you are, the world is. So your problem is the world's
problem. Surely, this is a simple and basic fact, is it not? In
our relationship with the one or the many we seem somehow
to overlook this point all the time. We want to bring about
alteration through a system or through a revolution in ideas
or values based on a system, forgetting that it is you and I
who create society, who bring about confusion or order by the
way in which we live. So we must begin near, that is we must
concern ourselves with our daily existence, with our daily
thoughts and feelings and actions which are revealed in the
manner of earning our livelihood and in our relationship
with ideas or beliefs. This is our daily existence, is it not? We
are concerned with livelihood, getting jobs, earning money;
we are concerned with the relationship with our family or
with our neighbours, and we are concerned with ideas and
with beliefs. Now, if you examine our occupation, it is fundamentally based on envy, it is not just a means of earning a
livelihood. Society is so constructed that it is a process of
constant conflict, constant becoming; it is based on greed, on
envy, envy of your superior, the clerk wanting to become the
manager, which shows that he is not just concerned with

earning a livelihood, a means of subsistence, but with acquiring position and prestige. This attitude naturally creates havoc in society, in relationship, but if you and I were only concerned with livelihood we should find out the right means of earning it, a means not based on envy. Envy is one of the most destructive factors in relationship because envy indicates the desire for power, for position, and it ultimately leads to politics; both are closely related. The clerk, when he seeks to become a manager, becomes a factor in the creation of power-politics which produce war; so he is directly responsible for war.

What is our relationship based on? The relationship between yourself and myself, between yourself and another – which is society – what is it based on? Surely not on love, though we talk about it. It is not based on love, because if there were love there would be order, there would be peace, happiness, between you and me. But in that relationship between you and me there is a great deal of ill-will which assumes the form of respect. If we were both equal in thought, in feeling, there would be no respect, there would be no ill-will, because we would be two individuals meeting, not as disciple and teacher, not as the husband dominating the wife, not as the wife dominating the husband. When there is ill-will there is a desire to dominate which arouses jealousy, anger, passion, all of which in our relationship creates constant conflict from which we try to escape, and this produces further chaos, further misery.

Now as regards ideas which are part of our daily existence, beliefs, and formulations, are they not distorting our minds? For what is stupidity? Stupidity is the giving of wrong values to those things which the mind creates, or to those things which the hands produce. Most of our thoughts spring from the self-protective instinct, do they not? Our ideas, oh, so many of them, do they not receive the wrong significance, one which they have not in themselves? Therefore when we believe in any form, whether religious, economic or social, when we believe in God, in ideas, in a social system which separates man from man, in nationalism and so on, surely we are giving a wrong significance to belief, which indicates stupidity, for belief divides people. So we see that by the way we live we can produce order or chaos, peace or conflict, happiness or misery.

So our problem is, is it not?, whether there can be a society which is static, and at the same time an individual in whom this constant revolution is taking place. That is, revolution in society must begin with the inner, psychological transformation of the individual. Most of us want to see a radical transformation in the social structure. That is the whole battle that is going on in the world – to bring about a social revolution through communistic or any other means. Now if there is a social revolution – that is, an action with regard to the outer structure of man – however radical that social revolution may be, its very nature is static if there is no inward revolution of the individual, no psychological transformation. Therefore to bring about a society that is not repetitive, nor static, not disintegrating, a society that is constantly alive, it is imperative that there should be a revolution in the psychological structure of the individual, for without inward, psychological revolution, mere transformation of the outer has very little significance. Society is always becoming crystallized, static, and is therefore always disintegrating. However much and however wisely legislation may be promulgated, society is always in the process of decay because revolution must take place within, not merely outwardly.

I think it is important to understand this and not slur over it. Outward action, when accomplished, is over, is static; if the relationship between individuals, which is society, is not the outcome of inward revolution, then the social structure, being static, absorbs the individual and therefore makes him equally static, repetitive. Realizing this, realizing the extraordinary significance of this fact, there can be no question of agreement or disagreement. It is a fact that society is always crystallizing and absorbing the individual and that constant, creative revolution can only be in the individual, not in society, not in the outer. That is,

creative revolution can take place only in individual relationship, which is society. We see how the structure of the present
society in India, in Europe, in America, in every part of the
world, is rapidly disintegrating; and we know it within our
own lives. We can observe it as we go down the streets. We
do not need great historians to tell us the fact that our society
is crumbling; and there must be new architects, new builders,
to create a new society. The structure must be built on a new
foundation, on newly discovered facts and values. Such
architects do not yet exist. There are no builders, none who,
observing, becoming aware of the fact that the structure is
collapsing, are transforming themselves into architects.
That is our problem. We see society crumbling, disintegrating; and it is we, you and I, who have to be the architects.
You and I have to rediscover the values and build on a more
fundamental, lasting foundation; because if we look to the
professional architects, the political and religious builders,
we shall be precisely in the same position as before.

Because you and I are not creative, we have reduced
society to this chaos, so you and I have to be creative because
the problem is urgent; you and I must be aware of the
causes of the collapse of society and create a new structure
based not on mere imitation but on our creative understanding. Now this implies, does it not?, negative thinking. Negative thinking is the highest form of understanding. That is,
in order to understand what is creative thinking, we must
approach the problem negatively, because a positive approach to the problem – which is that you and I must become
creative in order to build a new structure of society – will be
imitative. To understand that which is crumbling, we must
investigate it, examine it negatively – not with a positive
system, a positive formula, a positive conclusion.

Why is society crumbling, collapsing, as it surely is? One
of the fundamental reasons is that the individual, you, has
ceased to be creative. I will explain what I mean. You and I
have become imitative, we are copying, outwardly and inwardly. Outwardly, when learning a technique, when com-
municating with each other on the verbal level, naturally

there must be some imitation, copy. I copy words. To become an engineer, I must first learn the technique, then use the technique to build a bridge. There must be a certain amount of imitation, copying, in outward technique, but when there is inward, psychological, imitation surely we cease to be creative. Our education, our social structure, our so-called religious life, are all based on imitation; that is, I fit into a particular social or religious formula. I have ceased to be a real individual; psychologically, I have become a mere repetitive machine with certain conditioned responses, whether those of the Hindu, the Christian, the Buddhist, the German, or the Englishman. Our responses are conditioned according to the pattern of society, whether it is eastern or western, religious or materialistic. So one of the fundamental causes of the disintegration of society is imitation, and one of the disintegrating factors is the leader, whose very essence is imitation.

In order to understand the nature of disintegrating society is it not important to inquire whether you and I, the individual, can be creative? We can see that when there is imitation there must be disintegration; when there is authority there must be copying. And since our whole mental, psychological, make-up is based on authority, there must be freedom from authority, to be creative. Have you not noticed that in moments of creativeness, those rather happy moments of vital interest, there is no sense of repetition, no sense of copying? Such moments are always new, fresh, creative, happy. So we see that one of the fundamental causes of the disintegration of society is copying, which is the worship of authority.

III

SELF-KNOWLEDGE

THE problems of the world are so colossal, so very
complex, that to understand and so to resolve them one must
approach them in a very simple and direct manner; and
simplicity, directness, do not depend on outward circumstances nor on our particular prejudices and moods. The
solution is not to be found through conferences, blue-prints,
or through the substitution of new leaders for old, and so on.
The solution obviously lies in the creator of the problem, in
the creator of the mischief, of the hate and of the enormous
misunderstanding that exists between human beings. The
creator of this mischief, the creator of these problems, is the
individual, you and I, not the world as we think of it. The
world is your relationship with another. The world is not
something separate from you and me; the world, society, is
the relationship that we establish or seek to establish between each other.

So you and I are the problem, and not the world, because
the world is the projection of ourselves and to understand
the world we must understand ourselves. The world is not
separate from us; we are the world, and our problems are the
world's problems. This cannot be repeated too often, because
we are so sluggish in our mentality that we think the world's
problems are not our business, that they have to be resolved
by the United Nations or by substituting new leaders for the
old. It is a very dull mentality that thinks like that, because
we are responsible for this frightful misery and confusion in
the world, this ever-impending war. To transform the world,
we must begin with ourselves; and what is important in
beginning with ourselves is the intention. The intention
must be to understand ourselves and not to leave it to others
to transform themselves or to bring about a modified change
through revolution, either of the left or of the right. It is
important to understand that this is our responsibility, yours

and mine; because, however small may be the world we live in, if we can transform ourselves, bring about a radically different point of view in our daily existence, then perhaps we shall affect the world at large, the extended relationship with others.

So we are going to try and find out the process of understanding ourselves, which is not an isolating process. It is not withdrawal from the world, because you cannot live in isolation. *To be* is to be related, and there is no such thing as living in isolation. It is the lack of right relationship that brings about conflicts, misery and strife; however small our world may be, if we can transform our relationship in that narrow world, it will be like a wave extending outward all the time. I think it is important to see that point, that the world is our relationship, however narrow; and if we can bring a transformation there, not a superficial but a radical transformation, then we shall begin actively to transform the world. Real revolution is not according to any particular pattern, either of the left or of the right, but it is a revolution of values, a revolution from sensate values to the values that are not sensate or created by environmental influences. To find these true values which will bring about a radical revolution, a transformation or a regeneration, it is essential to understand oneself. Self-knowledge is the beginning of wisdom, and therefore the beginning of transformation or regeneration. To understand oneself there must be the intention to understand – and that is where our difficulty comes in. Although most of us are discontented, and we desire to bring about a sudden change, our discontent is canalized merely to achieve a certain result; being discontented, we either seek a different job or merely succumb to environment. Discontent, instead of setting us aflame, causing us to question life, the whole process of existence, is canalized, and thereby we become mediocre, losing that drive, that intensity, to find out the whole significance of existence. Therefore it is important to discover these things for ourselves, because self-knowledge cannot be given to us by another, it is not to be found through any book. We must discover, and to discover there must be the intention, the search, the inquiry. So long as that intention to find out, to inquire deeply, is weak or does not exist, mere assertion or a casual wish to find out about oneself is of very little significance.

Thus the transformation of the world is brought about by the transformation of oneself, because the self is the product and a part of the total process of human existence. To transform oneself, self-knowledge is essential; without knowing what you are, there is no basis for right thought, and without knowing yourself there cannot be transformation. One must know oneself as one is, not as one wishes to be which is merely an ideal and therefore fictitious, unreal; it is only that which *is* that can be transformed, not that which you wish to be. To know oneself as one is requires an extraordinary alertness of mind, because what *is* is constantly undergoing transformation, change, and to follow it swiftly the mind must not be tethered to any particular dogma or belief, to any particular pattern of action. If you would follow anything it is no good being tethered. To know yourself, there must be the awareness, the alertness of mind in which there is freedom from all beliefs, from all idealization, because beliefs and ideals only give you a colour, perverting true perception. If you want to know what you are you cannot imagine or have belief in something which you are not. If I am greedy, envious, violent, merely having an ideal of non-violence, of non-greed, is of little value. But to know that one is greedy or violent, to know and understand it, requires an extraordinary perception, does it not? It demands honesty, clarity of thought, whereas to pursue an ideal away from what *is* is an escape; it prevents you from discovering and acting directly upon what you are.

The understanding of what you are, whatever it be – ugly or beautiful, wicked or mischievous – the understanding of what you are, without distortion, is the beginning of virtue. Virtue is essential, for it gives freedom. It is only in virtue that you can discover, that you can live – not in the *cultivation* of a virtue, which merely brings about respectability. There is a difference between being virtuous and becoming virtuous. Being virtuous comes through the understanding of what *is*, whereas becoming virtuous is postponement, the covering up of what *is* with what you would like to be. Therefore in becoming virtuous you are avoiding action directly upon what *is*. This process of avoiding what *is* through the cultivation of the ideal is considered virtuous; but if you look at it closely and directly you will see that it is nothing of the kind. It is merely a postponement of coming face to face with what *is*. Virtue is not the becoming of what is not; virtue is the understanding of what *is* and therefore the freedom from what *is*. Virtue is essential in a society that is rapidly disintegrating. In order to create a new world, a new structure away from the old, there must be freedom to discover; and to be free, there must be virtue, for without virtue there is no freedom. Can the immoral man who is striving to become virtuous ever know virtue? The man who is not moral can never be free, and therefore he can never find out what reality is. Reality can be found only in understanding what *is*; and to understand what *is*, there must be freedom, freedom from the fear of what *is*.

To understand that process there must be the intention to know what *is*, to follow every thought, feeling and action; and to understand what *is* is extremely difficult, because what *is* is never still, never static, it is always in movement. The what *is* is what you are, not what you would like to be; it is not the ideal, because the ideal is fictitious, but it is actually what you are doing, thinking and feeling from moment to moment. What *is* is the actual, and to understand the actual requires awareness, a very alert, swift mind. But if we begin to condemn what *is*, if we begin to blame or resist it, then we shall not understand its movement. If I want to understand somebody, I cannot condemn him: I must observe, study him. I must love the very thing I am studying. If you want to understand a child, you must love and not condemn him. You must play with him, watch his movements, his idiosyncrasies, his ways of behaviour; but if you merely condemn, resist or blame him, there is no comprehension of the child. Similarly, to understand what *is*, one must observe what one thinks, feels and does from moment to moment. That is the actual. Any other action, any ideal or ideological action, is not the actual; it is merely a wish, a fictitious desire to be something other than what *is*.

To understand what *is* requires a state of mind in which there is no identification or condemnation, which means a mind that is alert and yet passive. We are in that state when we really desire to understand something; when the intensity of interest is there, that state of mind comes into being. When one is interested in understanding what *is*, the actual state of the mind, one does not need to force, discipline, or control it; on the contrary, there is passive alertness, watchfulness. This state of awareness comes when there is interest, the intention to understand.

The fundamental understanding of oneself does not come through knowledge or through the accumulation of experiences, which is merely the cultivation of memory. The understanding of oneself is from moment to moment; if we merely accumulate knowledge of the self, that very knowledge prevents further understanding, because accumulated knowlege and experience becomes the centre through which thought focuses and has its being. The world is not different from us and our activities because it is what we are which creates the problems of the world; the difficulty with the majority of us is that we do not know ourselves directly, but seek a system, a method, a means of operation by which to solve the many human problems.

Now is there a means, a system, of knowing oneself? Any clever person, any philosopher, can invent a system, a method; but surely the following of a system will merely produce a result created by that system, will it not? If I follow a particular method of knowing myself, then I shall have the result which that system necessitates; but the result will obviously not be the understanding of myself. That is, by following a method, a system, a means through which to know myself, I shape my thinking, my activities, according to a pattern; but the following of a pattern is not the understanding of oneself.

Therefore there is no method for self-knowledge. Seeking a method invariably implies the desire to attain some result – and that is what we all want. We follow authority – if not that of a person, then of a system, of an ideology – because we want a result which will be satisfactory, which will give us security. We really do not want to understand ourselves, our impulses and reactions, the whole process of our thinking, the conscious as well as the unconscious; we would rather pursue a system which assures us of a result. But the pursuit of a system is invariably the outcome of our desire for security, for certainty, and the result is obviously not the understanding of oneself. When we follow a method, we must have authorities – the teacher, the *guru*, the saviour, the Master – who will guarantee us what we desire; and surely that is not the way to self-knowledge.

Authority prevents the understanding of oneself, does it not? Under the shelter of an authority, a guide, you may have temporarily a sense of security, a sense of well-being, but that is not the understanding of the total process of oneself. Authority in its very nature prevents the full awareness of oneself and therefore ultimately destroys freedom; in freedom alone can there be creativeness. There can be creativeness only through self-knowledge. Most of us are not creative; we are repetitive machines, mere gramophone records playing over and over again certain songs of experience, certain conclusions and memories, either our own or those of another. Such repetition is not creative being – but it is what we want. Because we want to be inwardly secure, we are constantly seeking methods and means for this security, and thereby we create authority, the worship of another, which destroys comprehension, that spontaneous tranquillity of mind in which alone there can be a state of creativeness.

Surely our difficulty is that most of us have lost this sense of creativeness. To be creative does not mean that we must paint pictures or write poems and become famous. That is not creativeness – it is merely the capacity to express an idea, which the public applauds or disregards. Capacity and creativeness should not be confused. Capacity is not creativeness. Creativeness is quite a different state of being, is it not? It is a state in which the self is absent, in which the mind is no longer a focus for our experiences, our ambitions, our pursuits and our desires. Creativeness is not a continuous state, it is new from moment to moment, it is a movement in which there is not the 'me', the 'mine', in which the thought is not focused on any particular experience, ambition, achievement, purpose and motive. It is only when the self is not that there is creativeness – that state of being in which alone there can be reality, the creator of all things. But that state cannot be conceived or imagined, it cannot be formulated or copied, it cannot be attained through any system, through any philosophy, through any discipline; on the contrary, it comes into being only through understanding the total process of oneself.

The understanding of oneself is not a result, a culmination; it is seeing oneself from moment to moment in the mirror of relationship – one's relationship to property, to things, to people, and to ideas. But we find it difficult to be alert, to be aware, and we prefer to dull our minds by following a method, by accepting authorities, superstitions and gratifying theories; so our minds become weary, exhausted and insensitive. Such a mind cannot be in a state of creativeness. That state of creativeness comes only when the self, which is the process of recognition and accumulation, ceases to be; because, after all, consciousness as the 'me' is the centre of recognition, and recognition is merely the process of the accumulation of experience. But we are all afraid to be nothing, because we all want to be something. The little man wants to be a big man, the unvirtuous wants to be virtuous, the weak and obscure crave power, position, and authority. This is the incessant activity of the mind. Such a mind cannot be quiet and therefore can never understand the state of creativeness.

In order to transform the world about us, with its misery, wars, unemployment, starvation, class divisions, and utter confusion, there must be a transformation in ourselves. The revolution must begin within oneself – but not according to any belief or ideology, because revolution based on an idea, or in conformity to a particular pattern, is obviously no revolution at all. To bring about a fundamental revolution in oneself, one must understand the whole process of one's thought and feeling in relationship. That is the only solution to all our problems – not to have more disciplines, more beliefs, more ideologies, and more teachers. If we can understand ourselves as we are from moment to moment without the process of accumulation, then we shall see how there comes a tranquillity that is not a product of the mind, a tranquillity that is neither imagined nor cultivated; and only in that state of tranquillity can there be creativeness.

IV

ACTION AND IDEA

I SHOULD like to discuss the problem of action. This may be rather abstruse and difficult at the beginning but I hope that by thinking it over we shall be able to see the issue clearly, because our whole existence, our whole life, is a process of action.

Most of us live in a series of actions, of seemingly unrelated, disjointed actions, leading to disintegration, to frustration. It is a problem that concerns each one of us, because we live by action and without action there is no life, there is no experience, there is no thinking. Thought is action; and merely to pursue action at one particular level of consciousness, which is the outer, merely to be caught up in outward action without understanding the whole process of action itself, will inevitably lead us to frustration, to misery.

Our life is a series of actions or a process of action at different levels of consciousness. Consciousness is experiencing, naming and recording. That is, consciousness is challenge and response, which is experiencing, then terming or naming, and then recording, which is memory. This process is action, is it not? Consciousness is action; and without challenge, response, without experiencing, naming, or terming, without recording, which is memory, there is no action.

Now action creates the actor. That is, the actor comes into being when action has a result, an end in view. If there is no result in action, then there is no actor; but if there is an end or a result in view, then action brings about the actor. Thus actor, action, and end or result, is a unitary process, a single process, which comes into being when action has an end in view. Action towards a result is will; otherwise there is no will, is there? The desire to achieve an end brings about will, which is the actor – I want to achieve, I want to write a book, I want to be a rich man, I want to paint a picture.

We are familiar with these three states: the actor, the action, and the end. That is our daily existence. I am just explaining what *is*; but we will begin to understand how to transform what *is* only when we examine it clearly, so that there is no illusion or prejudice, no bias with regard to it. Now these three states which constitute experience – the actor, the action, and the result – are surely a process of becoming. Otherwise there is no becoming, is there? If there is no actor, and if there is no action towards an end, there is no becoming; and life as we know it, our daily life, is a process of becoming. I am poor and I act with an end in view, which is to become rich. I am ugly and I want to become beautiful. Therefore my life is a process of becoming something. The will to be is the will to become, at different levels of consciousness, in different states, in which there is challenge, response, naming and recording. Now this becoming is strife, this becoming is pain, is it not? It is a constant struggle: I am this, and I want to become that.

Therefore, then, the problem is: Is there not action without this becoming? Is there not action without this pain, without this constant battle? If there is no end, there is no actor, because action with an end in view creates the actor.

But can there be action without an end in view, and therefore no actor – that is, without the desire for a result? Such action is not a becoming, and therefore not a strife. There is a state of action, a state of experiencing, without the experiencer and the experience. This sounds rather philosophical but it is really quite simple.

In the moment of experiencing, you are not aware of yourself as the experiencer apart from the experience; you are in a state of experiencing. Take a very simple example: you are angry. In that moment of anger there is neither the experiencer nor the experience; there is only experiencing. But the moment you come out of it, a split second after the experiencing, there is the experiencer and the experience, the actor and the action with an end in view – which is to get rid of or to suppress the anger. We are in this state repeatedly, in the state of experiencing; but we always come out of it and give it a term, naming and recording it, and thereby giving continuity to becoming.

If we can understand action in the fundamental sense of the word then that fundamental understanding will affect our superficial activities also; but first we must understand the fundamental nature of action. Now is action brought about by an idea? Do you have an idea first and act afterwards? Or does action come first and then, because action creates conflict, you build around it an idea? Does action create the actor or does the actor come first?

It is very important to discover which comes first. If the idea comes first, then action merely conforms to an idea, and therefore it is no longer action but imitation, compulsion according to an idea. It is very important to realize this; because, as our society is mostly constructed on the intellectual or verbal level, the idea comes first with all of us and action follows. Action is then the handmaid of an idea, and the mere construction of ideas is obviously detrimental to action. Ideas breed further ideas, and when there is merely the breeding of ideas there is antagonism, and society becomes top-heavy with the intellectual process of ideation. Our social structure is very intellectual; we are cultivating the intellect at the expense of every other factor of our being and therefore we are suffocated with ideas.

Can ideas ever produce action, or do ideas merely mould thought and therefore limit action? When action is compelled by an idea, action can never liberate man. It is extraordinarily important for us to understand this point. If an idea shapes action, then action can never bring about the solution to our miseries. The investigation of ideation, of the building up of ideas, whether of the socialists, the capitalists, the communists, or of the various religions, is of the utmost importance, especially when our society is at the edge of a precipice, inviting another catastrophe, another excision. Those who are really serious in their intention to discover the human solution to our many problems must first understand this process of ideation.

What do we mean by an idea? How does an idea come into being? And can idea and action be brought together? Suppose I have an idea and I wish to carry it out; I seek a method of carrying it out, and we speculate, waste our time and energies in quarrelling over how the idea should be carried out. So, it is really very important to find out how ideas come into being; and after discovering the truth of that we can discuss the question of action. Without discussing ideas, merely to find out how to act has no meaning.

Now how do you get an idea – a very simple idea, it need not be philosophical, religious or economic? Obviously it is a process of thought, is it not? Idea is the outcome of a thought process. Without a thought process, there can be no idea. So I have to understand the thought process itself before I can understand its product, the idea. What do we mean by thought? When do you think? Obviously thought is the result of a response, neurological or psychological, is it not? It is the immediate response of the senses to a sensation, or it is psychological, the response of stored-up memory. There is the immediate response of the nerves to a sensation, and there is the psychological response of stored-up memory, the influence of race, group, *guru*, family, tradition, and so on – all of which you call thought. So the thought process is the response of memory, is it not? You would have no thoughts if you had no memory; and the response of memory to a certain experience brings the thought process into action. Say, for example, I have the stored-up memories of nationalism, calling myself a Hindu. That reservoir of memories of past responses, actions, implications, traditions, customs, responds to the challenge of a Mussulman, a Buddhist or a Christian, and the response of memory to the challenge inevitably brings about a thought process. Watch the thought process operating in yourself and you can test the truth of this directly. You have been insulted by someone, and that remains in your memory; it forms part of the background. When you meet the person, which is the challenge, the response is the memory of that insult. So the response of memory, which is the thought process, creates an idea; therefore the idea is always conditioned – and this is important to understand. That is to say the idea is the result of the thought process, the thought process is the response of memory, and memory is always conditioned. Memory is always in the past, and that memory is given life in the present by a challenge. Memory has no life in itself; it comes to life in the present when confronted by a challenge. And all memory, whether dormant or active, is conditioned, is it not?

Therefore there has to be quite a different approach. You have to find out for yourself, inwardly, whether you are acting on an idea, and if there can be action without ideation. Let us find out what that is: action which is not based on an idea.

When do you act without ideation? When is there an action which is not the result of experience? An action based on experience is, as we said, limiting, and therefore a hindrance. Action which is not the outcome of an idea is spontaneous when the thought process, which is based on experience, is not controlling action; which means that there is action independent of experience when the mind is not controlling action. That is the only state in which there is understanding: when the mind, based on experience, is not guiding action: when thought, based on experience, is not shaping action. What is action when there is no thought process? Can there be action without thought process? I want to build a bridge, a house; I know the technique, and the technique tells me how to build it. We call that action. There is the action of writing a poem, of painting, of governmental responsibilities, of social, environmental responses. All are based on an idea or previous experience, shaping action. But is there an action when there is no ideation?

Surely there is such action when the idea ceases; and the idea ceases only when there is love. Love is not memory, love is not experience, love is not the thinking about the person that one loves, for then it is merely thought. You cannot *think* of love. You can think of the person you love or are devoted to – your *guru*, your image, your wife, your husband; but the thought, the symbol, is not the real which is love. Therefore love is not an experience.

When there is love there is action, is there not?, and is that action not liberating? It is not the result of mentation, and there is no gap between love and action, as there is between idea and action. Idea is always old, casting its shadow on the present and we are ever trying to build a bridge between action and idea. When there is love – which is not mentation, which is not ideation, which is not memory, which is not the outcome of an experience, of a practised discipline – then that very love is action. That is the only thing that frees. So long as there is mentation, so long as there is the shaping of action by an idea which is experience, there can be no release; and so long as that process continues, all action is limited. When the truth of this is seen, the quality of love, which is not mentation, which you cannot think about, comes into being.

One has to be aware of this total process, of how ideas come into being, how action springs from ideas, and how ideas control action and therefore limit action, depending on sensation. It doesn't matter *whose* ideas they are, whether from the left or from the extreme right. So long as we cling to ideas, we are in a state in which there can be no experiencing at all; we are merely living in the field of time – in the past, which gives further sensation, or in the future, which is another form of sensation. It is only when the mind is free from idea that there can be experiencing.

Ideas are not truth; and truth is something that must be experienced directly, from moment to moment. It is not an experience which you *want* – which is then merely sensation. Only when one can go beyond the bundle of ideas – which is the 'me', which is the mind, which has a partial or complete continuity – only when one can go beyond that, when thought is completely silent, is there a state of experiencing. Then one shall know what truth is.

V

BELIEF

BELIEF and knowledge are very intimately related to desire; and perhaps, if we can understand these two issues, we can see how desire works and understand its complexities.

One of the things, it seems to me, that most of us eagerly accept and take for granted is the question of beliefs. I am not attacking beliefs. What we are trying to do is to find out why we accept beliefs; and if we can understand the motives, the causation of acceptance, then perhaps we may be able not only to understand why we do it, but also be free of it. One can see how political and religious beliefs, national and various other types of beliefs, do separate people, do create conflict, confusion, and antagonism – which is an obvious fact; and yet we are unwilling to give them up. There is the Hindu belief, the Christian belief, the Buddhist – innumerable sectarian and national beliefs, various political ideologies, all contending with each other, trying to convert each other. One can see, obviously, that belief is separating people, creating intolerance; is it possible to live without belief? One can find that out only if one can study oneself in relationship to a belief. Is it possible to live in this world without a belief – not change beliefs, not substitute one belief for another, but be entirely free from *all* beliefs, so that one meets life anew each minute? This, after all, is the truth: to have the capacity of meeting everything anew, from moment to moment, without the conditioning reaction of the past, so that there is not the cumulative effect which acts as a barrier between oneself and that which *is*.

If you consider, you will see that one of the reasons for the desire to accept a belief is fear. If we had no belief, what would happen to us? Shouldn't we be very frightened of what might happen? If we had no pattern of action, based on a belief – either in God, or in communism, or in socialism, or in imperialism, or in some kind of religious formula, some dogma in which we are conditioned – we should feel utterly lost, shouldn't we? And is not this acceptance of a belief the covering up of that fear – the fear of being really nothing, of being empty? After all, a cup is useful only when it is empty; and a mind that is filled with beliefs, with dogmas, with assertions, with quotations, is really an uncreative mind; it is merely a repetitive mind. To escape from that fear – that fear of emptiness, that fear of loneliness, that fear of stagnation, of not arriving, not succeeding, not achieving, not being something, not becoming something – is surely one of the reasons, is it not?, why we accept beliefs so eagerly and greedily. And, through acceptance of belief, do we understand ourselves? On the contrary. A belief, religious or political, obviously hinders the understanding of ourselves. It acts as a screen through which we are looking at ourselves. And can we look at ourselves without beliefs? If we remove those beliefs, the many beliefs that one has, is there anything left to look at? If we have no beliefs with which the mind has identified itself, then the mind, without identification, is capable of looking at itself as it is – and then, surely, there is the beginning of the understanding of one-self.

It is really a very interesting problem, this question of belief and knowledge. What an extraordinary part it plays

in our life! How many beliefs we have! Surely the more
intellectual, the more cultured, the more spiritual, if I can
use that word, a person is, the less is his capacity to understand. The savages have innumerable superstitions, even in
the modern world. The more thoughtful, the more awake,
the more alert are perhaps the less believing. Belief binds,
belief isolates; we see that is so throughout the world, the
economic and the political world, and also in the so-called
spiritual world. You believe there is a God, and perhaps I believe that there is no God; or you believe in the complete
State control of everything and of every individual, and I
believe in private enterprise; you believe that there is only
one Saviour and through him you can achieve your goal,
and I don't believe so. Thus you with your belief and I
with mine are asserting ourselves. Yet we both talk of love,
of peace, of unity of mankind, of one life – which means
absolutely nothing; because actually the very belief is a
process of isolation. You are a Brahmin, I a non-Brahmin;
you are a Christian, I am a Mussulman, and so on. You
talk of brotherhood and I also talk of the same brotherhood, love and peace; but in actuality we are separated, we
are dividing ourselves. A man who wants peace and who
wants to create a new world, a happy world, surely cannot
isolate himself through any form of belief. Is that clear? It
may be verbally, but, if you see the significance and validity
and the truth of it, it will begin to act.

We see that where there is a process of desire at work
there must be the process of isolation through belief, because
obviously you believe in order to be secure economically,
spiritually, and also inwardly. I am not talking of those
people who believe for economic reasons, because they are
brought up to depend on their jobs and therefore will be
Catholics, Hindus – it does not matter what – as long as there
is a job for them. We are also not discussing those people who
cling to a belief for the sake of convenience. Perhaps with
most of us it is equally so. For convenience, we believe in
certain things. Brushing aside these economic reasons, we
must go more deeply into it. Take the people who believe

strongly in anything, economic, social or spiritual; the process behind it is the psychological desire to be secure, is it not? And then there is the desire to continue. We are not discussing here whether there is or there is not continuity; we are only discussing the urge, the constant impulse to believe. A man of peace, a man who would really understand the whole process of human existence, cannot be bound by a belief, can he? He sees his desire at work as a means to being secure. Please do not go to the other side and say that I am preaching non-religion. That is not my point at all. My point is that as long as we do not understand the process of desire in the form of belief, there must be contention, there must be conflict, there must be sorrow, and man will be against man – which is seen every day. So if I perceive, if I am aware, that this process takes the form of belief, which is an expression of the craving for inward security, then my problem is not that I should believe this or that but that I should free myself from the desire to be secure. Can the mind be free from the desire for security? That is the problem – not what to believe and how much to believe. These are merely expressions of the inward craving to be secure psychologically, to be certain about something, when everything is so uncertain in the world.

Can a mind, can a conscious mind, can a personality, be free from this desire to be secure? We want to be secure and therefore need the aid of our estates, our property and our family. We want to be secure inwardly and also spiritually by erecting walls of belief, which are an indication of this craving to be certain. Can you as an individual be free from this urge, this craving to be secure, which expresses itself in the desire to believe in something? If we are not free of all that, we are a source of contention; we are not peace-making; we have no love in our hearts. Belief destroys; and this is seen in our everyday life. Can I see myself when I am caught in this process of desire, which expresses itself in clinging to a belief? Can the mind free itself from belief – not find a substitute for it but be entirely free from it? You cannot verbally answer 'yes' or 'no' to this; but you can definitely give an answer if your intention is to become free from belief. You then inevitably come to the point at which you are seeking the means to free yourself from the urge to be secure. Obviously there is no security inwardly which, as you like to believe, will continue. You like to believe there is a God who is carefully looking after your petty little interests, telling you whom you should see, what you should do and how you should do it. This is childish and immature thinking. You think the Great Father is watching every one of us. That is a mere projection of your own personal liking. It is obviously not true. Truth must be something entirely different.

Our next problem is that of knowledge. Is knowledge necessary to the understanding of truth? When I say, 'I know', the implication is that there is knowledge. Can such a mind be capable of investigating and searching out what is reality? And besides, what is it we know, of which we are so proud? Actually what is it we know? We know information; we are full of information and experience based on our conditioning, our memory and our capacities. When you say, 'I know', what do you mean? Either the acknowledgement that you know is the recognition of a fact, of certain information, or it is an experience that you have had. The constant accumulation of information, the acquisition of various forms of knowledge, all constitute the assertion 'I know'; and you start translating what you have read, according to your background, your desire, your experience. Your knowledge is a thing in which a process similar to the process of desire is at work. Instead of belief we substitute knowledge. 'I know; I have had experience; it cannot be refuted; my experience is that, on that I completely rely'; these are indications of that knowledge. But when you go behind it, analyse it, look at it more intelligently and carefully, you will find that the very assertion 'I know' is another wall separating you and me. Behind that wall you take refuge, seeking comfort, security. Therefore the more knowledge a mind is burdened with, the less capable it is of understanding.

I do not know if you have ever thought of this problem of acquiring knowledge – whether knowledge does ultimately help us to love, to be free from those qualities which produce conflict in ourselves and with our neighbours; whether knowledge ever frees the mind of ambition. Because ambition is, after all, one of the qualities that destroys relationship, that puts man against man. If we would live at peace with each other, surely ambition must completely come to an end – not only political, economic, social ambition, but also the more subtle and pernicious ambition, the spiritual ambition – to *be* something. Is it ever possible for the mind to be free from this accumulating process of knowledge, this desire to know?

It is a very interesting thing to watch how in our life these two, knowledge and belief, play an extraordinarily powerful part. Look how we worship those who have immense knowledge and erudition! Can you understand the meaning of it? If you would find something new, experience something which is not a projection of your imagination, your mind must be free, must it not? It must be capable of seeing something new. Unfortunately, every time you see something new you bring in all the information known to you already, all your knowledge, all your past memories; and obviously you become incapable of looking, incapable of receiving anything that is new, that is not of the old. Please don't immediately translate this into detail. If I do not know how to get back to my house, I shall be lost; if I do not know how to run a machine, I shall be of little use. That is quite a different thing. We are not discussing that here. We are discussing knowledge that is used as a means to security, the psychological and inward desire to be something. What do you get through knowledge – the authority of knowledge, the weight of knowledge, the sense of importance, dignity, the sense of vitality and what-not? A man who says, 'I know', 'There is', or, 'There is not', surely has stopped thinking, stopped pursuing this whole process of desire.

Our problem then, as I see it, is that we are bound, weighed down, by belief, by knowledge; and is it possible for a mind to be free from yesterday and from the beliefs that have been acquired through the process of yesterday? Do you understand the question? Is it possible for me as an individual and you as an individual to live in this society and yet be free from the beliefs in which we have been brought up? Is it possible for the mind to be free of all that knowledge, all that authority? We read the various scriptures, religious books. There they have very carefully described what to do, what not to do, how to attain the goal, what the goal is and what God is. You all know that by heart and you have pursued that. That is your knowledge, that is what you have acquired, that is what you have learnt; along that path you pursue. Obviously what you pursue and seek, you will find. But is it reality? Is it not the projection of your own knowledge? Is it possible to realize that *now* – not to-morrow, but now – and say, 'I see the truth of it', and let it go, so that your mind is not crippled by this process of imagination, of projection?

Is the mind capable of freedom from belief? You can only be free from it when you understand the inward nature of the causes that make you hold on to it, not only the conscious but the unconscious motives as well, that make you believe. After all, we are not merely a superficial entity functioning on the conscious level. We can find out the deeper conscious and unconscious activities if we give the unconscious mind a chance, because it is much quicker in response than the conscious mind. While your conscious mind is quietly thinking, listening and watching, the unconscious mind is much more active, much more alert and much more receptive; it can, therefore, have an answer. Can the mind which has been subjugated, intimidated, forced, compelled to believe, can such a mind be free to think? Can it look anew and remove the process of isolation between you and another? Please do not say that belief brings people to-gether. It does not. That is obvious. No organized religion has ever done that. Look at yourselves in your own country. You are all believers, but are you all together? Are you all united? You yourselves know you are not. You are divided into so many petty little parties, castes; you know the innumerable divisions. The process is the same right through the world whether in the east or in the west – Christians destroying Christians, murdering each other for petty little things, driving people into camps and so on, the whole horror of war. Therefore belief does not unite people. That is so clear. If that is clear and that is true, and if you see it, then it must be followed. But the difficulty is that most of us do not see, because we are not capable of facing that inward insecurity, that inward sense of being alone. We want something to lean on, whether it is the State, whether it is the caste, whether it is nationalism, whether it is a Master or a Saviour or anything else. And when we see the falseness of all this, the mind then is capable – it may be temporarily for a second – of seeing the truth of it; even though when it is too much for it, it goes back. But to see temporarily is sufficient; if you can see it for a fleeting second, it is enough; because you will then see an extraordinary thing taking place. The unconscious is at work, though the conscious may reject. It is not a progressive second; but that second is the only thing, and it will have its own results, even in spite of the conscious mind struggling against it.

So our question is: 'Is it possible for the mind to be free from knowledge and belief?' Is not the mind made up of knowledge and belief? Is not the structure of the mind belief and knowledge? Belief and knowledge are the processes of recognition, the centre of the mind. The process is enclosing, the process is conscious as well as unconscious. Can the mind be free of its own structure? Can the mind cease to be? That is the problem. Mind, as we know it, has belief behind it, has desire, the urge to be secure, knowledge, and accumulation of strength. If, with all its power and superiority, one cannot think for oneself, there can be no peace in the world. You may talk about peace, you may organize political parties, you may shout from the housetops; but you cannot have peace; because in the mind is the very essence which creates contradiction, which isolates and separates. A man of peace, a man of earnestness, cannot isolate himself and yet talk of brotherhood and peace. It is just a game, political or religious, a sense of achievement and ambition. A man who is really earnest about this, who wants to discover, has to face the problem of knowledge and belief; he has to go behind it, to discover the whole process of desire at work, the desire to be secure, the desire to be certain.

A mind that would be in a state in which the new can take place – whether it be the truth, whether it be God, or what you will – must surely cease to acquire, to gather; it must put aside all knowledge. A mind burdened with knowledge cannot possibly understand that which is real, which is not measurable.

VI

EFFORT

FOR most of us, our whole life is based on effort, some kind of volition. We cannot conceive of an action without volition, without effort. Our social, economic and so-called spiritual life is a series of efforts, always culminating in a certain result. And we think effort is essential, necessary.

Why do we make effort? Is it not, put simply, in order to achieve a result, to become something, to reach a goal? If we do not make an effort, we think we shall stagnate. We have an idea about the goal towards which we are constantly striving; and this striving has become part of our life. If we want to alter ourselves, if we want to bring about a radical change in ourselves, we make a tremendous effort to eliminate the old habits, to resist the habitual environmental influences and so on. So we are used to this series of efforts in order to find or achieve something, in order to live at all.

Is not all such effort the activity of the self? Is not effort self-centred activity? If we make an effort from the centre of the self, it must inevitably produce more conflict, more confusion, more misery. Yet we keep on making effort after effort. Very few of us realize that the self-centred activity of effort does not clear up any of the problems. On the contrary, it increases our confusion and our misery and our sorrow. We know this; and yet we continue hoping somehow to break through this self-centred activity of effort, the action of the will.

I think we shall understand the significance of life if we understand what it means to make an effort. Does happiness come through effort? Have you ever tried to be happy? It is impossible, is it not? You struggle to be happy and there is no happiness, is there? Joy does not come through suppression, through control or indulgence. You may indulge but there is bitterness at the end. You may suppress or control, but there is always strife in the hidden. Therefore happiness does not come through effort, nor joy through control and suppression; and still all our life is a series of suppressions, a series of controls, a series of regretful indulgences. Also there is a constant overcoming, a constant struggle with our passions, our greed and our stupidity. So do we not strive, struggle, make effort, in the hope of finding happiness, finding something which will give us a feeling of peace, a sense of love? Yet does love or understanding come by strife? I think it is very important to understand what we mean by struggle, strife or effort.

Does not effort mean a struggle to change what *is* into what is not, or into what it should be or should become? That is, we are constantly struggling to avoid facing what *is*, or we are trying to get away from it or to transform or modify what *is*. A man who is truly content is the man who understands what *is*, gives the right significance to what *is*. That is true contentment; it is not concerned with having few or many possessions but with the understanding of the whole significance of what *is*; and that can only come when you recognize what *is*, when you are aware of it, not when you are trying to modify it or change it.

So we see that effort is a strife or a struggle to transform that which *is* into something which you wish it to be. I am only talking about psychological struggle, not the struggle with a physical problem, like engineering or some discovery or transformation which is purely technical. I am only talking of that struggle which is psychological and which always overcomes the technical. You may build with great care a marvellous society, using the infinite knowledge science has given us. But so long as the psychological strife and struggle and battle are not understood and the psychological overtones and currents are not overcome, the structure of society is bound to crash, as has happened over and over again.

Effort is a distraction from what *is*. The moment I accept what *is* there is no struggle. Any form of struggle or strife is an indication of distraction; and distraction, which is effort, must exist so long as psychologically I wish to transform what *is* into something it is not.

First we must be free to see that joy and happiness do not come through effort. Is creation through effort, or is there creation only with the cessation of effort? When do you write, paint or sing? When do you create? Surely when there is no effort, when you are completely open, when on all levels you are in complete communication, completely integrated. Then there is joy and then you begin to sing or write a poem or paint or fashion something. The moment of creation is not born of struggle.

Perhaps in understanding the question of creativeness we shall be able to understand what we mean by effort. Is creativeness the outcome of effort, and are we aware in those moments when we are creative? Or is creativeness a sense of total self-forgetfulness, that sense when there is no turmoil, when one is wholly unaware of the movement of thought, when there is only a complete, full, rich being? Is that state the result of travail, of struggle, of conflict, of effort? I do not know if you have ever noticed that when you do something easily, swiftly, there is no effort, there is complete absence of struggle; but as our lives are mostly a series of battles, conflicts and struggles, we cannot imagine a life, a state of being, in which strife has fully ceased.

To understand the state of being without strife, that state of creative existence, surely one must inquire into the whole problem of effort. We mean by effort the striving to fulfil oneself, to become something, don't we? I am this, and I want to become that; I am not that, and I must become that. In becoming 'that', there is strife, there is battle, conflict, struggle. In this struggle we are concerned inevitably with fulfilment through the gaining of an end; we seek self-fulfilment in an object, in a person, in an idea, and that demands constant battle, struggle, the effort to become, to fulfil. So we have taken this effort as inevitable; and I wonder if it *is* inevitable – this struggle to become something? Why is there this struggle? Where there is the desire for fulfilment, in whatever degree and at whatever level, there must be struggle. Fulfilment is the motive, the drive behind the effort; whether it is the big executive, the housewife, or a poor man, there is this battle to become, to fulfil, going on.

Now why is there the desire to fulfil oneself? Obviously the desire to fulfil, to become something, arises when there is awareness of being nothing. Because I am nothing, because I am insufficient, empty, inwardly poor, I struggle to become something; outwardly or inwardly I struggle to fulfil myself in a person, in a thing, in an idea. To fill that void is the whole process of our existence. Being aware that we are empty, inwardly poor, we struggle either to collect things outwardly, or to cultivate inward riches. There is effort only when there is an escape from that inward void through action, through contemplation, through acquisition, through achievement, through power, and so on. That is our daily existence. I am aware of my insufficiency, my inward poverty, and I struggle to run away from it or to fill it. This running away, avoiding, or trying to cover up the void, entails struggle, strife, effort.

Now if one does not make an effort to run away, what happens? One lives with that loneliness, that emptiness; and in accepting that emptiness one will find that there comes a creative state which has nothing to do with strife, with effort. Effort exists only so long as we are trying to avoid that inward loneliness, emptiness, but when we look at it, observe it, when we accept what *is* without avoidance, we will find there comes a state of being in which all strife ceases. That state of being is creativeness and it is not the result of strife.

When there is understanding of what *is*, which is emptiness, inward insufficiency, when one lives with that insufficiency and understands it fully, there comes creative reality, creative intelligence, which alone brings happiness.

Therefore action as we know it is really reaction, it is a ceaseless becoming, which is the denial, the avoidance of what *is*; but when there is awareness of emptiness without choice, without condemnation or justification, then in that understanding of what *is* there is action, and this action is creative being. You will understand this if you are aware of yourself in action. Observe yourself as you are acting, not only outwardly but see also the movement of your thought and feeling. When you are aware of this movement you will see that the thought process, which is also feeling and action, is based on an idea of becoming. The idea of becoming arises only when there is a sense of insecurity, and that sense of insecurity comes when one is aware of the inward void. If you are aware of that process of thought and feeling, you will see that there is a constant battle going on, an effort to change, to modify, to alter what *is*. This is the effort to become, and becoming is a direct avoidance of what *is*. Through self-knowledge, through constant awareness, you will find that strife, battle, the conflict of becoming, leads to pain, to sorrow and ignorance. It is only if you are aware of inward insufficiency and live with it without escape, accepting it wholly, that you will discover an extraordinary tranquillity, a tranquillity which is not put together, made up, but a tranquillity which comes with understanding of what *is*. Only in that state of tranquillity is there creative being.

VII

THE FUNCTION OF THE MIND

When you observe your own mind you are observing not only the so-called upper levels of the mind but also watching the unconscious; you are seeing what the mind actually does, are you not? That is the only way you can investigate. Do not superimpose what it *should* do, how it *should* think or act, and so on; that would amount to making mere statements. That is, if you say the mind should be this or should not be that, then you stop all investigation and all thinking; or, if you quote some high authority, then you equally stop thinking, don't you? If you quote Buddha, Christ or XYZ, there is an end to all pursuit, to all thinking and all investigation. So one has to to guard against that. You must put aside all these subtleties of the mind if you would investigate this problem of the self together with me.

What is the function of the mind? To find that out, you must know what the mind is actually doing. What does your mind do? It is all a process of thinking, is it not? Otherwise, the mind is not there. So long as the mind is not thinking, consciously or unconsciously, there is no consciousness. We have to find out what the mind that we use in our everyday life, and also the mind of which most of us are unconscious, does in relation to our problems. We must look at the mind as it is and not as it should be.

Now what is mind as it is functioning? It is actually a process of isolation, is it not? Fundamentally that is what the process of thought is. It is thinking in an isolated form, yet remaining collective. When you observe your own thinking, you will see it is an isolated, fragmentary process. You are thinking according to your reactions, the reactions of your memory, of your experience, of your knowledge, of your belief. You are reacting to all that, aren't you? If I say that there must be a fundamental revolution, you immediately react. You will object to that word 'revolution' if you have

got good investments, spiritual or otherwise. So your reaction
is dependent on your knowledge, on your belief, on your
experience. That is an obvious fact. There are various forms
of reaction. You say, 'I must be brotherly', 'I must cooperate',
'I must be friendly', 'I must be kind', and so on. What are
these? These are all reactions; but the fundamental reaction of thinking is a process of isolation. You are watching
the process of your own mind, each one of you, which means
watching your own action, belief, knowledge, experience. All
these give security, do they not? They give security, give
strength to the process of thinking. That process only
strengthens the 'me', the mind, the self – whether you call
that self high or low. All our religions, all our social sanctions, all our laws are for the support of the individual, the
individual self, the separative action; and in opposition to
that there is the totalitarian state. If you go deeper into the
unconscious, there too it is the same process that is at work.
There, we are the collective influenced by the environment,
by the climate, by the society, by the father, the mother, the
grandfather. There again is the desire to assert, to dominate,
as an individual, as the 'me'.

Is not the function of the mind, as we know it and as we
function daily, a process of isolation? Aren't you seeking
individual salvation? You are going to be somebody in the
future; or in this very life you are going to be a great man,
a great writer. Our whole tendency is to be separated. Can
the mind do anything else but that? Is it possible for the
mind not to think separatively, in a self-enclosed manner,
fragmentarily? That is impossible. So we worship the
mind; the mind is extraordinarily important. Don't you
know, the moment you are a little bit cunning, a little bit
alert, and have a little accumulated information and knowledge, how important you become in society? You know how
you worship those who are intellectually superior, the
lawyers, the professors, the orators, the great writers,
the explainers and the expounders! You have cultivated
the intellect and the mind.

The function of the mind is to be separated; otherwise

your mind is not there. Having cultivated this process for centuries we find we cannot cooperate; we can only be urged, compelled, driven by authority, fear, either economic or religious. If that is the actual state, not only consciously but also at the deeper levels, in our motives, our intentions, our pursuits, how can there be cooperation? How can there be intelligent coming together to do something? As that is almost impossible, religions and organized social parties force the individual to certain forms of discipline. Discipline then becomes imperative if we want to come together, to do things together.

Until we understand how to transcend this separative thinking, this process of giving emphasis to the 'me' and the 'mine', whether in the collective form or in individual form, we shall not have peace; we shall have constant conflict and wars. Our problem is how to bring an end to the separative process of thought. Can thought ever destroy the self, thought being the process of verbalization and of reaction? Thought is nothing else but reaction; thought is not creative. Can such thought put an end to itself? That is what we are trying to find out. When I think along the lines: 'I must discipline', 'I must think properly', 'I must be this or that', thought is compelling itself, urging itself, disciplining itself to be something or not to be something. Is that not a process of isolation? It is not therefore that integrated intelligence which functions as a whole, from which alone there can be cooperation.

How are you to come to the end of thought? Or rather how is thought, which is isolated, fragmentary and partial, to come to an end? How do you set about it? Will your so-called discipline destroy it? Please examine the disciplining process, which is solely a thought process, in which there is subjection, repression, control, domination – all affecting the unconscious, which asserts itself later as you grow older. Having tried for such a long time to no purpose, you must have found that discipline is obviously not the process to destroy the self. The self cannot be destroyed through discipline, because discipline is a process of strengthening the self. Yet all your religions support it; all your meditations, your assertions, are based on this. Will knowledge destroy the self? Will belief destroy it? In other words, will anything that we are at present doing, any of the activities in which we are at present engaged in order to get at the root of the self, will any of that succeed? Is not all this a fundamental waste in a thought process which is a process of isolation, of reaction? What do you do when you realize fundamentally or deeply that thought cannot end itself? What happens? Watch yourself. When you are fully aware of this fact, what happens? You understand that any reaction is conditioned and that, through conditioning, there can be no freedom either at the beginning or at the end – and freedom is always at the beginning and not at the end.

When you realize that any reaction is a form of conditioning and therefore gives continuity to the self in different ways, what actually takes place? You must be very clear in this matter. Belief, knowledge, discipline, experience, the whole process of achieving a result or an end, ambition, becoming something in this life or in a future life – all these are a process of isolation, a process which brings destruction, misery, wars, from which there is no escape through collective action, however much you may be threatened with concentration camps and all the rest of it. Are you aware of that fact? What is the state of the mind which says, 'It is so', 'That is my problem', 'That is exactly where I am', 'I see what knowledge and discipline can do, what ambition does'? Surely, if you see all that, there is already a different process at work.

We see the ways of the intellect but we do not see the way of love. The way of love is not to be found through the intellect. The intellect, with all its ramifications, with all its desires, ambitions, pursuits, must come to an end for love to come into existence. Don't you know that when you love, you cooperate, you are not thinking of yourself? That is the highest form of intelligence – not when you love as a superior entity or when you are in a good position, which is nothing but fear. When your vested interests are there, there can be no love; there is only the process of exploitation, born of fear. So love can come into being only when the mind is not there. Therefore you must understand the whole process of the mind, the function of the mind.

It is only when we know how to love each other that there can be cooperation, that there can be intelligent functioning, a coming together over any question. Only then is it possible to find out what God is, what truth is. Now, we are trying to find truth through intellect, through imitation – which is idolatry. Only when you discard completely, through understanding, the whole structure of the self, can that which is eternal, timeless, immeasurable, come into being. You cannot go to it; it comes to you.

VIII

WHAT IS THE SELF?

Do we know what we mean by the self? By that, I mean the idea, the memory, the conclusion, the experience, the various forms of namable and unnamable intentions, the conscious endeavour to be or not to be, the accumulated memory of the unconscious, the racial, the group, the individual, the clan, and the whole of it all, whether it is projected outwardly in action or projected spiritually as virtue; the striving after all this is the self. In it is included the competition, the desire to be. The whole process of that is the self; and we know actually when we are faced with it that it is an evil thing. I am using the word 'evil' intentionally, because the self is dividing; the self is self-enclosing; its activities, however noble, are separative and isolating. We know all this. We also know those extraordinary moments when the self is not there, in which there is no sense of endeavour, of effort, and which happens when there is love.

It seems to me that it is important to understand how experience strengthens the self. If we are earnest, we should understand this problem of experience. Now what do we mean by experience? We have experience all the time, impressions; and we translate those impressions, and we react or act according to them; we are calculating, cunning, and so on. There is the constant interplay between what is seen objectively and our reaction to it, and interplay between the conscious and the memories of the unconscious.

According to my memories, I react to whatever I see, to whatever I feel. In this process of reacting to what I see, what I feel, what I know, what I believe, experience is taking place, is it not? Reaction, response to something seen, is experience. When I see you, I react; the naming of that reaction is experience. If I do not name that reaction it is not an experience. Watch your own responses and what is taking place about you. There is no experience unless there is a naming process going on at the same time. If I do not recognize you, how can I have the experience of meeting you? It sounds simple and right. Is it not a fact? That is, if I do not react according to my memories, according to my conditioning, according to my prejudices, how can I know that I have had an experience?

Then there is the projection of various desires. I desire to be protected, to have security inwardly; or I desire to have a Master, a *guru*, a teacher, a God; and I experience that which I have projected; that is, I have projected a desire which has taken a form, to which I have given a name; to that I react. It is my projection. It is my naming. That desire which gives me an experience makes me say: 'I have experienced', 'I have met the Master', or, 'I have not met the Master'. Desire is what you call experience, is it not?

When I desire silence of the mind, what is taking place? What happens? I see the importance of having a silent mind, a quiet mind, for various reasons; because the *Upanishads* have said so, religious scriptures have said so, saints have said so, and also occasionally I myself feel how good it is to be quiet, because my mind is so very chatty all the day. At times I feel how nice, how pleasurable, it is to have a peaceful mind, a silent mind. The desire is to experience silence. I want to have a silent mind, and so I ask, 'How can I get it?' I know what this or that book says about meditation, and the various forms of discipline, so through discipline I seek to experience silence. The self, the 'me', has therefore established itself in the experience of silence.

I want to understand what is truth; that is my desire, my longing; then there follows my projection of what I consider to be the truth, because I have read lots about it; I have heard many people talk about it; religious scriptures have described it. I want all that. What happens? The very want, the very desire, is projected, and I experience because I recognize that projected state. If I did not recognize that state, I would not call it truth. I recognize it and I experience it; and that experience gives strength to the self, to the 'me', does it not? So the self becomes entrenched in the experience. Then you say, 'I know', 'the Master exists', 'there is God' or 'there is no God'; you say that a particular political system is right and all others are wrong.

So experience is always strengthening the 'me'. The more you are entrenched in your experience, the more does the self get strengthened. As a result of this, you have a certain strength of character, strength of knowledge, of belief, which you display to other people because you know they are not as clever as you are, and because you have the gift of the pen or of speech and you are cunning. Because the self is still acting, so your beliefs, your Masters, your castes, your economic system are all a process of isolation, and they therefore bring contention. You must, if you are at all serious or earnest in this, dissolve this centre completely and not justify it. That is why we must understand the process of experience.

Is it possible for the mind, for the self, not to project, not to desire, not to experience? We see that all experiences of the self are a negation, a destruction, and yet we call them positive action, don't we? That is what we call the positive way of life. To undo this whole process is, to you, negation. Are you right in that? Can we, you and I, as individuals, go to the root of it and understand the process of the self?

Now what brings about dissolution of the self? Religious and other groups have offered identification, have they not? 'Identify yourself with the larger, and the self disappears', is what they say. But surely identification is still the process of the self; the larger is simply the projection of the 'me', which I experience and which therefore strengthens the 'me'.

All the various forms of discipline, belief and knowledge surely only strengthen the self. Can we find an element which will dissolve the self? Or is that a wrong question? That is what we want basically. We want to find something which will dissolve the 'me', do we not? We think there are various means, namely, identification, belief, etc.; but all of them are at the same level; one is not superior to the other, because all of them are equally powerful in strengthening the self, the 'me'. So can I see the 'me' wherever it functions, and see its destructive forces and energy? Whatever name I may give to it, it is an isolating force, it is a destructive force, and I want to find a way of dissolving it. You must have asked this yourself – 'I see the "I" functioning all the time and always bringing anxiety, fear, frustration, despair, misery, not only to myself but to all around me. Is it possible for that self to be dissolved, not partially but completely?' Can we go to the root of it and destroy it? That is the only way of truly functioning, is it not? I do not want to be partially intelligent but intelligent in an integrated manner. Most of us are intelligent in layers, you probably in one way and I in some other way. Some of you are intelligent in your business work, some others in your laboratory work, and so on; people are intelligent in different ways; but we are not integrally intelligent. To be integrally intelligent means to be without the self. Is it possible?

Now is it possible for the self to be completely absent? You know it is possible. What are the necessary ingredients, requirements? What is the element that brings it about? Can I find it? When I put that question 'Can I find it?' surely I am convinced that it is possible; so I have already created an experience in which the self is going to be strengthened, is it not? Understanding of the self requires a great deal of intelligence, a great deal of alertness, watching ceaselessly, so that it does not slip away. I, who am very earnest, want to dissolve the self. When I say that, I know it is possible to dissolve the self. The moment I say, 'I want to dissolve it', in that there is still the experiencing of the self; and so the self is strengthened. So how is it possible for the self not to experience? One can see that the state of creation is not at all the experience of the self. Creation is when the self is not there, because creation is not intellectual, is not of the mind, is not self-projected, is something beyond all experiencing. So is it possible for the mind to be quite still, in a state of non-recognition, or non-experiencing, to be in a state in which creation can take place, which means when the self is absent? The problem is this, is it not? Any movement of the mind, positive or negative, is an experience which actually strengthens the 'me'. Is it possible for the mind not to recognize? That can only take place when there is complete silence, but not the silence which is an experience of the self and which therefore strengthens the self.

Is there an entity apart from the self, which looks at the self and dissolves the self? Is there a spiritual entity which supersedes the self and destroys it, which puts it aside? We think there is, don't we? Most religious people think there is such an element. The materialist says, 'It is impossible for the self to be destroyed; it can be conditioned and restrained – politically, economically and socially; we can hold it firmly within a certain pattern and we can break it; and therefore it can be made to lead a high life, a moral life, and not to interfere with anything but to follow the social pattern, and to function merely as a machine'. That we know. There are other people, the so-called religious ones – they are not really religious, though we call them so – who say, 'Fundamentally, there is such an element. If we can get into touch with it, it will dissolve the self'.

Is there such an element to dissolve the self? Please see what we are doing. We are forcing the self into a corner.

If you allow yourself to be forced into the corner, you will see what will happen. We should like there to be an element which is timeless, which is not of the self, which, we hope, will come and intercede and destroy the self – and which we call God. Now is there such a thing which the mind can conceive? There may be or there may not be; that is not the point. But when the mind seeks a timeless spiritual state which will go into action in order to destroy the self, is that not another form of experience which is strengthening the 'me'? When you believe, is that not what is actually taking place? When you believe that there is truth, God, the timeless state, immortality, is that not the process of strengthening the self? The self has projected that thing which you feel and believe will come and destroy the self. So, having projected this idea of continuance in a timeless state as a spiritual entity, you have an experience; and such experience only strengthens the self; and therefore what have you done? You have not really destroyed the self but only given it a different name, a different quality; the self is still there, because you have experienced it. Thus our action from the beginning to the end is the same action, only we think it is evolving, growing, becoming more and more beautiful; but, if you observe inwardly, it is the same action going on, the same 'me' functioning at different levels with different labels, different names.

When you see the whole process, the cunning, extraordinary inventions, the intelligence of the self, how it covers itself up through identification, through virtue, through experience, through belief, through knowledge; when you see that the mind is moving in a circle, in a cage of its own making, what happens? When you are aware of it, fully cognizant of it, then are you not extraordinarily quiet – not through compulsion, not through any reward, not through any fear? When you recognize that every movement of the mind is merely a form of strengthening the self, when you observe it, see it, when you are completely aware of it in action, when you come to that point – not ideologically, verbally, not through projected experiencing, but when you are actually in that state – then you will see that the mind, being utterly still, has no power of creating. Whatever the mind creates is in a circle, within the field of the self. When the mind is non-creating there is creation, which is not a recognizable process.

Reality, truth, is not to be recognized. For truth to come, belief, knowledge, experiencing, the pursuit of virtue – all this must go. The virtuous person who is conscious of pursuing virtue can never find reality. He may be a very decent person; but that is entirely different from being a man of truth, a man who understands. To the man of truth, truth has come into being. A virtuous man is a righteous man, and a righteous man can never understand what is truth because virtue to him is the covering of the self, the strengthening of the self, because he is pursuing virtue. When he says, 'I must be without greed', the state of non-greed which he experiences only strengthens the self. That is why it is so important to be poor, not only in the things of the world but also in belief and in knowledge. A man with worldly riches or a man rich in knowledge and belief will never know anything but darkness, and will be the centre of all mischief and misery. But if you and I, as individuals, can see this whole working of the self, then we shall know what love is. I assure you that that is the only reformation which can possibly change the world. Love is not of the self. Self cannot recognize love. You say, 'I love'; but in the very saying of it, in the very experiencing of it, love is not. But, when you know love, self is not. When there is love, self is not.

IX

FEAR

WHAT is fear? Fear can exist only in relation to something, not in isolation. How can I be afraid of death, how can I be afraid of something I do not know? I can be afraid only of what I know. When I say I am afraid of death, am I really afraid of the unknown, which is death, or am I afraid of losing what I have known? My fear is not of death but of losing my association with things belonging to me. My fear is always in relation to the known, not to the unknown.

My inquiry now is how to be free from the fear of the known, which is the fear of losing my family, my reputation, my character, my bank account, my appetites and so on. You may say that fear arises from conscience; but your conscience is formed by your conditioning, so conscience is still the result of the known. What do I know? Knowledge is having ideas, having opinions about things, having a sense of continuity as in relation to the known, and no more. Ideas are memories, the result of experience, which is response to challenge. I am afraid of the known, which means I am afraid of losing people, things or ideas, I am afraid of discovering what I am, afraid of being at a loss, afraid of the pain which might come into being when I have lost or have not gained or have no more pleasure.

There is fear of pain. Physical pain is a nervous response, but psychological pain arises when I hold on to things that give me satisfaction, for then I am afraid of anyone or anything that may take them away from me. The psychological accumulations prevent psychological pain as long as they are undisturbed; I am a bundle of accumulations, experiences, which prevents any serious form of disturbance – and I do not want to be disturbed. Therefore I am afraid of anyone who disturbs them. Thus my fear is of the known; I am afraid of the accumulations, physical or psychological, that I have gathered as a means of warding off pain or preventing sorrow. But sorrow is in the very process of accumulating to ward off psychological pain. Knowledge also helps to prevent pain. As medical knowledge helps to prevent physical pain, so beliefs help to prevent psychological pain, and that is why I am afraid of losing my beliefs, though I have no perfect knowledge or concrete proof of the reality of such beliefs. I may reject some of the traditional beliefs that have been foisted on me because my own experience gives me strength, confidence, understanding; but such beliefs and the knowledge which I have acquired are basically the same – a means of warding off pain.

Fear exists so long as there is accumulation of the known, which creates the fear of losing. Therefore fear of the unknown is really fear of losing the accumulated known. The moment I say, 'I must not lose', there is fear. Though my intention in accumulating is to ward off pain, pain is inherent in the process of accumulation. The very things which I have create fear, which is pain.

The seed of defence brings offence. I want physical security; thus I create a sovereign government, which necessitates armed forces, which means war, which destroys security. Wherever there is a desire for self-protection, there is fear. When I see the fallacy of demanding security I do not accumulate any more. If you say that you see it but you cannot help accumulating, it is because you do not really see that, inherently, in accumulation there is pain.

Fear exists in the process of accumulation and belief in something is part of the accumulative process. My son dies, and I believe in reincarnation to prevent me psychologically from having more pain; but, in the very process of believing, there is doubt. Outwardly I accumulate things, and bring war; inwardly I accumulate beliefs, and bring pain. So long as I want to be secure, to have bank accounts, pleasures, and so on, so long as I want to become something, physiologically or psychologically, there must be pain. The very things I am doing to ward off pain bring me fear, pain.

Fear comes into being when I desire to be in a particular pattern. To live without fear means to live without a particular pattern. When I demand a particular way of living that in itself is a source of fear. My difficulty is my desire to live in a certain frame. Can I not break the frame? I can do so only when I see the truth: that the frame is causing fear and that this fear is strengthening the frame. If I say I must break the frame because I want to be free of fear, then I am merely following another pattern which will cause further fear. Any action on my part based on the desire to break the frame will only create another pattern, and therefore fear. How am I to break the frame without causing fear, that is without any conscious or unconscious action on my part with regard to it? This means that I must not act, I must make no movement to break the frame. What happens to me when I am simply looking at the frame without doing anything about it? I see that the mind itself is the frame; it lives in the habitual pattern which it has created for itself. Therefore, the mind itself is fear. Whatever the mind does goes towards strengthening an old pattern or furthering a new one. This means that whatever the mind does to get rid of fear causes fear.

Fear finds various escapes. The common variety is identification, is it not? – identification with the country, with the society, with an idea. Haven't you noticed how you respond when you see a procession, a military procession or a religious procession, or when the country is in danger of being invaded? You then identify yourself with the country, with a being, with an ideology. There are other times when you identify yourself with your child, with your wife, with a particular form of action or inaction, Indentification is a process of self-forgetfulness. So long as I am conscious of the 'me' I know there is pain, there is struggle, there is constant fear. But if I can identify myself with something greater, with something worth while, with beauty, with life, with truth, with belief, with knowledge, at least temporarily, there is an escape from the 'me', is there not? If I talk about 'my country' I forget myself temporarily, do I not? If I can say something about God, I forget myself. If I can identify myself with my family, with a group, with a particular party, with a certain ideology, then there is a temporary escape.

Identification therefore is a form of escape from the self, even as virtue is a form of escape from the self. The man who pursues virtue is escaping from the self and he has a narrow mind not a virtuous mind, for virtue is something which cannot be pursued. The more you try to become virtuous, the more strength you give to the self, to the 'me'. Fear, which is common to most of us in different forms, must always find a substitute and must therefore increase our struggle. The more you are identified with a substitute, the greater strength you have to hold on to that for which you are prepared to struggle, to die, because fear is at the back.

Do we now know what fear is? Is it not the non-acceptance of what is? We must understand the word 'acceptance'. I am not using that word as meaning the effort made to accept. There is no question of accepting when I perceive what *is*. When I do not see clearly what *is*, then I bring in the process of acceptance. Therefore fear is the non-acceptance of what *is*. How can I, who am a bundle of all these re-actions, responses, memories, hopes, depressions, frustrations, who am the result of the movement of consciousness blocked, go beyond? Can the mind, without this blocking and hindrance, be conscious? We know, when there is no hindrance, what extraordinary joy there is. Don't you know when the body is perfectly healthy there is a certain joy, well-being; and don't you know when the mind is completely free, without any block, when the centre of recognition as the 'me' is not there, you experience a certain joy? Haven't you experienced this state when the self is absent? Surely we all have.

There is understanding and freedom from the self only when I can look at it completely and integrally as a whole; and I can do that only when I understand the whole process of all activity born of desire which is the very expression of thought – for thought is not different from desire – without justifying it, without condemning it, without suppressing it; if I can understand that, then I shall know if there is the possibility of going beyond the restrictions of the self.

X

SIMPLICITY

I WOULD like to discuss what is simplicity, and perhaps from that arrive at the discovery of sensitivity. We seem to think that simplicity is merely an outward expression, a withdrawal: having few possessions, wearing a loin-cloth, having no home, putting on few clothes, having a small bank account. Surely that is not simplicity. That is merely an outward show. It seems to me that simplicity is essential; but simplicity can come into being only when we begin to understand the significance of self-knowledge.

Simplicity is not merely adjustment to a pattern. It requires a great deal of intelligence to be simple and not merely conform to a particular pattern, however worthy outwardly. Unfortunately most of us begin by being simple externally, in outward things. It is comparatively easy to have few things and to be satisfied with few things; to be content with little and perhaps to share that little with others. But a mere outward expression of simplicity in things, in possessions, surely does not imply the simplicity of inward being. Because, as the world is at present, more and more things are being urged upon us, outwardly, externally. Life is becoming more and more complex. In order to escape from that, we try to renounce or be detached from things – from cars, from houses, from organizations, from cinemas, and from the innumerable circumstances outwardly thrust upon us. We think we shall be simple by withdrawing. A great many saints, a great many teachers, have renounced the world; and it seems to me that such a renunciation on the part of any of us does not solve the problem. Simplicity which is fundamental, real, can only come into being inwardly; and from that there is an outward expression. How to be simple, then, is the problem; because that simplicity makes one more and more sensitive. A sensitive mind, a sensitive heart, is essential, for then it is capable of quick perception, quick reception.

One can be inwardly simple, surely, only by understanding the innumerable impediments, attachments, fears, in which one is held. But most of us *like* to be held – by people, by possessions, by ideas. We like to be prisoners. Inwardly we *are* prisoners, though outwardly we seem to be very simple. Inwardly we are prisoners of our desires, of our wants, of our ideals, of innumerable motivations. Simplicity cannot be found unless one is free inwardly. Therefore it must begin inwardly, not outwardly.

There is an extraordinary freedom when one understands the whole process of belief, why the mind is attached to a belief. When there is freedom from beliefs, there is simplicity. But that simplicity requires intelligence, and to be intelligent one must be aware of one's own impediments. To be aware, one must be constantly on the watch, not established in any particular groove, in any particular pattern of thought or action. After all, what one is inwardly does affect the outer. Society, or any form of action, is the projection of ourselves, and without transforming inwardly, mere legislation has very little significance outwardly; it bring about certain reforms, certain adjustments, but what one is inwardly always overcomes the outer. If one is inwardly greedy, ambitious, pursuing certain ideals, that inward complexity does eventually upset, overthrow outward society, however carefully planned it may be.

Therefore one must begin within – not exclusively, not rejecting the outer. You come to the inner, surely, by understanding the outer, by finding out how the conflict, the struggle, the pain, exists outwardly; as one investigates it more and more, naturally one comes to the psychological states which produce the outward conflicts and miseries. The outward expression is only an indication of our inward state, but to understand the inward state one must approach through the outer. Most of us do that. In understanding the inner – not exclusively, not by rejecting the outer, but by understanding the outer and so coming upon the inner – we will find that, as we proceed to investigate the inward complexities of our being, we become more and more sensitive, free. It is this inward simplicity that is so essential, because that simplicity creates sensitivity. A mind that is not sensitive, not alert, not aware, is incapable of any receptivity, any creative action. Conformity as a means of making ourselves simple really makes the mind and heart dull, insensitive. Any form of authoritarian compulsion, imposed by the government, by oneself, by the ideal of achievement, and so on – any form of conformity must make for insensitivity, for not being simple inwardly. Outwardly you may conform and give the appearance of simplicity, as so many religious people do. They practise various disciplines, join various organizations, meditate in a particular fashion, and so on – all giving an appearance of simplicity, but such conformity does not make for simplicity. Compulsion of any kind can never lead to simplicity. On the contrary, the more you suppress, the more you substitute, the more you sublimate, the less there is simplicity, whereas the more you understand the process of sublimation, suppression, substitution, the greater the possibility of being simple.

Our problems – social, environmental, political, religious – are so complex that we can solve them only by being simple, not by becoming extraordinarily erudite and clever. A simple person sees much more directly, has a more direct experience, than the complex person. Our minds are so crowded with an infinite knowledge of facts, of what others have said, that we have become incapable of being simple and having direct experience ourselves. These problems demand a new approach; and they can be so approached only when we are inwardly really simple. That simplicity comes only through self-knowledge, through understanding ourselves; the ways of our thinking and feeling; the movements of our thoughts; our responses; how we conform, through fear, to public opinion, to what others say, what the Buddha, the Christ, the great saints have said – all of which indicates our nature to conform, to be safe, to be secure. When one is seeking security, one is obviously in a state of fear and therefore there is no simplicity.

Without being simple, one cannot be sensitive – to the trees, to the birds, to the mountains, to the wind, to all the things which are going on about us in the world; if one is not simple one cannot be sensitive to the inward intimation of things. Most of us live so superficially, on the upper level of our consciousness; there we try to be thoughtful or intelligent, which is synonymous with being religious; there we try to make our minds simple, through compulsion, through discipline. But that is not simplicity. When we force the upper mind to be simple, such compulsion only hardens the mind, does not make the mind supple, clear, quick. To be simple in the whole, total process of our consciousness is extremely arduous; because there must be no inward reservation, there must be an eagerness to find out, to inquire into the process of our being, which means to be awake to every intimation, to every hint; to be aware of our fears, of our hopes, and to investigate and to be free of them more and more and more. Only then, when the mind and the heart are really simple, not encrusted, are we able to solve the many problems that confront us.

Knowledge is not going to solve our problems. You may know, for example, that there is reincarnation, that there is a continuity after death. You *may* know, I don't say you do; or you may be convinced of it. But that does not solve the problem. Death cannot be shelved by your theory, or by information, or by conviction. It is much more mysterious, much deeper, much more creative than that.

One must have the capacity to investigate all these things anew; because it is only through *direct experience* that our problems are solved, and to have direct experience there must be simplicity, which means there must be sensitivity. A mind is made dull by the weight of knowledge. A mind is made dull by the past, by the future. Only a mind that is capable of adjusting itself to the present, continually, from moment to moment, can meet the powerful influences and pressures constantly put upon us by our environment.

Thus a religious man is not really one who puts on a robe or a loin-cloth, or lives on one meal a day, or has taken innumerable vows to be this and not to be that, but one who is inwardly simple, who is not *becoming* anything. Such a mind is capable of extraordinary receptivity, because there is no barrier, there is no fear, there is no going towards something; therefore it is capable of receiving grace, God, truth, or what you will. But a mind that is *pursuing* reality is not a simple mind. A mind that is seeking out, searching, groping, agitated, is not a simple mind. A mind that conforms to any pattern of authority, inward or outward, cannot be sensitive. And it is only when a mind is really sensitive, alert, aware of all its own happenings, responses, thoughts, when it is no longer becoming, is no longer shaping itself to *be* something – only then is it capable of receiving that which is truth. It is only then that there can be happiness, for happiness is not an end – it is the result of reality. When the mind and the heart have become simple and therefore sensitive – not through any form of compulsion, direction, or imposition – then we shall see that our problems can be tackled very simply. However complex our problems, we shall be able to approach them freshly and see them differently. That is what is wanted at the present time: people who are capable of meeting this outward confusion, turmoil, antagonism anew, creatively, simply – not with theories nor formulas, either of the left or of the right. You *cannot* meet it anew if you are not simple.

A problem can be solved only when we approach it thus. We cannot approach it anew if we are thinking in terms of certain patterns of thought, religious, political or otherwise. So we must be free of all these things, to be simple. That is why it is so important to be aware, to have the capacity to understand the process of our own thinking, to be cognizant of ourselves totally; from that there comes a simplicity, there comes a humility, which is not a virtue or a practice. Humility that is gained ceases to be humility. A mind that makes itself humble is no longer a humble mind. It is only when one has humility, not a cultivated humility, that one is able to meet the things of life that are so pressing, because then one is not important, one doesn't look through one's own pressures and sense of importance; one looks at the problem for itself and then one is able to solve it.

XI

AWARENESS

To know ourselves means to know our relationship with the world – not only with the world of ideas and people, but also with nature, with the things we possess. That is, our life – life being relationship to the whole. Does the understanding of that relationship demand specialization? Obviously not. What it demands is awareness to meet life as a whole. How is one to be aware? That is our problem. How is one to have that awareness – if I may use this word without making it mean specialization? How is one to be capable of meeting life as a whole? – which means not only personal relationship with your neighbour but also with nature, with the things that you possess, with ideas, and with the things that the mind manufactures as illusion, desire and so on. How is one to be aware of this whole process of relationship? Surely that is our life, is it not? There is no life without relationship; and to understand this relationship does not mean isolation. On the contrary, it demands a full recognition or awareness of the total process of relationship.

How is one to be aware? How are we aware of anything? How are you aware of your relationship with a person? How are you aware of the trees, the call of a bird? How are you aware of your reactions when you read a newspaper? Are we aware of the superficial responses of the mind, as well as the inner responses? How are we aware of anything? First we are aware, are we not?, of a response to a stimulus; that is an obvious fact; I see something beautiful, and there is a response, then sensation, contact, identification and desire. That is the ordinary process, isn't it? We can observe what actually takes place, without studying any books.

So through identification you have pleasure and pain. And our 'capacity' is this concern with pleasure and the avoidance of pain, is it not? If you are interested in something, if it gives you pleasure, there is 'capacity' immediately; there is an awareness of that fact immediately; and if it is painful the 'capacity' is developed to avoid it. So long as we are looking to 'capacity' to understand ourselves, I think we shall fail; because the understanding of ourselves does not depend on capacity. It is not a technique that you develop, cultivate and increase through time, through constantly sharpening. This awareness of oneself can be tested, surely, in the action of relationship; it can be tested in the way we talk, the way we behave. Watch yourself without any identification, without any comparison, without any condemnation; just watch, and you will see an extraordinary thing taking place. You not only put an end to an activity which is unconscious – because most of our activities are unconscious – you not only bring that to an end, but, further, you are aware of the motives of that action, without inquiry, without digging into it.

When you are aware, you see the whole process of your thinking and action; but it can happen only when there is no condemnation. When I condemn something, I do not understand it, and it is one way of avoiding any kind of understanding. I think most of us do that purposely; we condemn immediately and we think we have understood. If we do not condemn but regard it, are aware of it, then the content, the significance of that action begins to open up. Experiment with this and you will see for yourself. Just be aware – without any sense of justification – which may appear rather negative but is not negative. On the contrary, it has the quality of passivity which is direct action; and you will discover this, if you experiment with it.

After all, if you want to understand something, you have to be in a passive mood, do you not? You cannot keep on thinking about it, speculating about it or questioning it. You have to be sensitive enough to receive the content of it. It is like being a sensitive photographic plate. If I want to understand you, I have to be passively aware; then you begin to tell me all your story. Surely that is not a question of capacity or specialization. In that process we begin to understand ourselves – not only the superficial layers of our consciousness, but the deeper, which is much more important; because *there* are all our motives and intentions, our hidden, confused demands, anxieties, fears, appetites. Outwardly we may have them all under control but inwardly they are boiling. Until those have been completely understood through awareness, obviously there cannot be freedom, there cannot be happiness, there is no intelligence.

Is intelligence a matter of specialization? – intelligence being the total awareness of our process. And is that intelligence to be cultivated through any form of specialization? Because that is what is happening, is it not? The priest, the doctor, the engineer, the industrialist, the business man, the professor – we have the mentality of all that specialization.

To realize the highest form of intelligence – which is truth, which is God, which cannot be described – to realize that, we think we have to make ourselves specialists. We study, we grope, we search out; and, with the mentality of the specialist or looking to the specialist, we study ourselves in order to develop a capacity which will help to unravel our conflicts, our miseries.

Our problem is, if we are at all aware, whether the conflicts and the miseries and the sorrows of our daily existence can be solved by another; and if they cannot, how is it possible for us to tackle them? To understand a problem obviously requires a certain intelligence, and that intelligence cannot be derived from or cultivated through specialization. It comes into being only when we are passively aware of the whole process of our consciousness, which is to be aware of ourselves without choice, without choosing what is right and what is wrong. When you are passively aware, you will see that out of that passivity – which is not idleness, which is not sleep, but extreme alertness – the problem has quite a different significance; which means there is no longer identification with the problem and therefore there is no judgement and hence the problem begins to reveal its content. If you are able to do that constantly, continuously, then every problem can be solved fundamentally, not superficially. That is the difficulty, because most of us are incapable of being passively aware, letting the problem tell the story without our interpreting it. We do not know how to look at a problem dispassionately. We are not capable of it, unfortunately, because we want a result from the problem, we want an answer, we are looking to an end; or we try to translate the problem according to our pleasure or pain; or we have an answer already on how to deal with the problem. Therefore we approach a problem, which is always new, with the old pattern. The challenge is always the new, but our response is always the old; and our difficulty is to meet the challenge adequately, that is fully. The problem is always a problem of relationship – with things, with people or with ideas; there is no other problem; and to meet the problem of relationship, with its constantly varying demands – to meet it rightly, to meet it adequately – one has to be aware passively. This passivity is not a question of determination, of will, of discipline; to be aware that we are *not* passive is the beginning. To be aware that we want a particular answer to a particular problem – surely that is the beginning: to know ourselves in relationship to the problem and how we deal with the problem. Then as we begin to know ourselves in relationship to the problem – how we respond, what are our various prejudices, demands, pursuits, in meeting that problem – this awareness will reveal the process of our own thinking, of our own inward nature; and in that there is a release.

What is important, surely, is to be aware without choice, because choice brings about conflict. The chooser is in confusion, therefore he chooses; if he is not in confusion, there is no choice. Only the person who is confused chooses what he shall do or shall not do. The man who is clear and simple does not choose; what is, is. Action based on an idea is obviously the action of choice and such action is not liberating; on the contrary, it only creates further resistance, further conflict, according to that conditioned thinking.

The important thing, therefore, is to be aware from moment to moment without accumulating the experience which awareness brings; because, the moment you accumulate, you are aware only according to that accumulation, according to that pattern, according to that experience. That is, your awareness is conditioned by your accumulation and therefore there is no longer observation but merely translation. Where there is translation, there is choice, and choice creates conflict; in conflict there can be no understanding.

Life is a matter of relationship; and to understand that relationship, which is not static, there must be an awareness which is pliable, an awareness which is alertly passive, not aggressively active. As I said, this passive awareness does not come through any form of discipline, through any practice. It is to be just aware, from moment to moment, of our thinking and feeling, not only when we are awake; for we shall see, as we go into it more deeply, that we begin to dream, that we begin to throw up all kinds of symbols which we translate as dreams. Thus we open the door into the hidden, which becomes the known; but to find the unknown, we must go beyond the door – surely, that is our difficulty. Reality is not a thing which is knowable by the mind, because the mind is the result of the known, of the past; therefore the mind must understand itself and its functioning, its truth, and only then is it possible for the unknown to *be*.

XII

DESIRE

FOR most of us, desire is quite a problem: the desire for property, for position, for power, for comfort, for immortality, for continuity, the desire to be loved, to have something permanent, satisfying, lasting, something which is beyond time. Now, what *is* desire? What is this thing that is urging, compelling us? I am not suggesting that we should be satisfied with what we have or with what we are, which is merely the opposite of what we want. We are trying to see what desire is, and if we can go into it tentatively, hesitantly, I think we shall bring about a transformation which is not a mere substitution of one object of desire for another object of desire. This is generally what we mean by 'change', is it not? Being dissatisfied with one particular object of desire, we find a substitute for it. We are everlastingly moving from one subject of desire to another which we consider to be higher, nobler, more refined; but, however refined, desire is still desire, and in this movement of desire there is endless struggle, the conflict of the opposites.

Is it not, therefore, important to find out what is desire and whether it can be transformed? What is desire? Is it not the symbol and its sensation? Desire is sensation with the object of its attainment. Is there desire without a symbol and its sensation? Obviously not. The symbol may be a picture, a person, a word, a name, an image, an idea which gives me a sensation, which makes me feel that I like or dislike it; if the sensation is pleasurable, I want to attain, to possess, to hold on to its symbol, and continue in that pleasure. From time to time, according to my inclinations and intensities, I change the picture, the image, the object. With one form of pleasure I am fed up, tired, bored, so I seek a new sensation, a new idea, a new symbol. I reject the old sensation and take on a new one, with new words, new significances, new experiences. I resist the old and yield to the new which I consider to be higher, nobler, more satisfying. Thus in desire there is a resistance and a yielding, which involves temptation; and of course in yielding to a particular symbol of desire there is always the fear of frustration.

If I observe the whole process of desire in myself I see that there is always an object towards which my mind is directed for further sensation, and that in this process there is involved resistance, temptation and discipline. There is perception, sensation, contact and desire, and the mind becomes the mechanical instrument of this process, in which symbols, words, objects are the centre around which all desire, all pursuits, all ambitions are built; that centre is the 'me'. Can I dissolve that centre of desire – not one particular desire, one particular appetite or craving, but the whole structure of desire, of longing, hoping, in which there is always the fear of frustration? The more I am frustrated, the more strength I give to the 'me'. So long as there is hoping, longing, there is always the background of fear, which again strengthens that centre. And revolution is possible only at that centre, not on the surface, which is merely a process of distraction, a superficial change leading to mischievous action.

When I am aware of this whole structure of desire, I see how my mind has become a dead centre, a mechanical process of memory. Having tired of one desire, I automatically want to fulfil myself in another. My mind is always experiencing in terms of sensation, it is the instrument of sensation. Being bored with a particular sensation, I seek a new sensation, which may be what I call the realization of God; but it is still sensation. I have had enough of this world and its travail and I want peace, the peace that is everlasting; so I meditate, control, I shape my mind in order to experience that peace. The experiencing of that peace is still sensation. So my mind is the mechanical instrument of sensation, of memory, a dead centre from which I act, think. The objects I pursue are the projections of the mind as symbols from which it derives sensations. The word 'God', the word 'love', the word 'communism', the word 'democracy', the word 'nationalism' – these are all symbols which give sensations to the mind, and therefore the mind clings to them. As you and I know, every sensation comes to an end, and so we proceed from one sensation to another; and every sensation strengthens the habit of seeking further sensation. Thus the mind becomes merely an instrument of sensation and memory, and in that process we are caught. So long as the mind is seeking further experience it can think only in terms of sensation; and any experience that may be spontaneous, creative, vital, strikingly new, it immediately reduces to sensation and pursues that sensation, which then becomes a memory. Therefore the experience is dead and the mind becomes merely a stagnant pool of the past.

If we have gone into it at all deeply we are familiar with this process; and we seem to be incapable of going beyond. We *want* to go beyond, because we are tired of this endless routine, this mechanical pursuit of sensation; so the mind projects the idea of truth, of God; it dreams of a vital change and of playing a principal part in that change, and so on and on and on. Hence there is never a creative state. In myself I see this process of desire going on, which is mechanical, repetitive, which holds the mind in a process of routine and makes of it a dead centre of the past in which there is no creative spontaneity. Also there are sudden moments of creation, of that which is not of the mind, which is not of memory, which is not of sensation or of desire.

Our problem, therefore, is to understand desire – not how far it should go or where it should come to an end, but to understand the whole process of desire, the cravings, the longings, the burning appetites. Most of us think that possessing very little indicates freedom from desire – and how we worship those who have but few things! A loincloth, a robe, symbolizes our desire to be free from desire; but that again is a very superficial reaction. Why begin at the superficial level of giving up outward possessions when your mind is crippled with innumerable wants, innumerable desires, beliefs, struggles? Surely it is *there* that the revolution must take place, not in how much you possess or what clothes you wear or how many meals you eat. But we are impressed by these things because our minds are very superficial.

Your problem and my problem is to see whether the mind can ever be free from desire, from sensation. Surely creation has nothing to do with sensation; reality, God, or what you will, is not a state which can be experienced as sensation. When you have an experience, what happens? It has given you a certain sensation, a feeling of elation or depression. Naturally, you try to avoid, put aside, the state of depression; but if it is a joy, a feeling of elation, you pursue it. Your experience had produced a pleasurable sensation and you want more of it; and the 'more' strengthens the dead centre of the mind, which is ever craving further experience. Hence the mind cannot experience anything new, it is *incapable* of experiencing anything new, because its approach is always through memory, through recognition; and that which is recognized through memory is not truth, creation, reality. Such a mind cannot experience reality; it can only experience sensation, and creation is not sensation; creation is something that is everlastingly new from moment to moment.

Now I realize the state of my own mind; I see that it is the instrument of sensation and desire, or rather that it *is* sensation and desire, and that it is mechanically caught up in routine. Such a mind is incapable of ever receiving or feeling out the new; for the new must obviously be something beyond sensation, which is always the old. So, this mechanical process with its sensations has to come to an end, has it not? The wanting more, the pursuit of symbols, words, images, with their sensation – all that has to come to an end. Only then is it possible for the mind to be in that state of creativeness in which the new can always come into being. If you will understand without being mesmerized by words, by habits, by ideas, and see how important it is to have the new constantly impinging on the mind, then, perhaps, you will understand the process of desire, the routine, the boredom, the constant craving for experience. Then I think you will begin to see that desire has very little significance in life for a man who is really seeking. Obviously there are certain physical needs: food, clothing, shelter, but they never become psychological appetites, things on which the mind builds itself as a centre of desire. Beyond the physical needs, *any* form of desire – for greatness, for truth, for virtue – becomes a psychological process by which the mind builds the idea of the 'me' and strengthens itself at the centre.

When you see this process, when you are really aware of it without opposition, without a sense of temptation, without resistance, without justifying or judging it, then you will discover that the mind is capable of receiving the new and that the new is never a sensation; therefore it can never be recognized, re-experienced. It is a state of being in which creativeness comes without invitation, without memory; and that is reality.

XIII

RELATIONSHIP AND ISOLATION

LIFE is experience, experience in relationship. One cannot live in isolation; so life is relationship and relationship is action. And how can one have that capacity for understanding relationship which is life? Does not relationship mean not only communion with people but intimacy with things and ideas? Life is relationship, which is expressed through contact with things, with people and with ideas. In understanding relationship we shall have capacity to meet life fully, adequately. So our problem is not capacity – for capacity is not independent of relationship – but rather the understanding of relationship, which will naturally produce the capacity for quick pliability, for quick adjustment, for quick response.

Relationship, surely, is the mirror in which you discover yourself. Without relationship you are not; to be is to be related; to be related is existence. You exist only in relationship; otherwise you do not exist, existence has no meaning. It is not because you *think* you are that you come into existence. You exist because you are related; and it is the lack of understanding of relationship that causes conflict.

Now there is no understanding of relationship, because we use relationship merely as a means of furthering achievement, furthering transformation, furthering becoming. But relationship is a means of self-discovery, because relationship is *to be*; it is existence. To understand myself, I must understand relationship. Relationship is a mirror in which I can see myself. That mirror can either be distorted, or it can be 'as is', reflecting that which *is*. But most of us see in relationship, in that mirror, things we would *rather* see; we do not see what *is*. We would rather idealize, escape, we would rather live in the future than understand that relationship in the immediate present.

Now if we examine our life, our relationship with another, we shall see that it is a process of isolation. We are really not concerned with another; though we talk a great deal about it, actually we are not concerned. We are related to someone only so long as that relationship gives us a refuge, so long as it satisfies us. But the moment there is a disturbance in the relationship which produces discomfort in ourselves, we discard that relationship. In other words, there is relationship only so long as we are gratified. This may sound harsh, but if you really examine your life very closely you will see it is a fact; and to avoid a fact is to live in ignorance, which can never produce right relationship. If we look into our lives and observe relationship, we see it is a process of building resistance against another, a wall over which we look and observe the other; but we always retain the wall and remain behind it, whether it be a psychological wall, a material wall, an economic wall or a national wall. So long as we live in isolation, behind a wall, there is no relationship with another; and we live enclosed because it is much more gratifying, we think it is much more secure. The world is so disruptive, there is so much sorrow, so much pain, war, destruction, misery, that we want to escape and live within the walls of security of our own psychological being. So, relationship with most of us is actually a process of isolation, and obviously such relationship builds a society which is also isolating. That is exactly what is happening throughout the world: you remain in your isolation and stretch your hand over the wall, calling it nationalism, brotherhood or what you will, but actually sovereign governments, armies, continue. Still clinging to your own limitations, you think you can create world unity, world peace – which is impossible. So long as you have a frontier, whether national, economic, religious or social, it is an obvious fact that there cannot be peace in the world.

The process of isolation is a process of the search for power; whether one is seeking power individually or for a racial or national group there must be isolation, because the very desire for power, for position, is separatism. After all, that is what each one wants, is it not? He wants a powerful position in which he can dominate, whether at home, in the office, or in a bureaucratic régime. Each one is seeking power, and in seeking power he will establish a society which is based on power, military, industrial, economic, and so on – which again is obvious. Is not the desire for power in its very nature isolating? I think it is very important to understand this, because the man who wants a peaceful world in which there are no wars, no appalling destruction, no catastrophic misery on an immeasurable scale, must understand this fundamental question, must he not? A man who is affectionate, who is kindly, has no sense of power, and therefore such a man is not bound to any nationality, to any flag. He has no flag.

There is no such thing as living in isolation – no country, no people, no individual, can live in isolation; yet, because you are seeking power in so many different ways, you breed isolation. The nationalist is a curse because through his very nationalistic, patriotic spirit, he is creating a wall of isolation. He is so identified with his country that he builds a wall against another. What happens when you build a wall against something? That something is constantly beating against your wall. When you resist something, the very resistance indicates that you are in conflict with the other. So nationalism, which is a process of isolation, which is the outcome of the search for power, cannot bring about peace in the world. The man who is a nationalist and talks of brotherhood is telling a lie; he is living in a state of contradiction.

Can one live in the world without the desire for power, for position, for authority? Obviously one can. One does it when one does not identify oneself with something greater. This identification with something greater – the party, the country, the race, the religion, God – is the search for power. Because you in yourself are empty, dull, weak, you like to identify yourself with something greater. That desire to identify yourself with something greater is the desire for power.

Relationship is a process of self-revelation, and, without knowing oneself, the ways of one's own mind and heart, merely to establish an outward order, a system, a cunning formula, has very little meaning. What is important is to understand oneself in relationship with another. Then relationship becomes not a process of isolation but a movement in which you discover your own motives, your own thoughts, your own pursuits; and that very discovery is the beginning of liberation, the beginning of transformation.

XIV

THE THINKER AND THE THOUGHT

In all our experiences, there is always the experiencer, the observer, who is gathering to himself more and more or denying himself. Is that not a wrong process and is that not a pursuit which does not bring about the creative state? If it is a wrong process, can we wipe it out completely and put it aside? That can come about only when I experience, not as a thinker experiences, but when I am aware of the false process and see that there is only a state in which the thinker is the thought.

So long as I am experiencing, so long as I am becoming,

there must be this dualistic action, there must be the thinker and the thought, two separate processes at work; there is no integration, there is always a centre which is operating through the will of action to be or not to be – collectively, individually, nationally and so on. Universally, this is the process. So long as effort is divided into the experiencer and the experience, there must be deterioration. Integration is only possible when the thinker is no longer the observer. That is, we know at present there are the thinker and the thought, the observer and the observed, the experiencer and the experienced; there are two different states. Our effort is to bridge the two.

The will of action is always dualistic. Is it possible to go beyond this will which is separative and discover a state in which this dualistic action is not? That can only be found when we directly experience the state in which the thinker is the thought. We now think the thought is separate from the thinker; but is that so? We would like to think it is, because then the thinker can explain matters through his thought. The effort of the thinker is to become more or become less; and therefore, in that struggle, in that action of the will, in 'becoming', there is always the deteriorating factor; we are pursuing a false process and not a true process.

Is there a division between the thinker and the thought? So long as they are separate, divided, our effort is wasted; we are pursuing a false process which is destructive and which is the deteriorating factor. We think the thinker is separate from his thought. When I find that I am greedy, possessive, brutal, I think I should not be all this. The thinker then tries to alter his thoughts and therefore effort is made to 'become'; in that process of effort he pursues the false illusion that there are two separate processes, whereas there is only one process. Therein, I think, lies the fundamental factor of deterioration.

Is it possible to experience that state when there is only one entity and not two separate processes, the experiencer and the experience? Then perhaps we shall find out what it is to be creative, and what the state is in which there is no deterioration at any time, in whatever relationship man may be.

I am greedy. I and greed are not two different states; there is only one thing and that is greed. If I am aware that I am greedy, what happens? I make an effort not to be greedy, either for sociological reasons or for religious reasons; that effort will always be in a small limited circle; I may extend the circle but it is always limited. Therefore the deteriorating factor is there. But when I look a little more deeply and closely, I see that the maker of effort is the cause of greed and he is greed itself; and I also see that there is no 'me' and greed, existing separately, but that there is only greed. If I realize that I am greedy, that there is not the observer who is greedy but I am myself greed, then our whole question is entirely different; our response to it is entirely different; then our effort is not destructive.

What will you do when your whole being is greed, when whatever action you do is greed? Unfortunately, we don't think along those lines. There is the 'me', the superior entity, the soldier who is controlling, dominating. To me that process is destructive. It is an illusion and we know why we do it. I divide myself into the high and the low in order to continue. If there is only greed, completely, not 'I' operating greed, what happens? Surely then there is a different process at work altogether, a different problem comes into being. It is that problem which is creative, in which there is no sense of 'I' dominating, becoming, positively or negatively. We must come to that state if we would be creative. In that state, there is no maker of effort. It is not a matter of verbalizing or of trying to find out what that state is; if you set about it in that way you will lose and you will never find. What is important is to see that the maker of effort and the object towards which he is making effort are the same. That requires enormously great understanding, watchfulness, to see how the mind divides itself into the high and the low – the high being the security, the permanent entity – but still remaining a process of thought and therefore of time. If we can understand this as direct experience, then you will see that quite a different factor comes into being.

XV

CAN THINKING SOLVE OUR PROBLEMS?

THOUGHT has not solved our problems and I don't think it ever will. We have relied on the intellect to show us the way out of our compexity. The more cunning, the more hideous, the more subtle the intellect is the greater the variety of systems, of theories, of ideas. And ideas do not solve any of our human problems; they never have and they never will. The mind is not the solution; the way of thought is obviously not the way out of our difficulty. It seems to me that we should first understand this process of thinking, and perhaps be able to go beyond – for when thought ceases, perhaps we shall be able to find a way which will help us to solve our problems, not only the individual but also the collective.

Thinking has not solved our problems. The clever ones, the philosophers, the scholars, the political leaders, have not really solved any of our human problems – which are the relationship between you and another, between you and myself. So far we have used the mind, the intellect, to help us investigate the problem and thereby are hoping to find a solution. Can thought ever dissolve our problems? Is not thought, unless it is in the laboratory or on the drawing-board, always self-protecting, self-perpetuating, conditioned? Is not its activity self-centred? And can such thought ever resolve any of the problems which thought itself has created? Can the mind, which has created the problems, resolve those things that it has itself brought forth?

Surely thinking is a reaction. If I ask you a question, you respond to it – you respond according to your memory, to your prejudices, to your upbringing, to the climate, to the whole background of your conditioning; you reply accordingly, you think accordingly. The centre of this background is the 'me' in the process of action. So long as that background is not understood, so long as that thought process, that self which creates the problem, is not understood and put an end to, we are bound to have conflict, within and without, in thought, in emotion, in action. No solution of any kind, however clever, however well thought out, can ever put an end to the conflict between man and man, between you and me. Realizing this, being aware of how thought springs up and from what source, then we ask, 'Can thought ever come to an end?'

That is one of the problems, is it not? Can thought resolve our problems? By thinking over the problem, have you resolved it? Any kind of problem – economic, social, religious – has it ever been really solved by thinking? In your daily life, the more you think about a problem, the more complex, the more irresolute, the more uncertain it becomes. Is that not so in our actual, daily life? You may, in thinking out certain facets of the problem, see more clearly another person's point of view, but thought cannot see the completeness and fullness of the problem – it can see only partially and a partial answer is not a complete answer, therefore it is not a solution.

The more we think over a problem, the more we investigate, analyse and discuss it, the more complex it becomes. So is it possible to look at the problem comprehensively, wholly? How is this possible? Because that, it seems to me, is our major difficulty. Our problems are being multiplied – there is imminent danger of war, there is every kind of disturbance in our relationships – and how can we understand all that comprehensively, as a whole? When is that possible? Surely it is only possible when the process of thinking – which has its source in the 'me', the self, in the background of tradition, of conditioning, of prejudice, of hope, of despair – has come to an end. Can we understand this self, not by analysing, but by seeing the thing as it is, being aware of it as a fact and not as a theory? – not seeking to dissolve the self in order to achieve a result but seeing the activity of the self, the 'me', constantly in action? Can we *look* at it, without any movement to destroy or to encourage? That is the problem, is it not? If, in each one of us, the centre of the 'me' is non-existent, with its desire for power, position, authority, continuance, self-preservation, surely our problems will come to an end!

The self is a problem that thought cannot resolve. There must be an awareness which is not of thought. To be aware, without condemnation or justification, of the activities of the self – just to be aware – is sufficient. If you are aware in order to find out *how* to resolve the problem, in order to transform it, in order to produce a result, then it is still within the field of the self, of the 'me'. So long as we are seeking a result, whether through analysis, through awareness, through constant examination of every thought, we are still within the field of thought, which is within the field of the 'me', of the ego.

As long as the activity of the mind exists, surely there can be no love. When there is love, we shall have no social problems. But love is not something to be acquired. The mind can seek to acquire it, like a new thought, a new gadget, a new way of thinking; but the mind cannot be in a state of love so long as thought is acquiring love. So long as the mind is seeking to be in a state of non-greed, surely it is still greedy, is it not? Similarly, so long as the mind wishes, desires, and practises in order to be in a state in which there is love, surely it denies that state, does it not?

Seeing this problem, this complex problem of living, and being aware of the process of our own thinking and realizing that it actually leads nowhere – when we deeply realize that, then surely there is a state of intelligence which is not individual or collective. Then the problem of the relationship of the individual to society, of the individual to the community, of the individual to reality, ceases; because then there is only intelligence, which is neither personal nor impersonal. It is this intelligence alone, I feel, that can solve our immense problems. That cannot be a result; it comes into being only when we understand this whole total process of thinking, not only at the conscious level but also at the deeper, hidden levels of consciousness.

To understand any of these problems we have to have a very quiet mind, a very still mind, so that the mind can look at the problem without interposing ideas or theories, without any distraction. That is one of our difficulties – because thought has become a distraction. When I want to understand, look at something, I don't have to think about it – I *look* at it. The moment I begin to think, to have ideas, opinions about it, I am already in a state of distraction, looking away from the thing which I must understand. So thought, when you have a problem, becomes a distraction – though being an idea, opinion, judgement, comparison – which prevents us from looking and thereby understanding and resolving the problem. Unfortunately for most of us thought has become so important. You say, 'How can I exist, be, without thinking? How can I have a blank mind?' To have a blank mind is to be in a state of stupor, idiocy or what you will, and your instinctive reaction is to reject it. But surely a mind that is very quiet, a mind that is not distracted by its own thought, a mind that is open, can look at the problem very directly and very simply. And it is this capacity to look without any distraction at our problems that is the only solution. For that there must be a quiet, tranquil mind.

Such a mind is not a result, is not an end-product of a practice, of meditation, of control. It comes into being through no form of discipline or compulsion or sublimation, without any effort of the 'me', of thought; it comes into being when I understand the whole process of thinking – when I can see a fact without any distraction. In that state of tranquillity of a mind that is really still there is love. And it is love alone that can solve all our human problems.

XVI

TIME AND TRANSFORMATION

I WOULD like to talk a little about what is time, because I
think the enrichment, the beauty and significance of that
which is timeless, of that which is true, can be experienced
only when we understand the whole process of time. After
all, we are seeking, each in his own way, a sense of happiness, of enrichment. Surely a life that has significance, the
riches of true happiness, is not of time. Like love, such a life
is timeless; and to understand that which is timeless, we
must not approach it through time but rather understand
time. We must not utilize time as a means of attaining,
realizing, apprehending the timeless. That is what we are
doing most of our lives: spending time in trying to grasp
that which is timeless, so it is important to understand what
we mean by time, because I think it is possible to be free of
time. It is very important to understand time as a whole
and not partially.

It is interesting to realize that our lives are mostly spent
in time – time, not in the sense of chronological sequence,
of minutes, hours, days and years, but in the sense of
psychological memory. We live by time, we are the result
of time. The present is merely the passage of the past to the
future. Our minds, our activities, our being, are founded on
time; without time we cannot think, because thought is the
result of time, thought is the product of many yesterdays
and there is no thought without memory. Memory is time;
for there are two kinds of time, the chronological and the
psychological. There is time as yesterday by the watch and
as yesterday by memory. You cannot reject chronological
time; it would be absurd – you would miss your train. But
is there really any time at all apart from chronological
time? Is there time as the mind thinks of it? Is there time
apart from the mind? Surely time, psychological time, is the
product of the mind. Without the foundation of thought

there is no time – time merely being memory as yesterday in conjunction with today, which moulds tomorrow. That is, memory of yesterday's experience in response to the present is creating the future – which is still the process of thought, a path of the mind. The thought process brings about psychological progress in time but is it real, as real as chronological time? And can we use that time which is of the mind as a means of understanding the eternal, the timeless? As I said, happiness is not of yesterday, happiness is not the product of time, happiness is always in the present, a timeless state. I do not know if you have noticed that when you have ecstasy, a creative joy, a series of bright clouds surrounded by dark clouds, in that moment there is no time: there is only the immediate present. The mind, coming in after the experiencing in the present, remembers and wishes to continue it, gathering more and more to itself, thereby creating time. So time is created by the 'more'; time is acquisition and time is also detachment, which is still an acquisition of the mind. Therefore merely disciplining the mind in time, conditioning thought within the framework of time, which is memory, surely does not reveal that which is timeless.

Is transformation a matter of time? Most of us are accustomed to think that time is necessary for transformation: I am something, and to change what I am into what I should be requires time. I am greedy, with greed's results of confusion, antagonism, conflict, and misery; to bring about the transformation, which is non-greed, we think time is necessary. That is to say time is considered as a means of evolving into something greater, of becoming something. The problem is this: One is violent, greedy, envious, angry, vicious or passionate. To transform what *is*, is time necessary? First of all, why do we want to change what *is*, or bring about a transformation? Why? Because what we are dissatisfies us; it creates conflict, disturbance, and, disliking that state, we want something better, something nobler, more idealistic. Therefore we desire transformation because there is pain, discomfort, conflict. Is conflict overcome by time? If you say it will be overcome by time, you are still in conflict. You may say it will take twenty days or twenty years to get rid of conflict, to change what you are, but during that time you are still in conflict and therefore time does not bring about transformation. When we use time as a means of acquiring a quality, a virtue or a state of being, we are merely postponing or avoiding what *is*; and I think it is important to understand this point. Greed or violence causes pain, disturbance in the world of our relationship with another, which is society; and being conscious of this state of disturbance, which we term greed or violence, we say to ourselves, 'I will get out of it in time; I will practise non-violence, I will practise non-envy, I will practise peace.' Being in a state of conflict you want to achieve a state in which there is no conflict. Now is that state of no conflict the result of time, of a duration? Obviously not; because, while you are achieving a state of non-violence, you are still being violent and are therefore still in conflict.

Our problem is, can a conflict, a disturbance, be overcome in a period of time, whether it be days, years or lives? What happens when you say, 'I am going to practise non-violence during a certain period of time'? The very practice indicates that you are in conflict, does it not? You would not practice if you were not resisting conflict; you say the resistance to conflict is necessary in order to overcome conflict and for that resistance you must have time. But the very resistance to conflict is itself a form of conflict. You are spending your energy in resisting conflict in the form of what you call greed, envy or violence but your mind is still in conflict, so it is important to see the falseness of the process of depending on time as a means of overcoming violence and thereby be free of that process. Then you are able to be what you are: a psychological disturbance which is violence itself.

To understand anything, any human or scientific problem, what is important, what is essential? A quiet mind, is it not?, a mind that is intent on understanding. It is not a mind that is exclusive, that is trying to concentrate – which again is an effort of resistance. If I really want to understand something, there is immediately a quiet state of mind. When you want to listen to music or look at a picture which you love, which you have a feeling for, what is the state of your mind? Immediately there is a quietness, is there not? When you are listening to music, your mind does not wander all over the place; you are listening. Similarly, when you want to understand conflict, you are no longer depending on time at all; you are simply confronted with what *is*, which is conflict. Then immediately there comes a quietness, a stillness of mind. When you no longer depend on time as a means of transforming what *is* because you see the falseness of that process, then you are confronted with what *is*, and as you are interested to understand what *is*, naturally you have a quiet mind. In that alert yet passive state of mind there is understanding. So long as the mind is in conflict, blaming, resisting, condemning, there can be no understanding. If I want to understand you, I must not condemn you, obviously. It is that quiet mind, that still mind, which brings about transformation. When the mind is no longer resisting, no longer avoiding, no longer discarding or blaming what *is* but is simply passively aware, then in that passivity of the mind you will find, if you really go into the problem, that there comes a transformation.

Revolution is only possible *now*, not in the future; regeneration is today, not tomorrow. If you will experiment with what I have been saying, you will find that there is immediate regeneration, a newness, a quality of freshness; because the mind is always still when it is interested, when it desires or has the intention to understand. The difficulty with most of us is that we have not the intention to understand, because we are afraid that if we understood it might bring about a revolutionary action in our life, and therefore we resist. It is the defence mechanism that is at work when we use time or an ideal as a means of gradual transformation.

Thus regeneration is only possible in the present, not in the future, not tomorrow. A man who relies on time as a means through which he can gain happiness or realize truth or God is merely deceiving himself; he is living in ignorance and therefore in conflict. A man who sees that time is not the way out of our difficulty and who is therefore free from the false, such a man naturally has the intention to understand; therefore his mind is quiet spontaneously, without compulsion, without practice. When the mind is still, tranquil, not seeking any answer or any solution, neither resisting nor avoiding – it is only then that there can be a regeneration, because then the mind is capable of perceiving what is true; and it is truth that liberates, not your effort to be free.

PART TWO

For the Young

I WONDER if we have ever asked ourselves what education means. Why do we go to school, why do we learn various subjects, why do we pass examinations and compete with each other for better grades? What does this so-called education mean, and what is it all about? This is really a very important question, not only for the students, but also for the parents, for the teachers, and for everyone who loves this earth. Why do we go through the struggle to be educated? Is it merely in order to pass some examinations and get a job? Or is it the function of education to prepare us while we are young to understand the whole process of life? Having a job and earning one's livelihood is necessary – but is that all? Are we being educated only for that? Surely, life is not merely a job, an occupation; life is something extraordinarily wide and profound, it is a great mystery, a vast realm in which we function as human beings. If we merely prepare ourselves to earn a livelihood, we shall miss the whole point of life; and to understand life is much more important than merely to prepare for examinations and become very proficient in mathematics, physics, or what you will.

So, whether we are teachers or students, is it not important to ask ourselves why we are educating or being educated? And what does life mean? Is not life an extraordinary thing? The birds, the flowers, the flourishing trees, the heavens, the stars, the rivers and the fish therein – all this is life. Life is the poor and the rich; life is the constant battle between groups, races and nations; life is meditation; life is what we call religion, and it is also the subtle, hidden things of the mind – the envies, the ambitions, the passions, the fears, fulfilments and anxieties. All this and much more is life. But we generally prepare ourselves to understand only one small corner of it. We pass certain examinations, find a job, get married, have children, and then become more and more like machines. We remain fearful, anxious, frightened of life. So, is it the function of education to help us understand the whole process of life, or is it merely to prepare us for a vocation, for the best job we can get?

What is going to happen to all of us when we grow to be men and women? Have you ever asked yourselves what you are going to do when you grow up? In all likelihood you will get married, and before you know where you are you will be mothers and fathers; and you will then be tied to a job, or to the kitchen, in which you will gradually wither away. Is that all that *your* life is going to be? Have you ever asked yourselves this question? Should you not ask it? If your family is wealthy you may have a fairly good position already assured, your father may give you a comfortable job, or you may get richly married; but there also you will decay, deteriorate.

Surely, education has no meaning unless it helps you to understand the vast expanse of life with all its subtleties, with its extraordinary beauty, its sorrows and joys. You may win degrees, you may have a series of letters after your name and land a very good job; but then what? What is the point of it all if in the process your mind becomes dull, weary, stupid? So, while you are young, must you not seek to find out what life is all about? And is it not the true function of education to cultivate in you the intelligence which will try to find the answer to all these problems? Do you know what intelligence is? It is the capacity, surely, to think freely, without fear, without a formula, so that you begin to discover for yourself what is real, what is true; but if you are frightened you will never be intelligent. Any form of ambition, spiritual or mundane, breeds anxiety, fear; therefore ambition does not help to bring about a mind that is clear, simple, direct, and hence intelligent.

You know, it is really very important while you are young to live in an environment in which there is no fear. Most of us, as we grow older, become frightened; we are afraid of living, afraid of losing a job, afraid of tradition, afraid of what the neighbours, or what the wife or husband will say, afraid of death. Most of us have fear in one form or another;

and where there is fear there is no intelligence. And is it not possible for all of us, while we are young, to be in an environment where there is no fear but rather an atmosphere of freedom – freedom, not just to do what we like, but to understand the whole process of living? Life is really very beautiful, it is not this ugly thing that we have made of it; and you can appreciate its richness, its depth, its extraordinary loveliness only when you revolt against everything – against organized religion, against tradition, against the present rotten society – so that you as a human being find out for yourself what is true. Not to imitate but to discover – *that* is education, is it not? It is very easy to conform to what your society or your parents and teachers tell you. That is a safe and easy way of existing; but that is not living, because in it there is fear, decay, death. To live is to find out for yourself what is true, and you can do this only when there is freedom, when there is continuous revolution inwardly, within yourself.

But you are not encouraged to do this; no one tells you to question, to find out for yourself what God is, because if you were to rebel you would become a danger to all that is false. Your parents and society want you to live safely, and you also want to live safely. Living safely generally means living in imitation and therefore in fear. Surely, the function of education is to help each one of us to live freely and without fear, is it not? And to create an atmosphere in which there is no fear requires a great deal of thinking on your part as well as on the part of the teacher, the educator.

Do you know what this means – what an extraordinary thing it would be to create an atmosphere in which there is no fear? And we *must* create it, because we see that the world is caught up in endless wars; it is guided by politicians who are always seeking power; it is a world of lawyers, policemen and soldiers, of ambitious men and women all wanting position and all fighting each other to get it. Then there are the so-called saints, the religious *gurus* with their followers; they also want power, position, here or in the next life. It is a mad world, completely confused, in which the communist is fighting the capitalist, the socialist is resisting both, and everybody is against somebody, struggling to arrive at a safe place, a position of power or comfort. The world is torn by conflicting beliefs, by caste and class distinctions, by separative nationalities, by every form of stupidity and cruelty – and this is the world you are being educated to fit into. You are encouraged to fit into the framework of this disastrous society; your parents want you to do that, and you also want to fit in.

Now, is it the function of education merely to help you to conform to the pattern of this rotten social order, or is it to give you freedom – complete freedom to grow and create a different society, a new world? We want to have this freedom, not in the future, but now, otherwise we may all be destroyed. We must create immediately an atmosphere of freedom so that you can live and find out for yourselves what is true, so that you become intelligent, so that you are able to face the world and understand it, not just conform to it, so that inwardly, deeply, psychologically, you are in constant revolt; because it is only those who are in constant revolt who discover what is true, not the man who conforms, who follows some tradition. It is only when you are constantly inquiring, constantly observing, constantly learning, that you find truth, God, or love; and you cannot inquire, observe, learn, you cannot be deeply aware, if you are afraid. So the function of education, surely, is to eradicate, inwardly as well as outwardly, this fear that destroys human thought, human relationship and love.

II

PERHAPS we can approach the problem of fear from another angle. Fear does extraordinary things to most of us. It creates all kinds of illusions and problems. Until we go into it very deeply and really understand it, fear will always distort our actions. Fear twists our ideas and makes crooked the way of our life; it creates barriers between people, and it certainly destroys love. So the more we go into fear, the more we understand and are really free of it, the greater will be our contact with all that is around us. At present our vital contacts with life are very few, are they not? But if we can free ourselves of fear we shall have wide contacts, deep understanding, real sympathy, loving consideration, and great will be the extension of our horizon. So let us see if we can talk about fear from a different point of view.

I wonder if you have noticed that most of us want some kind of psychological safety. We want security, somebody on whom to lean. As a small child holds on to the mother's hand, so we want something to cling to; we want somebody to love us. Without a sense of security, without a mental safeguard, we feel lost, do we not? We are used to leaning on others, looking to others to guide and help us, and without this support we feel confused, afraid, we do not know what to think, how to act. The moment we are left to ourselves, we feel lonely, insecure, uncertain. From this arises fear, does it not?

So we want something to give us a sense of certainty, and we have safeguards of many different kinds. We have inward as well as outward protections. When we close the windows and doors of our house and stay inside, we feel very secure, we feel safe, unmolested. But life is not like that. Life is constantly knocking at our door, trying to push open our windows that we may see more; and if out of fear we lock the doors, bolt all the windows, the knocking only grows louder. The closer we cling to security in any form, the more life comes and pushes us. The more we are afraid and enclose ourselves, the greater is our suffering, because life won't leave us alone. We want to be secure but life says we cannot be; and so our struggle begins. We seek security in society, in tradition, in our relationship with our fathers and mothers, with our wives or husbands; but life always breaks through the walls of our security.

We also seek security or comfort in ideas, do we not? Have you observed how ideas come into being and how the mind clings to them? You have an idea of something beautiful you saw when you were out for a walk, and your mind goes back to that idea, that memory. You read a book and you get an idea to which you cling. So you must see how ideas arise, and how they become a means of inward comfort, security, something to which the mind clings.

Have you ever thought about this question of ideas? If you have an idea and I have an idea, and each of us thinks that his own idea is better than the other's, we struggle, don't we? I try to convince you, and you try to convince me. The whole world is built on ideas and the conflict between them; and if you go into it, you will find that merely clinging to an idea has no meaning. But have you noticed how your father, your mother, your teachers, your aunts and uncles all cling hard to what they think?

Now, how does an idea come into being? How do you get an idea? When you have the idea of going out for a walk, for example, how does it arise? It is very interesting to find out. If you observe – you will see how an idea of that kind arises, and how your mind clings to it, pushing everything else aside. The idea of going out for a walk is a response to a sensation, is it not? You have gone out for a walk before and it has left a pleasurable feeling or sensation; you want to do it again, so the idea is created and then put into action. When you see a beautiful car, there is a sensation, is there not? The sensation comes from the very looking at the car. The seeing creates the sensation. From the sensation there is born the idea, 'I want that car, it is my car', and the idea then becomes very dominant.

We seek security in outward possessions and relationships, and also in inward ideas or beliefs. I believe in God, in rituals, I believe that I should be married in a certain way, I believe in reincarnation, in life after death, and so on. These beliefs are all created by my desires, by my prejudices, and to these beliefs I cling. I have external securities, outside the skin as it were, and also inward securities; remove or question them, and I am afraid; I will push you away, I will battle with you if you threaten my security.

Now, is there any such thing as security? Do you understand? We have ideas about security. We may feel safe with our parents, or in a particular job. The way we think, the way of our life, the way we look at things – with all this we may feel satisfied. Most of us are very content to be enclosed in safe ideas. But can we ever be safe, can we ever be secure, however many outward or inward safeguards we may have? Outwardly, one's bank may fail tomorrow, one's father or mother may die, there may be a revolution. And is there any safety in ideas? We like to think we are safe in our ideas, in our beliefs, in our prejudices; but are we? They are walls which are not real; they are merely our conceptions, our sensations. We like to believe there is a God who is looking after us, or that we are going to be reborn richer, more noble than we are now. That may be, or it may not be. So we can see for ourselves, if we look into both the outward and the inward securities, that there is no safety in life at all.

Seeing all this, a really thoughtful person begins to free himself from every kind of security, inward or outward. This is extremely difficult, because it means that you are alone – alone in the sense that you are not dependent. The moment you depend, there is fear; and where there is fear, there is no love. When you love, you are not lonely. The sense of loneliness arises only when you are frightened of being alone and of not knowing what to do. When you are controlled by ideas, isolated by beliefs, then fear is inevitable; and when you are afraid, you are completely blind.

So, the teachers and the parents together have to solve this problem of fear. But unfortunately your parents are afraid of what you might do if you don't get married, or if you don't get a job. They are afraid of your going wrong, or of what people might say, and because of this fear they want to make you do certain things. Their fear is clothed in what they call love. They want to look after you, therefore you must do this or that. But if you go behind the wall of their so-called affection and consideration, you will find there is fear for your safety, for your respectability; and you also are afraid because you have depended on other people for so long.

That is why it is very important that you should, from the tenderest age, begin to question and break down these feelings of fear so that you are not isolated by them, and are not enclosed in ideas, in traditions, in habits, but are a free human being with creative vitality.

III

Is it not very important, while we are young, to be loved, and also to know what it means to love? But it seems to me that most of us do not love, nor are we loved. And I think it is essential, while we are young, to go into this problem very seriously and understand it; for then perhaps we can be sensitive enough to feel love, to know its quality, its perfume, so that when we grow older it will not be entirely destroyed. So let us consider this question.

What does it mean to love? Is it an ideal, something far away, unattainable? Or can love be felt by each one of us at odd moments of the day? To have the quality of sympathy, of understanding, to help someone naturally, without any motive, to be spontaneously kind, to care for a plant or a dog, to be sympathetic to the villager, generous to your friend, to a neighbour – is this not what we mean by love? Is not love a state in which there is no sense of resentment, but everlasting forgiveness? And is it not possible, while we are young to feel it?

While we are young many of us do experience this feeling – a sudden out-going sympathy for the villager, for a dog, for those who are little or helpless. And should it not be constantly tended? Should you not always give some part of the day to aiding another, to caring for a tree or a garden, to helping in the house, so that, as you grow to maturity you will know what it means to be considerate naturally, without enforcement, without motive? Should you not have this quality of real affection?

Real affection cannot be brought into being artificially, you have to *feel* it; and your guardian, your parents, your teachers must also feel it. Most people have no real affection; they are too concerned with their achievements, their longings, their knowledge, their success. They give such colossal importance to what they have done and want to do that it ultimately destroys them.

That is why it is very important, while you are young, to help look after the rooms, or to care for a number of trees which you yourself have planted, or to go to the assistance of a sick friend, so that there is a subtle feeling of sympathy, of concern, of generosity – real generosity which is not just of the mind, and which makes you want to share with somebody whatever you may have, however little. If you do not have this feeling of love, of generosity, of kindness, of gentleness, while you are young, it will be very difficult to have it when you are older; but if you begin to have it now, then perhaps you can awaken it in others.

To have sympathy and affection implies freedom from fear, does it not? But you see, it is very difficult to grow up in this world without fear, without having some personal motive in action. The older people have never thought about this problem of fear, or they have thought about it only abstractly, without acting upon it in daily existence. You are still very young, you are watching, inquiring, learning, but if you do not see and understand what causes fear, you will become as they are. Like some hidden weed, fear will grow and spread and twist your mind. You should therefore be aware of everything that is happening around you and within yourself – how the teachers talk, how your parents behave, and how you respond – so that this question of fear is seen and understood.

Most grown-up people think that some kind of discipline is necessary. Do you know what discipline is? It is a process of making you do something which you do not want to do. Where there is discipline, there is fear; so discipline is not the way of love. That is why discipline at all costs should be avoided – discipline being coercion, resistance, compulsion, making you do something which you really do not understand, or persuading you to do it by offering you a reward. If you don't understand something, don't do it, and don't be compelled to do it. Ask for an explanation; don't just be obstinate, but try to find out the truth of the matter so that no fear is involved and your mind becomes very pliable, very supple.

When you do not understand and are merely compelled by the authority of grown-up people, you are suppressing your own mind, and then fear comes into being; and that fear pursues you like a shadow throughout life. That is why it is so important not to be disciplined according to any particular type of thought or pattern of action. But most older people can think only in those terms. They want to make you do something for your so-called good. This very process of making you do something for your own 'good', destroys your sensitivity, your capacity to understand, and therefore your love. To refuse to be coerced or compelled is very difficult, because the world about us is so strong; but if we merely give in and do things without understanding, we fall into a habit of thoughtlessness, and then it becomes still more difficult for us to break away.

So, in your school, should you have authority, discipline? Or should you be encouraged by your teachers to discuss these questions, go into them, understand them, so that, when you are grown up and go out into the world, you will be a mature human being who is capable of meeting intelligently the world's problems? You cannot have that deep intelligence if there is any kind of fear. Fear only makes you dull, it curbs your initiative, it destroys that flame which we call sympathy, generosity, affection, love. So do not allow yourself to be disciplined into a pattern of action, but find out – which means that you must have the time to question, to inquire; and the teachers must also have the time; if there is no time, then time must be made. Fear is a source of corruption, it is the beginning of degeneration, and to be free of fear is more important than any examination or any scholastic degree.

IV

WE have been discussing how essential it is to have love, and we saw that one cannot acquire or buy it; yet without love, all our plans for a perfect social order in which there is no exploitation, no regimentation, will have no meaning at all, and I think it is very important to understand this while we are young.

Wherever one goes in the world, it does not matter where, one finds that society is in a perpetual state of conflict. There are always the powerful, the rich, the well-to-do on the one hand, and the labourers on the other; and each one is enviously competing, each one wants a higher position, a bigger salary, more power, greater prestige. That is the state of the world, and so there is always war going on both within and without.

Now, if you and I want to bring about a complete revolution in the social order, the first thing we have to understand is this instinct for the acquisition of power. Most of us want power in one form or another. We see that through wealth and power we shall be able to travel, associate with important people and become famous; or we dream of bringing about a perfect society. We think we shall achieve that which is good through power; but the very pursuit of power – power for ourselves, power for our country, power for an ideology – is evil, destructive, because it inevitably creates opposing powers, and so there is always conflict.

Is it not right, then, that education should help you, as you grow up, to perceive the importance of bringing about a world in which there is no conflict either within or without, a world in which you are not in conflict with your neighbour or with any group of people, because the drive of ambition, which is the desire for position and power, has utterly ceased? And is it possible to create a society in which there will be no inward or outward conflict? Society is the relationship between you and me; and if our relationship is based on ambition, each one of us wanting to be more powerful than the other, then obviously we shall always be in conflict. So, can this cause of conflict be removed? Can we all educate ourselves not to be competitive, not to compare ourselves with somebody else, not to want this or that position – in a word, not to be ambitious at all?

When you go outside the school with your parents, when you read the newspapers or talk to people, you must have noticed that almost everybody wants to bring about a change in the world. And have you not also noticed that these very people are always in conflict with each other over something or other – over ideas, property, race, caste or religion? Your parents, your neighbours, the ministers and bureaucrats – are they not all ambitious, struggling for a better position, and therefore always in conflict with somebody? Surely, it is only when all this competitiveness is removed that there will be a peaceful society in which all of us can live happily, creatively.

Now, how is this to be done? Can regulations, legislation, or the training of your mind not to be ambitious, do away with ambition? Outwardly you may be trained not to be ambitious, socially you may cease to compete with others; but inwardly you will still be ambitious, will you not? And is it possible to sweep away completely this ambition, which is bringing so much misery to human beings? Probably you have not thought about it before, because nobody has talked to you like this; but now that somebody is talking to you about it, don't you want to find out if it is possible to live in this world richly, fully, happily, creatively, without the destructive drive of ambition, without competition? Don't you want to know how to live so that your life will not destroy another or cast a shadow across his path?

You see, we think this is a Utopian dream which can never be brought about in fact; but I am not talking about Utopia, that would be nonsense. Can you and I, who are simple, ordinary people, live creatively in this world without the drive of ambition which shows itself in various ways as the desire for power, position? You will find the right answer when you love what you are doing. If you are an engineer merely because you must earn a livelihood, or because your father or society expects it of you, that is another form of compulsion; and compulsion in any form creates a contradiction, conflict. Whereas, if you really love to be an engineer, or a scientist, or if you can plant a tree, or paint a picture, or write a poem, not to gain recognition but just because you love to do it, then you will find that you never compete with another. I think this is the real key: to love what you do.

But when you are young it is often very difficult to know what you love to do, because you want to do so many things. You want to be an engineer, an air pilot zooming along in the blue skies; or perhaps you want to be a famous orator or politician. You may want to be an artist, a chemist, a poet or a carpenter. You may want to work with your head, or do something with your hands. Are any of these things what you really love to do, or is your interest in them merely a reaction to social pressures? How can you find out? And is not the true purpose of education to *help* you to find out, so that as you grow up you can begin to give your whole mind, heart and body to that which you really love to do?

To find out what you love to do demands a great deal of intelligence; because, if you are afraid of not being able to earn a livelihood, or of not fitting into this rotten society, then you will never find out. But, if you are not frightened, if you refuse to be pushed into the groove of tradition by your parents, by your teachers, by the superficial demands of society, then there is a possibility of discovering what it is you really love to do. So, to discover, there must be no fear of not surviving.

But most of us are afraid of not surviving; we say, 'What will happen to me if I don't do as my parents say, if I don't fit into this society?' Being frightened, we do as we are told, and in that there is no love, there is only contradiction; and this inner contradiction is one of the factors that brings about destructive ambition.

So, it is a basic function of education to help you to find out what you really love to do, so that you can give your whole mind and heart to it, because that creates human dignity, that sweeps away mediocrity, the petty bourgeois mentality. That is why it is very important to have the right teachers, the right atmosphere, so that you will grow up with the love which expresses itself in what you are doing. Without this love your examinations, your knowledge, your capacities, your position and possessions are just ashes, they have no meaning; without this love your actions are going to bring more wars, more hatred, more mischief and destruction.

All this may mean nothing to you, because outwardly you are still very young, but I hope it will mean something to your teachers – and also to you, somewhere inside.

V

I DO not think we shall understand the complex problem of love till we understand the equally complex problem which we call the mind. Have you noticed, when we are very young, how inquisitive we are? We want to know, and we see many more things than the older people do. If we are at all awake, we observe things that the older people do not even notice. The mind, when we are young, is much more alert, much more curious. That is why we learn so easily mathematics, geography, or whatever it is. As we grow older, the mind becomes more and more crystallized, heavy, dull. Have you noticed how prejudiced most older people are? Their minds are not open, they approach everything from a fixed point of view. You are young now; but if you are not very watchful, your mind also will become like that.

Is it not then very important to understand the mind, and to see whether, instead of gradually becoming dull, you can be supple, capable of instant adjustments, of extraordinary initiative, of deep research and understanding in every department of life? Must you not know the ways of the mind to understand the way of love? Because it is the mind that destroys love. People who are merely clever, cunning, do not know what love is, because their minds, although sharp, are superficial; they live on the surface, and love is not a thing that exists on the surface.

What is the mind? I do not mean just the brain, the physical organism which reacts to stimuli through various nervous responses, and about which any physiologist can tell you. Rather we are going to find out what the mind is. The mind which says, 'I think'; 'it is mine'; 'I am hurt'; 'I am jealous'; 'I love'; 'I hate'; 'I am an Indian'; 'I am a Moslem'; 'I believe in this and I do not believe in that'; 'I know and you do not know'; 'I respect'; 'I despise'; 'I want'; 'I do not want' – what is this thing? Unless you begin now to understand and make yourself thoroughly familiar with the whole process of thinking which is called the mind, unless you are fully aware of it in yourself, you will gradually, as you grow older, become hard, crystallized, dull, fixed in a certain pattern of thought.

What is this thing which we call the mind? It is the way of our thinking, is it not? I am talking of *your* mind, not somebody else's mind – the way you think and feel, the way you look at the trees, at the fishermen, the way you consider other people. Your mind, as you grow older, gradually becomes warped or fixed in a certain pattern. You want something, you crave it, you desire to be or become something, and this desire sets a pattern; that is, your mind creates a pattern and gets caught in it. Your desire crystallizes your mind.

Say, for example, you want to be a very rich man. The desire to be wealthy creates a pattern, and your thinking then gets caught in it; you can think only in those terms, and you cannot go beyond them. Therefore your mind slowly becomes crystallized, it gets hard, dull. Or, if you believe in something – in God, in Communism, in a certain political system – that very belief sets the pattern, because it is the outcome of your desire; and your desire strengthens the walls of the pattern. Gradually your mind becomes incapable of quick adjustment, of deep penetration, of real clarity, because you are caught in the labyrinth of your own desires.

So, until we begin to investigate this process which we call the mind, until we are familiar with and understand our own ways of thinking, we cannot possibly find out what love is. There can be no love as long as our minds desire certain things of love, or demand that it act in a certain way. When we imagine what love should be and give to it certain motives, we gradually create a pattern of action with regard to love; but that is not love, it is merely our idea of what love should be.

Say, for example, I possess my wife or husband, as you possess a dress or a coat. If somebody took away your coat, you would be anxious, irritated, angry. Why? Because you regard that coat as your property; you possess it, and through its possession you feel enriched, don't you? Through possessing many clothes you feel enriched, not only physically but inwardly; and when somebody takes away your coat, you feel irritated because inwardly you are being deprived of that feeling of richness, that sense of possession.

Now, the feeling of possession creates a barrier with regard to love, does it not? If I own you, possess you, is that love? I possess you as I possess a car, a coat, a dress, because in possessing, I feel very gratified, and I depend on that feeling; it is very important to me inwardly. This sense of owning, possessing someone, this emotional dependence on another, is what we call love; but if you examine it, you will find that, behind the word 'love', the mind is taking satisfaction in possession.

So, in desiring, wanting, the mind creates a pattern, and in that pattern it gets caught; and then it grows weary, dull, stupid, thoughtless. The mind is the centre of this feeling of possession, the feeling of the 'me' and the 'mine': 'I own something', 'I am a big man', 'I am a little man', 'I am insulted', 'I am flattered', 'I am clever', 'I am very beautiful', 'I want to be somebody', 'I am the son or the daughter of somebody'. This feeling of the 'me' and the 'mine' is the very core of the mind, it is the mind itself. The more the mind has this feeling of being somebody, of being great, or very clever, or very stupid, and so on, the more it builds walls around itself and becomes enclosed, dull. Then it suffers, for in that enclosure inevitably there is pain. Because it is suffering, the mind says, 'What am I to do?' But instead of removing the enclosing walls by awareness, by careful thought, by going into and understanding the whole process by which they are created, it struggles to find something else outside with which to enclose itself again. So the mind gradually becomes a barrier to love; and without understanding what the mind is, which is to understand the ways of our own thinking, the inner source from which there is action, we cannot possibly find out what love is.

Is not the mind also an instrument of comparison? You know what it means to compare. You say, 'This is better than that'; you compare yourself with somebody who is more beautiful, or less clever. There is comparison when you say, 'I remember a river which I saw a year ago, and it is still more beautiful than this one'. You compare yourself with a saint or a hero, with the ultimate ideal. This comparative judgement makes the mind dull; it does not quicken the mind, it does not make the mind comprehensive, inclusive. When you are constantly comparing, what happens? When you see the sunset and immediately compare it with a previous sunset, or when you say, 'That mountain is beautiful, but I saw a still more beautiful mountain two years ago', you are really not looking at the beauty which is there before you. So comparison prevents you from looking fully. If, in looking at you, I say, 'I know a much nicer person', I am not really looking at you, am I? My mind is occupied with something else. To really look at a sunset, there must be no comparison, to really look at you, I must not compare you with someone else. It is only when I look at you fully, not with comparative judgement, that I can understand you. When I compare you with another, I do not understand you, I merely judge you, I say you are this or that. So, stupidity arises when there is comparison, because in comparing you with somebody else there is a lack of human dignity. But when I look at you without comparing, then my only concern is to understand you, and in that very concern, which is not comparative, there is intelligence, there is human dignity.

As long as the mind is comparing, there is no love; and the mind is always comparing, weighing, judging, is it not? It is always looking to find out where the weakness is; so there is no love. When the mother and father love their children, they do not compare one child with another. But you compare yourself with someone better, nobler, richer; you are all the time concerned with yourself in relation to somebody else, so you create in yourself a lack of love. In this way the mind becomes more and more comparative, more and more possessive, more and more dependent, thereby establishing a pattern in which it gets caught. Because it cannot look at anything anew, afresh, it destroys the very perfume of life, which is love.

VI

WHEN you are young you are curious to know all about everything, why the sun shines, what the stars are, all about the moon and the world around us; but as we grow older, knowledge becomes a mere collection of information without any feeling. We become specialists, we know much about this or that subject, and we take very little interest in the things around us, the beggar in the street, the rich man passing by in his car. If we want to know why there are riches and poverty in the world, we can find an explanation. There is an explanation for everything, and explanation seems to satisfy most of us. The same holds true of religion. We are satisfied with explanations; and explaining everything away we call knowledge. And is this what we mean by education? Are we learning to find out, or are we merely asking for explanations, definitions, conclusions, in order to put our minds at rest so that we need not inquire further?

Our elders may have explained everything to us, but our interest has generally been deadened thereby. As we grow older life becomes more complex and very difficult. There are so many things to know, there is so much misery and suffering; and seeing all this complexity, we think we have resolved it all by explaining it away. Someone dies, and it is explained away; so suffering is deadened through explanation. Perhaps we revolt against the idea of war when we are young, but as we grow older we accept the explanation of war, and our minds become dull.

When we are young what is more important is not to be satisfied with explanations, but to find out how to be intelligent and thereby discover the truth of things; and we cannot be intelligent if we are not free. It is said that freedom comes only when we are old and wise, but surely there must be freedom while we are still very young – not freedom to do what we like, but freedom to understand very deeply our own instincts and urges. There must be a freedom in which there is no fear, but one cannot be free from fear through an explanation. We are aware of death and the fear of death. By explaining death, can we know what dying is, or be free from the fear of death?

As we grow older it is important to have the capacity to think very simply. What is simplicity? Who is a simple person? A man who lives a hermit's life, who has very few belongings – is he really simple? Is not simplicity something entirely different? Simplicity is of the mind and heart. Most of us are very complex, we have many wants and desires. For example, you want to pass your examinations, you want to get a good job, you have ideals and want to develop a good character, and so on. The mind has so many demands; and does that make for simplicity? Is it not very important to find out?

A complex mind cannot find out the truth of anything, it cannot find out what is real – and that is our difficulty. From childhood we are trained to conform, and we do not know how to reduce complexity to simplicity. It is only the very simple and direct mind that can find the real, the true. We know more and more, but our minds are never simple; and it is only the simple mind that is creative.

When you paint a picture of a tree, what is it you are painting? Are you just painting a picture of the tree as it looks, with its leaves, its branches, its trunk, complete in every detail, or are you painting from the feeling which the tree has awakened in you? If the tree tells you something and you paint from that inner experience, though your feeling may be very complex, the picture that you paint will be the outcome of a great simplicity. It is necessary when you are young to keep your mind very simple, uncontaminated, although you may have all the information you want.

VII

I WOULD like to discuss with you the problem of freedom. It is a very complex problem, needing deep study and understanding. We hear much talk about freedom, religious freedom, and the freedom to do what one would like to do. Volumes have been written on all this by scholars. But I think we can approach it very simply and directly, and perhaps that will bring us to the real solution.

I wonder if you have ever stopped to observe the marvellous glow in the west as the sun sets, with the shy young moon just over the trees? Often at that hour the river is very calm, and then everything is reflected on its surface: the bridge, the train that goes over it, the tender moon, and presently, as it grows dark, the stars. It is all very beautiful. And to observe, to watch, to give your whole attention to something beautiful, your mind must be free of preoccupations, must it not? It must not be occupied with problems, with worries, with speculations. It is only when the mind is very quiet that you can really observe, for then the mind is sensitive to extraordinary beauty; and perhaps here is a clue to our problem of freedom.

Now, what does it mean to be free? Is freedom a matter of doing what happens to suit you, going where you like, thinking what you will? This you do anyhow. Merely to have independence, does that mean freedom? Many people in the world are independent, but very few are free. Freedom implies great intelligence, does it not? To be free is to be intelligent, but intelligence does not come into being by just wishing to be free; it comes into being only when you begin to understand your whole environment, the social, religious, parental and traditional influences that are continually closing in on you. But to understand the various influences – the influence of your parents, of your government, of society, of the culture to which you belong, of your beliefs, your gods and superstitions, of the tradition to which you conform unthinkingly – to understand all these and become free from them requires deep insight; but you generally give in to them because inwardly you are frightened. You are afraid of not having a good position in life; you are afraid of what your priest will say; you are afraid of not following tradition, of not doing the right thing. But freedom is really a state of mind in which there is no fear or compulsion, no urge to be secure.

Don't most of us want to be safe? Don't we want to be told what marvellous people we are, how lovely we look, or what extraordinary intelligence we have? Otherwise we would not put letters after our names. All that kind of thing gives us self-assurance, a sense of importance. We all want to be famous people – and the moment we want to *be* something, we are no longer free.

Please see this, for it is the real clue to the understanding of the problem of freedom. Whether in this world of politicians, power, position and authority, or in the so-called spiritual world where you aspire to be virtuous, noble, saintly, the moment you want to be somebody you are no longer free. But the man or the woman who sees the absurdity of all these things and whose heart is therefore innocent, and therefore not moved by the desire to be somebody – such a person is free. If you understand the simplicity of it you will also see its extraordinary beauty and depth.

After all, examinations are for that purpose: to give you a position, to make you somebody. Titles, position and knowledge encourage you to be something. Have you not noticed that your parents and teachers tell you that you must amount to something in life, that you must be successful like your uncle or your grandfather? Or you try to imitate the example of some hero, to be like the Masters, the saints; so you are never free. Whether you follow the example of a Master, a saint, a teacher, a relative, or stick to a particular tradition, it all implies a demand on your part to *be* something; and it is only when you really understand this fact that there is freedom.

The function of education, then, is to help you from childhood not to imitate anybody, but to be yourself all the time. And this is a most difficult thing to do: whether you are ugly or beautiful, whether you are envious or jealous, always to be what you are, but understand it. To be yourself is very difficult, because you think that what you are is ignoble, and that if you could only change what you are into something noble it would be marvellous; but that never happens. Whereas, if you look at what you actually are and understand it, then in that very understanding there is a transformation. So freedom lies, not in trying to become something different, nor in doing whatever you happen to feel like doing, nor in following the authority of tradition, of your parents, of your teacher, but in understanding what you are from moment to moment.

You see, you are not educated for this; your education encourages you to become something or other – but that is not the understanding of yourself. Your 'self' is a very complex thing; it is not merely the entity that goes to school, that quarrels, that plays games, that is afraid, but it is also something hidden, not obvious. It is made up, not only of all the thoughts that you think, but also of all the things that have been put into your mind by other people, by books, by the newspapers, by your leaders; and it is possible to understand all that only when you don't want to be somebody, when you don't imitate, when you don't follow – which means, really, when you are in revolt against the whole tradition of trying to become something. That is the only true revolution, leading to extraordinary freedom. To cultivate this freedom is the real function of education.

Your parents, your teachers and your own desires want you to be identified with something or other in order to be happy, secure. But to be intelligent, must you not break through all the influences that enslave and crush you?

The hope of a new world is in those of you who begin to see what is false and revolt against it, not just verbally but actually. And that is why you should seek the right kind of education; for it is only when you grow in freedom that you can create a new world not based on tradition or shaped according to the idiosyncrasy of some philosopher or idealist. But there can be no freedom as long as you are merely trying to become somebody, or imitate a noble example.

VIII

PERHAPS some of you do not wholly understand all that I have been saying about freedom; but it is very important to be exposed to ideas, to something to which you may not be accustomed. It is good to see what is beautiful, but you must also observe the ugly things of life, you must be awake to everything. Similarly, you must be exposed to things which you perhaps don't quite understand, for the more you think and ponder over these matters which may be somewhat difficult for you, the greater will be your capacity to live richly.

I don't know if any of you have noticed, early in the morning, the sunlight on the waters. How extraordinarily soft is the light, and how the dark waters dance, with the morning star over the trees, the only star in the sky. Do you ever notice any of that? Or are you so busy, so occupied with the daily routine, that you forget or have never known the rich beauty of this earth – this earth on which all of us have to live? Whether we call ourselves communists or capitalists, Hindus or Buddhists, Moslems or Christians, whether we are blind, lame, or well and happy, this earth is ours. Do you understand? It is our earth, not somebody else's; it is not only the rich man's earth, it does not belong exclusively to the powerful rulers, to the nobles of the land, but it is our earth, yours and mine. We are nobodies, yet we also live on this earth, and we all have to live together. It is the world of the poor as well as of the rich, of the unlettered as well as of the learned; it is *our* world, and I think it is very important to feel this and to love the earth, not just occasionally on a peaceful morning, but all the time. We can feel that it is our world and love it only when we understand what freedom is.

There is no such thing as freedom at the present time, we don't know what it means. We would like to be free but, if you notice, everybody – the teacher, the parent, the lawyer, the policeman, the soldier, the politician, the business man – is doing something in his own little corner to prevent that freedom. To be free is not merely to do what you like, or to break away from outward circumstances which bind you, but to understand the whole problem of dependence. Do you know what dependence is? You depend on your parents, don't you? You depend on your teachers, you depend on the cook, on the postman, on the man who brings you milk, and so on. That kind of dependence one can understand fairly easily. But there is a far deeper kind of dependence which one must understand before one can be free: the dependence on another for one's happiness. Do you know what it means to depend on somebody for your happiness? It is not the mere physical dependence on another which is so binding, but the inward, psychological dependence from which you derive so-called happiness; for when you depend on somebody in that way, you become a slave. If, as you grow older, you depend emotionally on your parents, on your wife or husband, on a *guru*, or on some idea, there is already the beginning of bondage. We don't understand this – although most of us, especially when we are young, want to be free.

To be free we have to revolt against all inward dependence,

and we cannot revolt if we don't understand why we are dependent. Until we understand and really break away from all inward dependence we can never be free, for only in that understanding can there be freedom. But freedom is not a mere reaction. Do you know what a reaction is? If I say something that hurts you, if I call you an ugly name and you get angry with me, that is a reaction – a reaction born of dependence; and independence is a further reaction. But freedom is not a reaction, and until we understand reaction and go beyond it, we are never free.

Do you know what it means to love somebody? Do you know what it means to love a tree, or a bird, or a pet animal, so that you take care of it, feed it, cherish it, though it may give you nothing in return, though it may not offer you shade, or follow you, or depend on you? Most of us don't love in that way, we don't know what that means at all because our love is always hedged about with anxiety, jealousy, fear – which implies that we depend inwardly on another, we want to be loved. We don't just love and leave it there, but we ask something in return; and in that very asking we become dependent.

So freedom and love go together. Love is not a reaction. If I love you because you love me, that is mere trade, a thing to be bought in the market; it is not love. To love is not to ask anything in return, not even to feel that you are giving something – and it is only such love that can know freedom. But, you see, you are not educated for this. You are educated in mathematics, in chemistry, geography, history, and there it ends, because your parents' only concern is to help you get a good job and be successful in life. If they have money they may send you abroad, but like the rest of the world their whole purpose is that you should be rich and have a respectable position in society; and the higher you climb the more misery you cause for others, because to get there you have to compete, be ruthless. So parents send their children to schools where there is ambition, competition, where there is not love at all, and that is why a society such as ours is continually decaying, in constant strife; and though the politicians, the judges, the so-called nobles of the land talk about peace, it does not mean a thing.

Now, you and I have to understand this whole problem of freedom. We must find out for ourselves what it means to love; because if we don't love we can never be thoughtful, attentive; we can never be considerate. Do you know what it means to be considerate? When you see a sharp stone on a path trodden by many bare feet, you remove it, not because you have been asked, but because you feel for another – it does not matter who he is, and you may never meet him. To plant a tree and cherish it, to look at the river and enjoy the fullness of the earth, to observe a bird on the wing and see the beauty of its flight, to have sensitivity and be open to this extraordinary movement called life – for all this there must be freedom; and to be free you must love. Without love there is no freedom; without love, freedom is merely an idea which has no value at all. So it is only for those who understand and break away from inner dependence, and who therefore know what love is, that there can be freedom; and it is they alone who will bring about a new civilization, a different world.

IX

AMONG so many other things in life, have you ever considered why it is that most of us are rather sloppy – sloppy in our dress, in our manners, in our thoughts, in the way we do things? Why are we unpunctual and, so, inconsiderate of others? And what is it that brings about order in everything, order in our dress, in our thoughts, in our speech, in the way we walk, in the way we treat those who are less fortunate than ourselves? What brings about this curious order that comes without compulsion, without planning, without deliberate mentation? Have you ever considered it? Do you know what I mean by order? It is to sit quietly without pressure, to eat elegantly without rush, to be leisurely and yet precise, to be clear in one's thinking and yet expansive. What brings about this order in life? It is really a very important point, and I think that, if one could be educated to discover the factor that produces order, it would have great significance.

Surely, order comes into being only through virtue; for unless you are virtuous, not merely in the little things, but in all things, your life becomes chaotic, does it not? Being virtuous has very little meaning in itself; but because you are virtuous there is precision in your thought, order in your whole being, and that is the function of virtue.

But what happens when a man tries to *become* virtuous, when he disciplines himself to be kind, efficient, thoughtful, considerate, when he attempts not to hurt people, when he spends his energies in trying to establish order, in struggling to be good? His efforts only lead to respectability, which brings about mediocrity of mind; therefore he is not virtuous.

Have you ever looked very closely at a flower? How astonishingly precise it is, with all its petals; yet there is an extraordinary tenderness, a perfume, a loveliness about it. Now, when a man *tries* to be orderly, his life may be very precise, but it has lost that quality of gentleness which comes into being only when, like with the flower, there is no effort. So our difficulty is to be precise, clear and expansive without effort.

You see, the *effort* to be orderly or tidy has such a narrowing influence. If I deliberately try to be orderly in my room, if I am careful to put everything in its place, if I am always watching myself, where I put my feet, and so on, what happens? I become an intolerable bore to myself and to others. It is a tiresome person who is always trying to be something, whose thoughts are very carefully arranged, who chooses one thought in preference to another. Such a person may be very tidy, clear, he may use words precisely, he may be very attentive and considerate, but he has lost the creative joy of living.

So, what is the problem? How can one have this creative joy of living, be expansive in one's feeling, wide in one's thinking, and yet be precise, clear, orderly in one's life? I think most of us are not like that because we never feel anything intensely, we never give our hearts and minds to anything completely. I remember watching two red squirrels, with long bushy tails and lovely fur, chase each other up and down a tall tree for about ten minutes without stopping – just for the joy of living. But you and I cannot know that joy if we do not feel things deeply, if there is no passion in our lives – passion, not for doing good or bringing about some reform, but passion in the sense of feeling things very strongly; and we can have that vital passion only when there is a total revolution in our thinking, in our whole being.

Have you noticed how few of us have deep feeling about anything? Do you ever rebel against your teachers, against your parents, not just because you don't like something, but because you have a deep, ardent feeling that you don't want to do certain things? If you feel deeply and ardently about something, you will find that this very feeling in a curious way brings a new order into your life.

Orderliness, tidiness, clarity of thinking are not very important in themselves, but they become important to a man who is sensitive, who feels deeply, who is in a state of perpetual inward revolution. If you feel very strongly about the lot of the poor man, about the beggar who receives dust in his face as the rich man's car goes by, if you are extraordinarily receptive, sensitive to everything, then that very sensitivity brings orderliness, virtue; and I think this is very important for both the educator and the student to understand.

In this country, unfortunately, as all over the world, we care so little, we have no deep feeling about anything. Most of us are intellectuals – intellectuals in the superficial sense of being very clever, full of words and theories about what is right and what is wrong, about how we should think, what we should do. Mentally we are highly developed, but inwardly there is very little substance or significance; and it is this inward substance that brings about true action, which is not action according to an idea.

That is why you should have very strong feelings – feelings

of passion, anger – and watch them, play with them, find out the truth of them; for if you merely suppress them, if you say, 'I must not get angry, I must not feel passionate, because it is wrong', you will find that your mind is gradually being encased in an idea and thereby becomes very shallow. You may be immensely clever, you may have encyclopaedic knowledge, but, if there is not the vitality of strong and deep feeling, your comprehension is like a flower that has no perfume.

It is very important for you to understand all these things while you are young, because then, when you grow up, you will be real revolutionaries – revolutionaries, not according to some ideology, theory or book, but revolutionaries in the total sense of the word, right through as integrated human beings, so that there is not a spot left in you which is contaminated by the old. Then your mind is fresh, innocent, and is therefore capable of extraordinary creativeness. But if you miss the significance of all this, your life will become very drab, for you will be overwhelmed by society, by your family, by your wife or husband, by theories, by religious or political organizations. That is why it is so urgent for you to be rightly educated – which means that you must have teachers who can help you to break through the crust of so-called civilization and be, not repetitive machines, but individuals who really have a song inside them and are therefore happy, creative human beings.

X

HAVE you ever sat very quietly without any movement? You try it, sit really still, with your back straight, and observe what your mind is doing. Don't try to control it, don't say it should not jump from one thought to another, from one interest to another, but just be aware of how your mind is jumping. Don't do anything about it, but watch it as from the banks of a river you watch the water flow by. In the flowing river there are so many things – fishes, leaves, dead animals – but it is always living, moving, and your mind is like that. It is everlastingly restless, flitting from one thing to another like a butterfly.

When you listen to a song, how do you listen to it? You may like the person who is singing, he may have a nice face, and you may follow the meaning of the words; but behind all that, when you listen to a song, you are listening to the tones and to the silence between the tones, are you not? In the same way, try sitting very quietly without fidgeting, without moving your hands or even your toes, and just watch your mind. It is great fun. If you try it as fun, as an amusing thing, you will find that the mind begins to settle down without any effort on your part to control it. There is then no censor, no judge, no evaluator; and when the mind is thus very quiet of itself, spontaneously still, you will discover what it is to be gay. Do you know what gaiety is? It is just to laugh, to take delight in anything or nothing, to know the joy of living, smiling, looking straight into the face of another without any sense of fear.

Have you ever really looked anybody in the face? Have you ever looked into the face of your teacher, of your parent, of the big official, of the servant, and seen what happens? Most of us are afraid to look directly into the face of another; and others don't want us to look at them in that way, because they also are frightened. Nobody wants to reveal himself; we are all on guard, hiding behind various layers of misery, suffering, longing, hope, and there are very few who can look you straight in the face and smile. And it is very important to smile, to be happy; because, you see, without a song in one's heart life becomes very dull. One may go from temple to temple, from one husband or wife to another, or one may find a new teacher or *guru*; but if there is not this inward joy, life has very little meaning. And to find this inward joy is not easy, because most of us are only superficially discontented.

Do you know what it means to be discontented? It is very difficult to understand discontent, because most of us canalize discontent in a certain direction and thereby smother it. That is, our only concern is to establish ourselves in a secure position with well-established interests and prestige, so as not to be disturbed. It happens in homes and in schools too. The teachers don't want to be disturbed, and that is why they follow the old routine; because the moment one is really discontented and begins to inquire, to question, there is bound to be disturbance. But it is only through real discontent that one has initiative.

Do you know what initiative is? You have initiative when you initiate or start something without being prompted. It need not be anything very great or extraordinary – that may come later; but there is the spark of initiative when you plant a tree on your own, when you are spontaneously kind, when you smile at a man who is carrying a heavy load, when you remove a stone from the path, or pat an animal along the way. That is a small beginning of the tremendous initiative you must have if you are to know this extraordinary thing called creativeness. Creativeness has its roots in the initiative which comes into being only when there is deep discontent.

Don't be afraid of discontent, but give it nourishment until the spark becomes a flame and you are everlastingly discontented with everything – with your jobs, with your families, with the traditional pursuit of money, position, power – so that you really begin to think, to discover. But as you grow older you will find that to maintain this spirit of discontent is very difficult. You have children to provide for and the demands of your job to consider; the opinion of your neighbours, of society closing in upon you, and soon you begin to lose this burning flame of discontent. When you feel discontented you turn on the radio, you go to a *guru*, say your prayers, join a club, drink, run after women – anything to smother the flame. But, you see, without this flame of discontent you will never have the initiative which is the beginning of creativeness. To find out what is true you must be in revolt against the established order; but the more money your parents have, and the more secure your teachers are in their jobs, the less they want you to revolt.

Creativeness is not merely a matter of painting pictures or writing poems, which is good to do, but which is very little in itself. What is important is to be wholly discontented, for such total discontent is the beginning of the initiative which becomes creative as it matures; and that is the only way to find out what is truth, what is God, because the creative state is God.

So one must have this total discontent – but with joy. Do you understand? One must be wholly discontented, not complainingly, but with joy, with gaiety, with love. Most people who are discontented are terrible bores; they are always complaining that something or other is not right, or wishing they were in a better position, or wanting circumstances to be different, because their discontent is very superficial. And those who are not discontented at all are already dead.

If you can be in revolt while you are young, and as you grow older keep your discontent alive with the vitality of joy and great affection, then that flame of discontent will have an extraordinary significance because it will build, it will create, it will bring new things into being. For this you must have the right kind of education, which is not the kind that merely prepares you to get a job or to climb the ladder of success, but the education that helps you to think and gives you space – space, not in the form of a larger bedroom or a higher roof, but space for your mind to grow so that it is not bound by any belief, by any fear.

XI

MOST of us cling to some small part of life, and think that through that part we shall discover the whole. Without leaving the room we hope to explore the whole length and width of the river and perceive the richness of the green pastures along its banks. We live in a little room, we paint on a little canvas, thinking that we have grasped life by the hand or understood the significance of death; but we have not. To do that we must go outside. And it is extraordinarily difficult to go outside, to leave the room with its narrow window and see everything as it is without judging, without condemning, without saying, 'This I like and that I don't like'; because most of us think that through the part we shall understand the whole. Through a single spoke we hope to understand the wheel; but one spoke does not make a wheel, does it? It takes many spokes, as well as a hub and a rim, to make the thing called a wheel, and we need to see the whole wheel in order to comprehend it. In the same way we must perceive the whole process of living if we are really to understand life.

I hope you are following all this, because education should help you to understand the whole of life and not just prepare you to get a job and carry on in the usual way with your marriage, your children, your insurance, and your little gods. But to bring about the right kind of education requires a great deal of intelligence, insight, and that is why it is so important for the educator himself to be educated to understand the whole process of life and not merely to teach you according to some formula, old or new.

Life is an extraordinary mystery – not the mystery in books, not the mystery that people talk about, but a mystery that one has to discover for oneself; and that is why it is so grave a matter that you should understand the little, the narrow, the petty, and go beyond it.

If you don't begin to understand life while you are young, you will grow up inwardly hideous; you will be dull, empty inside, though outwardly you may have money, ride in expensive cars, put on airs. That is why it is very important to leave your little room and perceive the whole expanse of the heavens. But you cannot do that unless you have love – not bodily love or divine love, but just love; which is to love the birds, the trees, the flowers, your teachers, your parents, and beyond your parents, humanity.

Will it not be a great tragedy if you don't discover for yourselves what it is to love? If you don't know love now, **you** will never know it, because as you grow older, what is called love will become something very ugly – a possession, a form of merchandise to be bought and sold. But if you begin now to have love in your heart, if you love the tree you plant, the stray animal you pat, then as you grow up you will not remain in your small room with its narrow window, but will leave it and love the whole of life.

Love is factual, it is not emotional, something to be cried over; it is not sentiment. Love has no sentimentality about it at all. And it is a very grave and important matter that you should know love while you are young. Your parents and teachers perhaps don't know love, and that is why they have created a terrible world, a society which is perpetually at war within itself and with other societies. Their religions, their philosophies and ideologies are all false because they have no love. They perceive only a part; they are looking out of a narrow window from which the view may be pleasant and extensive, but it is not the whole expanse of life. Without this feeling of intense love you can never have the perception of the whole; therefore you will always be miserable and at the end of your life you will have nothing but ashes, a lot of empty words.

XII

I THINK it is a very rare thing, after leaving school, to find happiness in the latter part of one's life. When you leave here, you will be facing extraordinary problems, the problem of war, the problems of personal relationship, the problems of citizens, the problem of religion, and the constant conflict within society; and it seems to me that it would be a false education which did not prepare you to face these problems and bring about a true and happier world. Surely it is the function of education, especially in a school where you have the opportunity of creative expression, to help the students not to be caught in those social and environmental influences which will narrow their minds and therefore limit their outlook and their happiness; and it seems to me that those who are about to enter college should know for themselves the many problems that confront us all. It is very important, especially in the world that you are going to face, to have an extraordinarily clear intelligence, and that intelligence is not brought about by any outside influence, or through books. It comes, I think, when one is aware of these problems and is able to meet them, not in any personal or limited sense, not as an American, or a Hindu, or a Communist, but as a human being capable of bearing the responsibility of seeing the true worth of things as they are and not interpreting them according to any particular ideology or pattern of thought.

Is it not important that education should prepare each one of us to understand and face our human problems, and not merely give us knowledge or technological training? Because, you see, life is not so very easy. You may have had a happy time, a creative time, a time in which you have ripened; but when you leave the school, things will begin to happen and enclose you; you will be limited, not only by personal relationships, but by social influences, by your own fears, and by the inevitable ambition to succeed.

I think it is a curse to be ambitious Ambition is a form of self-interest, self-enclosure, and therefore it breeds mediocrity of mind. To live in a world that is full of ambition without being ambitious means, really, to love something for itself without seeking a reward, a result; and that is very difficult, because the whole world, all your friends, your relations, everyone is struggling to succeed, to fulfil, to become somebody. But to understand and be free of all this, and to do something which you really love – no matter what it is, or however lowly and unrecognized – *that*, I think awakens the spirit of greatness which never seeks approbation, recompense, which does things for their own sake and therefore has the strength and the capacity not to be caught in the influence of mediocrity.

I think it is very important to see this while you are young;

because magazines, newspapers, television and radio constantly emphasize the worship of success, thereby encouraging ambition and competitiveness which breed mediocrity of mind. When you are ambitious you are merely adjusting to a particular pattern of society, whether in America, Russia, or India, and therefore you are living on a very superficial level.

When you leave school and enter college, and later face the world, it seems to me that what is important is not to succumb, not to bow your heads to various influences, but to meet and understand these as they are and see their true significance and their worth, in a gentle spirit with great inward strength which will not create further discord in the world.

So, I think that a real school through its students should bring a blessing to the world. For the world needs a blessing, it is in a terrible state; and the blessing can come only when we as individuals are not seeking power, when we are not trying to fulfil our personal ambitions, but have a clear understanding of the vast problems with which we are confronted. This demands great intelligence, which means, really, a mind that does not think according to any particular pattern, but is free in itself and is therefore capable of seeing what is true and putting aside that which is false.

XIII

I AM sure we all have sometime or other experienced a great sense of tranquillity and beauty coming to us from the green fields, the setting sun, the still waters, or the snow-capped peaks. But what is beauty? Is it merely the appreciation that we feel, or is beauty a thing apart from perception? If you have good taste in clothes, if you use colours that harmonize, if you have dignified manners, if you speak quietly and hold yourself erect, all that makes for beauty, does it not? But that is merely the outward expression of an inward state, like a poem you write or a picture you paint. You can look at the green field reflected in the river and experience no sense of beauty, just pass it by. If, like the fisherman, you see every day the swallows flying low over the water, it probably means very little to you; but if you are aware of the extraordinary beauty of something like that, what is it that happens within you and makes you say, 'How very beautiful'? What goes to make up this inward sense of beauty?

Surely, to have this inward beauty, there must be complete abandonment; the sense of not being held, of no restraint, no defence, no resistance; but abandonment becomes chaotic if there is no austerity with it. And do we know what it means to be austere, to be satisfied with little and not to think in terms of 'the more'? There must be this abandonment with deep inward austerity – the austerity that is extraordinarily simple because the mind is not acquiring, gaining, not thinking in terms of 'the more'. It is the simplicity born of abandonment with austerity that brings about the state of creative beauty. But if there is no love you cannot be simple, you cannot be austere. You may talk about simplicity and austerity, but without love they are merely a form of compulsion, and therefore there is no abandonment. Only he has love who abandons himself, forgets himself completely, and thereby brings about the state of creative beauty.

Beauty obviously includes beauty of form; but without inward beauty, the mere sensual appreciation of beauty of form leads to degradation, disintegration. There is inward beauty only when you feel real love for people and for all the things of the earth; and with that love there comes a tremendous sense of consideration, watchfulness, patience. You may have perfect technique, as a singer or a poet, you may know how to paint or put words together, but without this creative beauty inside, your talent will have very little significance.

Unfortunately, most of us are becoming mere technicians. We pass examinations, acquire this or that technique in order to earn a livelihood; but to acquire technique or develop capacity without paying attention to the inner state, brings about ugliness and chaos in the world. If we awaken creative beauty inwardly, it expresses itself outwardly, and then there is order. But that is much more difficult than acquiring a technique, because it means abandoning ourselves completely, being without fear, without restraint, without resistance, without defence; and we can thus abandon ourselves only when there is austerity, a sense of great inward simplicity. Outwardly we may be simple, we may have but few clothes and be satisfied with one meal a day; but that is not austerity. There is austerity when the mind is capable of infinite experience – when it has experience, and yet remains very simple. But that state can come into being only when the mind is no longer thinking in terms of 'the more', in terms of having or becoming something through time.

What I am talking about may be difficult for you to understand, but it is really quite important. You see, technicians are not creators; and there are more and more technicians in the world, people who know what to do and how to do it, but who are not creators. In America there are calculating machines capable of solving in a few minutes mathematical problems which would take a man a hundred years to solve. These extraordinary machines are being developed. But machines can never be creators – and human beings are becoming more and more like machines. Even when they rebel, their rebellion is within the limits of the machine and is therefore no rebellion at all.

So it is very important to find out what it is to be creative. You can be creative only when there is abandonment – which means, really, when there is no sense of compulsion, no fear of not being, of not gaining, of not arriving. Then there is great austerity, simplicity, and with it there is love. The whole of that is beauty, the state of creativeness.

XIV

HAVE you ever sat very quietly with closed eyes and watched the movement of your own thinking? Have you watched your mind working – or rather, has your mind watched itself in operation, just to see what your thoughts are, what your feelings are, how you look at the trees, at the flowers, at the birds, at people, how you respond to a suggestion or react to a new idea? Have you ever done this? If you have not, you are missing a great deal. To know how one's mind works is a basic purpose of education. If you don't know how your mind reacts, if your mind is not aware of its own activities, you will never find out what society is. You may read books on sociology, study social sciences, but if you don't know how your own mind works you cannot actually understand what society is, because your mind is part of society; it *is* society. Your reactions, your beliefs, your going to the temple, the clothes you wear, the things you do and don't do and what you think – society is made up of all this, it is the replica of what is going on in your own mind. So your mind is not apart from society, it is not distinct from your culture, from your religion, from your various class divisions, from the ambitions and conflicts of the many. All this is society, and you are part of it. There is no 'you' separate from society.

Now, society is always trying to control, to shape, to mould the thinking of the young. From the moment you are born and begin to receive impressions, your father and mother are constantly telling you what to do and what not to do, what to believe and what not to believe; you are told that there is God, or that there is no God but the State and that some dictator is its prophet. From childhood these things are poured into you, which means that your mind – which is very young, impressionable, inquisitive, curious to know, wanting to find out – is gradually being encased, conditioned, shaped so that you will fit into the pattern of a particular society and not be a revolutionary. Since the habit of pat-

terned thinking has already been established in you, even if
you do 'revolt' it is within the pattern. It is like prisoners
revolting in order to have better food, more amenities –
but always within the prison. When you seek God, or try to
find out what is right government, it is always within the
pattern of society, which says, 'This is true and that is false,
this is good and that is bad, this is the right leader and
these are the saints'. So your revolt, like the so-called revolution brought about by ambitious or very clever people, is
always limited by the past. That is not revolt, that is not
revolution: it is merely heightened activity, a more valiant
struggle within the pattern. Real revolt, true revolution, is to
break away from the pattern and to inquire outside of it.

You see, all reformers – it does not matter *who* they are –
are merely concerned with bettering the conditions within
the prison. They never tell you not to conform, they never
say, 'Break through the walls of tradition and authority,
shake off the conditioning that holds the mind'. And that
is real education: not merely to require you to pass examinations for which you have crammed, or to write out something which you have learnt by heart, but to help you to see
the walls of this prison in which the mind is held. Society
influences all of us, it constantly shapes our thinking, and
this pressure of society from the outside is gradually trans-
lated as the inner; but, however deeply it penetrates, it is
still from the outside, and there is no such thing as the inner
as long as you do not break through this conditioning. You
must know what you are thinking, and whether you are
thinking as a Hindu, or a Moslem, or a Christian; that is,
in terms of the religion you happen to belong to. You must
be conscious of what you believe or do not believe. All this
is the pattern of society and, unless you are aware of the
pattern and break away from it, you are still a prisoner
though you may think you are free.

But you see, most of us are concerned with revolt within
the prison; we want better food, a little more light, a larger
window so that we can see a little more of the sky. We are
concerned with whether the outcaste should enter the temple

or not; we want to break down this particular caste, and in the very breaking down of one caste we create another, a 'superior' caste; so we remain prisoners, and there is no freedom in prison. Freedom lies outside the walls, outside the pattern of society; but to be free of that pattern you have to understand the whole content of it, which is to understand your own mind. It is the mind that has created the present civilization, this tradition-bound culture or society and, without understanding your own mind, merely to revolt as a communist, a socialist, this or that, has very little meaning. That is why it is very important to have self-knowledge, to be aware of all your activities, your thoughts and feelings; and this is education, is it not? Because when you are fully aware of yourself your mind becomes very sensitive, very alert.

You try this – not someday in the far-away future, but to-morrow or this afternoon. If there are too many people in your room, if your home is crowded, then go away by yourself, sit under a tree or on the river bank and quietly observe how your mind works. Don't correct it, don't say, 'This is right, that is wrong', but just watch it as you would a film. When you go to the cinema you are not taking part in the film; the actors and actresses are taking part, you are only watching. In the same way, watch how your mind works. It is really very interesting, far more interesting than any film, because your mind is the residue of the whole world and it contains all that human beings have experienced. Do you understand? Your mind is humanity, and when you perceive this, you will have immense compassion. Out of this understanding comes great love; and then you will know, when you see lovely things, what beauty is.

XV

We have been discussing the question of revolt within the prison: how all reformers, idealists, and others who are incessantly active in producing certain results, are always revolting within the walls of their own conditioning, within the walls of their own social structure, within the cultural pattern of civilization which is an expression of the collective will of the many. I think it would now be worth while if we could see what confidence is and how it comes about.

Through initiative there comes about confidence; but initiative within the pattern only brings *self*-confidence, which is entirely different from confidence without the self. Do you know what it means to have confidence? If you do something with your own hands, if you plant a tree and see it grow, if you paint a picture, or write a poem, or, when you are older build a bridge or run some administrative job extremely well, it gives you confidence that you are able to do something. But, you see, confidence as we know it now is always within the prison, the prison which society – whether communist, Hindu, or Christian – has built around us. Initiative within the prison does create a certain confidence, because you feel you can do things; you can design a motor, be a very good doctor, an excellent scientist, and so on. But this feeling of confidence which comes with the capacity to succeed within the social structure, or to reform, to give more light, to decorate the interior of the prison is really *self*-confidence; you know you can do something, and you feel important in doing it. Whereas, when through investigating, through understanding, you break away from the social structure of which you are a part, there comes an entirely different kind of confidence which is without the sense of self-importance; and if we can understand the difference between these two – between self-confidence, and confidence without the self – I think it will have great significance in our life.

When you play a game very well, like badminton, cricket,

or football, you have a certain sense of confidence, have you not? It gives you the feeling that you are pretty good at it. If you are quick at solving mathematical problems, that also breeds a sense of self-assurance. When confidence is born of action within the social structure, there always goes with it a strange arrogance, does there not? The confidence of a man who can do things, who is capable of achieving results, is always coloured by this arrogance of the self, the feeling, 'It is I who do it'. So, in the very act of achieving a result, of bringing about a social reform within the prison, there is the arrogance of the self, the feeling that *I* have done it, that *my* ideal is important, that *my* group has succeeded. This sense of the 'me' and the 'mine' always goes with the confidence that expresses itself within the social prison.

Have you not noticed how arrogant idealists are? The political leaders who bring about certain results, who achieve great reforms – have you not noticed that they are full of themselves, puffed up with their ideals and their achievements? In their own estimation they are very important. Read a few of the political speeches, watch some of these people who call themselves reformers, and you will see that in the very process of reformation they are cultivating their own ego; their reforms, however extensive, are still within the prison, therefore they are destructive and ultimately bring more misery and conflict to man.

Now, if you can see through this whole social structure, the cultural pattern of the collective will which we call civilization – if you can understand all that and break away from it, break through the prison walls of your particular society, whether Hindu, communist, or Christian, then you will find that there comes a confidence which is not tainted with the sense of arrogance. It is the confidence of innocence. It is like the confidence of a child who is so completely innocent he will try anything. It is this innocent confidence that will bring about a new civilization; but this innocent confidence cannot come into being as long as you remain within the social pattern.

Please do listen to this carefully. The speaker is not in the least important, but it is very important for you to understand the truth of what is being said. After all, that is education, is it not? The function of education is not to make you fit into the social pattern; on the contrary, it is to help you to understand completely, deeply, fully and thereby break away from the social pattern, so that you are an individual without that arrogance of the self, but yet have confidence because you are really innocent.

Is it not a great tragedy that almost all of us are only concerned either with how to fit into society, or how to reform it? Have you noticed that most of the questions you have asked reflect this attitude? You are saying, in effect, 'How can I fit into society? What will my father and mother say, and what will happen to me if I don't?' Such an attitude destroys whatever confidence, whatever initiative you have. And you leave school and college like so many automatons, highly efficient perhaps, but without any creative flame. That is why it is so important to understand the society, the environment in which one lives, and, in that very process of understanding, break away from it.

You see, this is a problem all over the world. Man is seeking a new response, a new approach to life, because the old ways are decaying, whether in Europe, in Russia, or here. Life is a continual challenge, and merely to try to bring about a better economic order is not a total response to that challenge, which is always new; and when cultures, peoples, civilizations are incapable of responding to the challenge of the new, they are destroyed.

Unless you are properly educated, unless you have this extraordinary confidence of innocence, you are inevitably going to be absorbed by the collective and lost in mediocrity. You will put some letters after your name, you will be married, have children, and that will be the end of you.

You see, most of us are frightened. Your parents are frightened, your educators are frightened, the governments and religions are frightened of your becoming a total individual, because they all want you to remain safely within the prison of environmental and cultural influences. But it is only the individuals who break through the social pattern by understanding it, and who are therefore not bound by the conditioning of their own minds – it is only such people who can bring about a new civilization, not the people who merely conform, or who resist one particular pattern because they are shaped by another. The search for God or truth does not lie within the prison, but rather in understanding the prison and breaking through its walls – and this very movement towards freedom creates a new culture, a different world.

XVI

Rain on dry land is an extraordinary thing, is it not? It washes the leaves clean, the earth is refreshed. And I think we all ought to wash our minds completely clean, as the trees are washed by the rain, because they are so heavily laden with the dust of many centuries, the dust of what we call knowledge, experience. If you and I would cleanse the mind every day, free it of yesterday's reminiscences, each one of us would then have a fresh mind, a mind capable of dealing with the many problems of existence.

Now, one of the great problems that is disturbing the world is what is called equality. In one sense there is no such thing as equality, because we all have many different capacities; but we are discussing equality in the sense that all people should be treated alike. In a school, for example, the positions of the principal, the teachers and the house parents are merely jobs, functions; but, you see, with certain jobs or functions goes what is called status, and status is respected because it implies, power, prestige, it means being in a position to tell people off, to order people about, to give jobs to one's friends and the members of one's family. So with function goes status; but if we could remove this whole idea of status, of power, of position, prestige, of giving benefits to others, the function would have quite a different and simple meaning, would it not? Then, whether people were governors, prime ministers, cooks, or poor teachers, they would all be treated with the same respect because they are all performing a different but necessary function in society.

Do you know what would happen, especially in a school, if we could really remove from function the whole sense of power, of position, prestige; the feeling, 'I am the Head, I am important'? We would all be living in quite a different atmosphere, would we not? There would be no authority in the sense of the high and the low, the big man and the little man, and therefore there would be freedom. And it is very important that we create such an atmosphere in the school, an atmosphere of freedom in which there is love, in which each one feels a tremendous sense of confidence; because, you see, confidence comes when you feel completely at home, secure. Do you feel at ease in your own home if your father, your mother and your grandmother are constantly telling you what to do so that you gradually lose all confidence in doing anything by yourself? As you grow up you must be able to discuss, to find out if what you think is true and stick to it. You must be able to stand by something which you feel is right, even though it brings pain, suffering, loss of money, and all the rest of it; and for that you must feel, while you are young, completely secure and at ease.

Most young people don't feel secure because they are frightened. They are afraid of their elders, of their teachers, of their mothers and fathers, so they never really feel at home. But when you *do* feel at home, there happens a very strange thing. When you can go to your room, lock the door and be there by yourself unnoticed, with no one telling you what to do, you feel completely secure; and then you begin to flower, to understand, to unfold. To help you unfold is the function of a school; and if it does not help you to unfold, it is no school at all.

When you feel at home in a place in the sense that you feel secure, not beaten down, not compelled to do this or that, when you feel very happy, completely at ease, then you are not naughty, are you? When you are really happy, you don't want to hurt anybody, you don't want to destroy anything. But to make the student feel completely happy is extraordinarily difficult, because he comes to the school with an idea that the Principal, the teachers and the house parents are going to tell him what to do and push him around, and hence there is fear.

Most of you come from homes or from schools in which you have been educated to respect status. Your father and mother have status, the Principal has status, so you come here with fear, respecting status. But we must create in the school a real atmosphere of freedom, and that can come about only when there is function without status, and therefore a feeling of equality. The real concern of right education is to help you to be a vital, sensitive human being, one who is not afraid and who has no false sense of respect because of status.

XVII

THE other morning I saw a dead body being carried away to be burnt. It was wrapped in bright magenta cloth and it swayed with the rhythm of the four mortals who were carrying it. I wonder what kind of impression a dead body makes on one. Don't you wonder why there is deterioration? You buy a brand new motor, and within a few years it is worn out. The body also wears out; but don't you inquire a little further to find out why the mind deteriorates? Sooner or later there is the death of the body, but most of us have minds which are already dead. Deterioration has already taken place; and why does the mind deteriorate? The body deteriorates because we are constantly using it and the physical organism wears out. Disease, accident, old age, bad food, poor heredity – these are the factors which cause the deterioration and death of the body. But why should the mind deteriorate, become old, heavy, dull?

When you see a dead body, have you never wondered about this? Though our bodies must die, why should the mind ever deteriorate? Has this question never occurred to you? For the mind *does* deteriorate – we see it not only in old people, but also in the young. We see in the young how the mind is already becoming dull, heavy, insensitive; and if we can find out why the mind deteriorates, then perhaps we shall discover something really indestructible. We may understand what is eternal life, the life that is unending, that is not of time, the life that is incorruptible, that does not decay like the body which is carried to the *ghats*, burnt and the remains thrown into the river.

Now, why does the mind deteriorate? Have you ever thought about it? Being still very young – and if you have not already been made dull by society, by your parents, by circumstances – you have a fresh, eager, curious mind. You want to know why the stars exist, why the birds die, why the leaves fall, how the jet plane flies; you want to know so many things. But that vital urge to inquire, to find out, is soon smothered, is it not? It is smothered by fear, by the weight of tradition, by our own incapacity to face this extraordinary thing called life. Haven't you noticed how quickly your eagerness is destroyed by a sharp word, by a disparaging gesture, by the fear of an examination or the threat of a parent – which means that sensitivity is already being pushed aside and the mind made dull?

Another cause of dullness is imitation. You are made to imitate by tradition. The weight of the past drives you to conform, toe the line, and through conformity the mind feels safe, secure; it establishes itself in a well-oiled groove so that it can run smoothly without disturbance, without a quiver of doubt. Watch the grown-up people about you and you will see that their minds do not want to be disturbed. They want peace, even though it is the peace of death; but real peace is something entirely different.

When the mind establishes itself in a groove, in a pattern, haven't you noticed that it is always prompted by the desire to be secure? That is why it follows an ideal, an example, a *guru*. It wants to be safe, undisturbed, therefore it imitates. When you read in your history books about great leaders, saints, warriors, don't you find yourself wanting to copy them? Not that there aren't great people in the world; but the instinct is to imitate great people, to try to become like them, and that is one of the factors of deterioration because the mind then sets itself in a mould.

Furthermore, society does not want individuals who are alert, keen, revolutionary, because such individuals will not fit into the established social pattern and they may break it up. That is why society seeks to hold your mind in its pattern, and why your so-called education encourages you to imitate, to follow, to conform.

Now, can the mind stop imitating? That is, can it cease to form habits? And can the mind, which is already caught in habit, be free of habit?

The mind is the result of habit, is it not? It is the result of tradition, the result of time – time being repetition, a continuity of the past. And can the mind, *your* mind, stop thinking in terms of what has been – and of what will be, which is really a projection of what has been? Can your mind be free from habits and from creating habits? If you go into this problem very deeply you will find that it can; and when the mind renews itself without forming new patterns, habits, without again falling into the groove of imitation, then it remains fresh, young, innocent, and is therefore capable of infinite understanding.

For such a mind there is no death because there is no longer a process of accumulation. It is the process of accumulation that creates habit, imitation, and for the mind that accumulates there is deterioration, death. But a mind that is not accumulating, not gathering, that is dying each day, each minute – for such a mind there is no death. It is in a state of infinite space.

So the mind must die to everything it has gathered – to all the habits, the imitated virtues, to all the things it has relied upon for its sense of security. Then it is no longer caught in the net of its own thinking. In dying to the past from moment to moment the mind is made fresh, therefore it can never deteriorate or set in motion the wave of darkness.

XVIII

I DON'T know if on your walks you have noticed a long, narrow pool beside the river. Some fishermen must have dug it, and it is not connected with the river. The river is flowing steadily, deep and wide, but this pool is heavy with scum because it is not connected with the life of the river, and there are no fish in it. It is a stagnant pool, and the deep river, full of life and vitality, flows swiftly along.

Now, don't you think human beings are like that? They dig a little pool for themselves away from the swift current of life, and in that little pool they stagnate, die; and this stagnation, this decay we call existence. That is, we all want a state of permanency; we want certain desires to last forever, we want pleasures to have no end. We dig a little hole and barricade ourselves in it with our families, with our ambitions, our cultures, our fears, our gods, our various forms of worship, and there we die, letting life go by – that life which is impermanent, constantly changing, which is so swift, which has such enormous depths, such extraordinary vitality and beauty.

Have you not noticed that if you sit quietly on the bank of the river you hear its song – the lapping of the water, the sound of the current going by? There is always a sense of movement, an extraordinary movement towards the wider and the deeper. But in the little pool there is no movement at all, its water is stagnant. And if you observe you will see that this is what most of us want: little stagnant pools of existence away from life. We say that our pool-existence is right, and we have invented a philosophy to justify it; we have developed social, political, economic and religious theories in support of it, and we don't want to be disturbed because, you see, what we are after is a sense of permanency.

Do you know what it means to seek permanency? It means wanting the pleasurable to continue indefinitely, and wanting that which is not pleasurable to end as quickly as possible. We want the name that we bear to be known and to continue through family, through property. We want a sense of permanency in our relationships, in our activities, which means that we are seeking a lasting, continuous life in the stagnant pool; we don't want any real changes there, so we have built a society which guarantees us the permanency of property, of name, of fame.

But you see, life is not like that at all; life is not permanent. Like the leaves that fall from a tree, all things are impermanent, nothing endures; there is always change and death. Have you ever noticed a tree standing naked against the sky, how beautiful it is? All its branches are outlined, and in its nakedness there is a poem, there is a song. Every leaf is gone and it is waiting for the spring. When the spring comes it again fills the tree with the music of many leaves, which in due season fall and are blown away; and that is the way of life.

But we don't want anything of that kind. We cling to our children, to our traditions, to our society, to our names and our little virtues, because we want permanency; and that is why we are afraid to die. We are afraid to lose the things we know. But life is not what we would like it to be; life is not permanent at all. Birds die, snow melts away, trees are cut down or destroyed by storms, and so on. But we want everything that gives us satisfaction to be permanent; we want our position, the authority we have over people, to endure. We refuse to accept life as it is in fact.

The fact is that life is like the river: endlessly moving on, ever seeking, exploring, pushing, overflowing its banks, penetrating every crevice with its water. But, you see, the mind won't allow that to happen to itself. The mind sees that it is dangerous, risky to live in a state of impermanency, insecurity, so it builds a wall around itself: the wall of tradition, of organized religion, of political and social theories. Family, name, property, the little virtues that we have cultivated – these are all within the walls, away from life. Life is moving, impermanent, and it ceaselessly tries to penetrate, to break down these walls, behind which there is confusion and misery. The gods within the walls are all false gods, and their writings and philosophies have no meaning because life is beyond them.

Now, a mind that has no walls, that is not burdened with its own acquisitions, accumulations, with its own knowledge, a mind that lives timelessly, insecurely – to such a mind, life is an extraordinary thing. Such a mind is life itself, because life has no resting place. But most of us want a resting place; we want a little house, a name, a position, and we say these things are very important. We demand permanency and create a culture based on this demand, inventing gods which are not gods at all but merely a projection of our own desires.

A mind which is seeking permanency soon stagnates; like that pool along the river, it is soon full of corruption, decay. Only the mind which has no walls, no foothold, no barrier, no resting place, which is moving completely with life, time-lessly pushing on, exploring, exploding – only such a mind can be happy, eternally new, because it is creative in itself.

Do you understand what I am talking about? You should because all this is part of real education and, when you understand it, your whole life will be transformed, your relationship with the world, with your neighbour, with your wife or husband, will have a totally different meaning. Then you won't try to fulfil yourself through anything, see-ing that the pursuit of fulfilment only invites sorrow and misery. That is why you should ask your teachers about all this and discuss it among yourselves. If you understand it, you will have begun to understand the extraordinary truth of what life is, and in that understanding there is great beauty and love, the flowering of goodness. But the efforts of a mind that is seeking a pool of security, of permanency, can only lead to darkness and corruption. Once established in the pool, such a mind is afraid to venture out, to seek, to explore; but truth, God, reality or what you will, lies beyond the pool.

Do you know what religion is? It is not in the chant, it is not in the performance of any ritual, it is not in the wor-ship of tin gods or stone images, it is not in the temples and churches, it is not in the reading of the Bible or the *Gita*, it is not in the repeating of a sacred name or in the following of some other superstition invented by men. None of this is religion.

Religion is the feeling of goodness, of that love which is like the river, living, moving everlastingly. In that state you will find there comes a moment when there is no longer any search at all; and this ending of search is the beginning of something totally different. The search for God, for truth, the feeling of being completely good – not the cultivation of goodness, of humility, but the seeking out of something beyond the inventions and tricks of the mind, which means having a feeling for that something, living in it, being it – *that* is true religion. But you can do that only when you leave the pool you have dug for yourself and go out into the river of life. Then life has an astonishing way of taking care of you, because then there is no taking care on your part. Life carries you where it will because you are part of itself; then there is no problem of security, of what people say or don't say, and that is the beauty of life.

XIX

I WONDER how many of you noticed the rainbow last evening? It was just over the water, and one came upon it suddenly. It was a beautiful thing to behold, and it gave one a great sense of joy, an awareness of the vastness and beauty of the earth. To communicate such joy one must have a knowledge of words, the rhythm and beauty of right language, mustn't one? But what is far more important is the feeling itself, the ecstasy that comes with the deep appreciation of something lovely; and this feeling cannot be awakened through the mere cultivation of knowledge or memory.

You see, we must have knowledge to communicate, to tell each other about something; and to cultivate knowledge there must be memory. Without knowledge you cannot fly an aircraft, you cannot build a bridge or a lovely house, you cannot construct great roads, look after trees, care for animals and do the many other things that a civilized man must do. To generate electricity, to work in the various sciences, to help man through medicine, and so on – for all this you must have knowledge, information, memory, and in these matters it is necessary to receive the best possible instruction. That is why it is very important that you should have technically first-class teachers to give you right information and help you to cultivate a thorough knowledge of various subjects.

But, you see, while knowledge is necessary at one level, at another level it becomes a hindrance. There is a great deal of knowledge available about physical existence, and it is being added to, all the time. It is essential to have such knowledge and to utilize it for the benefit of man. But is there not another kind of knowledge which, at the psychological level, becomes a hindrance to the discovery of what is true? After all, knowledge is a form of tradition, is it not? And tradition is the cultivation of memory. Tradition in mechanical affairs is essential, but when tradition is used as a means of guiding man inwardly, it becomes a hindrance to the discovery of greater things.

We rely on knowledge, on memory in mechanical things and in our everyday living. Without knowledge we would not be able to drive a car, we would be incapable of doing many things. But knowledge is a hindrance when it becomes a tradition, a belief which guides the mind, the psyche, the inward being; and it also divides people. Have you noticed how people all over the world are divided into groups, calling themselves Hindus, Moslems, Buddhists, Christians, and so on? What divides them? Not the ˙investigations of science, not the knowledge of agriculture, of how to build bridges or fly jet planes. What divides people is tradition.

So knowledge is a hindrance when it has become a tradition which shapes or conditions the mind to a particular pattern, because then it not only divides people and creates enmity between them, but it also prevents the deep discovery of what is truth, what is life, what is God. To discover what is God, the mind must be free of all tradition, of all accumulation, of all knowledge which it uses as a psychological safeguard.

The function of education is to give the student abundant knowledge in the various fields of human endeavour and at the same time to free his mind from all tradition so that he is able to investigate, to find out, to discover. Otherwise the mind becomes mechanical, burdened with the machinery of knowledge. Unless it is constantly freeing itself from the accumulations of tradition, the mind is incapable of discovering the Supreme, that which is eternal; but it must obviously acquire expanding knowledge and information so that it is capable of dealing with the things that man needs and must produce.

So knowledge, which is the cultivation of memory, is useful and necessary at a certain level, but at another level it becomes a detriment. To recognize the distinction – to see where knowledge is destructive and has to be put aside, and where it is essential and to be allowed to function with as much amplitude as possible – is the beginning of intelligence.

Now, what is happening in education at the present time? You are being given various kinds of knowledge, are you not? When you go to college you may become an engineer, a doctor, or a lawyer, you may take a Ph.D. in mathematics or in some other branch of knowledge, you may study domestic science and learn how to keep house, how to cook, and so on; but nobody helps you to be free of all traditions so that from the very beginning your mind is fresh, eager and therefore capable of discovering something totally new all the time. The philosophies, theories and beliefs which you acquire from books, and which become your tradition, are really a hindrance to the mind, because the mind uses these things as a means of its own psychological security and is therefore conditioned by that them. So it is necessary both to free the mind from all tradition, and at the same time to cultivate knowledge, technique; and this is the function of education.

The difficulty is to free the mind from the known so that it can discover what is new all the time. A great mathematician once told of how he had been working on a problem for a number of days and could not find the solution. One morning, as he was taking a walk as usual, he suddenly saw the answer. What had happened? His mind, being quiet, was free to look at the problem, and the problem itself revealed the answer. One must have information about a problem, but the mind must be free of that information to find the answer.

Most of us learn facts, gather information or knowledge, but the mind never learns how to be quiet, how to be free from all the turmoils of life, from the soil in which problems take root. We join societies, adhere to some philosophy, give ourselves over to a belief, but all this is utterly useless because it does not solve our human problems. On the contrary, it brings greater misery, greater sorrow. What is needed is not philosophy or belief, but for the mind to be free to investigate, to discover and to be creative.

You cram to pass examinations, you gather a lot of information and write it all out to get a degree, hoping to find a job and get married; and is that all? You have acquired knowledge, technique, but your mind is not free, so you become a slave to the existing system – which really means that you are not a creative human being. You may have children, you may paint a few pictures or write an occasional poem, but surely that is not creativeness. There must first be freedom of the mind for creativeness to take place, and then technique can be used to express that creativeness. But to have the technique is meaningless without a creative mind, without the extraordinary creativeness which comes with the discovery of what is true. Unfortunately most of us do not know this creativeness because we have burdened our minds with knowledge, tradition, memory, with what Shankara, Buddha, Marx or some other person has said. Whereas, if your mind is free to discover what is true, then you will find that there comes an abundant and incorruptible richness in which there is great joy. Then all one's relationships – with people, with ideas and with things – have quite a different meaning.

XX

THAT green field with mustard-yellow flowers and a stream running through it is a lovely thing to look upon, is it not? Yesterday evening I was watching it, and in seeing the extraordinary beauty and quietness of the countryside one invariably asks oneself what is beauty. There is an immediate response to that which is lovely and also to that which is ugly, the response of pleasure or of pain, and we put that feeling into words saying, 'This is beautiful' or 'This is ugly'. But what matters is not the pleasure or the pain; rather, it is to be in communion with everything, to be sensitive both to the ugly and to the beautiful.

Now, what is beauty? This is one of the most fundamental questions, it is not superficial, so don't brush it aside. To understand what beauty is, to have that sense of goodness which comes when the mind and heart are in communion with something lovely without any hindrance so that one feels completely at ease – surely, this has great significance in life; and until we know this response to beauty our lives will be very shallow. One may be surrounded by great beauty, by mountains and fields and rivers, but unless one is alive to it all one might just as well be dead.

You girls and boys and older people just put to yourselves this question: what is beauty? Cleanliness, tidiness of dress, a smile, a graceful gesture, the rhythm of walking, a flower in your hair, good manners, clarity of speech, thoughtfulness, being considerate of others, which includes punctuality – all this is part of beauty; but it is only on the surface, is it not? And is that all there is to beauty, or is there something much deeper?

There is beauty of form, beauty of design, beauty of life. Have you observed the lovely shape of a tree when it is in full foliage, or the extraordinary delicacy of a tree naked against the sky? Such things are beautiful to behold, but they are all the superficial expressions of something much deeper. So what is it that we call beauty?

You may have a beautiful face, clean-cut features, you may dress with good taste and have polished manners, you may paint well or write about the beauty of the landscape, but without this inward sense of goodness all the external appurtenances of beauty lead to a very superficial, sophisticated life, a life without much significance.

So we must find out what beauty really is, must we not? Mind you, I am not saying that we should avoid the outward expressions of beauty. We must all have good manners, we must be physically clean and dress tastefully, without ostentation, we must be punctual, clear in our speech, and all the rest of it. These things are necessary and they create a pleasant atmosphere; but by themselves they have not much significance.

It is inward beauty that gives grace, an exquisite gentleness to outward form and movement. And what is this inward beauty without which one's life is very shallow? Have you ever thought about it? Probably not. You are too busy, your minds are too occupied with study, with play, with talking, laughing and teasing each other. But to help you to discover what is inward beauty, without which outward form and movement have very little meaning, is one of the functions of right education; and the deep appreciation of beauty is an essential part of your own life.

Can a shallow mind appreciate beauty? It may talk about beauty; but can it experience this welling up of immense joy upon looking at something that is really lovely? When the mind is merely concerned with itself and its own activities, it is not beautiful; whatever it does, it remains ugly, limited, therefore it is incapable of knowing what beauty is. Whereas, a mind that is not concerned with itself, that is free of ambition, a mind that is not caught up in its own desires or driven by its own pursuit of success – such a mind is not shallow, and it flowers in goodness. Do you understand? It is this inward goodness that gives beauty, even to a so-called ugly face. When there is inward goodness, the ugly face is transformed, for inward goodness is really a deeply religious feeling.

Do you know what it is to be religious? It has nothing to do with temple bells, though they sound nice in the distance, nor with *pujas*, nor with the ceremonies of the priests and all the rest of the ritualistic nonsense. To be religious is to be sensitive to reality. Your total being – body, mind and heart – is sensitive to beauty and to ugliness, to the donkey tied to a post, to the poverty and filth in this town, to laughter and tears, to everything about you. From this sensitivity for the whole of existence springs goodness, love; and without this sensitivity there is no beauty, though you may have talent, be very well dressed, ride in an expensive car and be scrupulously clean.

Love is something extraordinary, is it not? You cannot love if you are thinking about yourself – which does not mean that you must think about somebody else. Love *is*, it has no object. The mind that loves is really a religious mind because it is in the movement of reality, of truth, of God, and it is only such a mind that can know what beauty is. The mind that is not caught in any philosophy, that is not enclosed in any system or belief, that is not driven by its own ambition and is therefore sensitive, alert, watchful – such a mind has beauty.

It is very important while you are young to learn to be tidy and clean, to sit well without restless movements, to have good table manners and to be considerate, punctual; but all these things, however necessary, are superficial, and if you merely cultivate the superficial without understanding the deeper thing, you will never know the real significance of beauty. A mind that does not belong to any nation, group or society, that has no authority, that is not motivated by ambition or held by fear – such a mind is always flowering in love and goodness. Because it is in the movement of reality, it knows what beauty is; being sensitive to both the ugly and the beautiful, it is a creative mind, it has limitless understanding.

XXI

A MAN in *sannyasi* robes used to come every morning to gather flowers from the trees in a nearby garden. His hands and his eyes were greedy for the flowers, and he picked every flower within reach. He was evidently going to offer them to some dead image, a thing made of stone. The flowers were lovely, tender things just opening to the morning sun, and he did not pick them gently, but tore them off, viciously stripping the garden of whatever it held. His god demanded lots of flowers – lots of living things for a dead stone image.

Another day I watched some young boys picking flowers. They were not going to offer the flowers to any god; they were talking and thoughtlessly tearing off the flowers, and throwing them away. Have you ever observed yourself doing this? I wonder why you do it? As you walk along you will break off a twig, strip away the leaves and drop it. Have you not noticed this thoughtless action on your part? The grown-up people do it too, they have their own way of expressing their inner brutality, this appalling disrespect for living things. They talk about harmlessness, yet everything they do is destructive.

One can understand your picking a flower or two to put in your hair, or to give to somebody with love; but why do you just tear at the flowers? The grown-ups are ugly in their ambition, they butcher each other in their wars and corrupt each other with money. They have their own forms of hideous action; and apparently the young people here as elsewhere are following in their footsteps.

The other day I was out walking with one of the boys and we came upon a stone lying on the road. When I removed it, he asked, 'Why did you do that?' What does this indicate? Is it not a lack of consideration, respect? You show respect out of fear, do you not? You promptly jump up when an elder comes into the room, but that is not respect, it is fear; because if you really felt respect you would not destroy the flowers, you would remove a stone from the road, you would tend the trees and help to take care of the garden. But, whether we are old or young, we have no real feeling of consideration. Why? Is it that we don't know what love is?

Do you understand what simple love is? Not the complexity of sexual love, nor the love of God, but just love, being tender, really gentle in one's whole approach to all things. At home you don't always get this simple love, your parents are too busy; at home there may be no real affection, no tenderness, so you come here with that background of insensitivity and you behave like everybody else. And how is one to bring about sensitivity? Not that you must have regulations against picking the flowers; for when you are merely restrained by regulations, there is fear. But how is there to come into being this sensitivity which makes you alert not to do any harm to people, to animals, to flowers?

Are you interested in all this? You should be. If you are not interested in being sensitive, you might as well be dead – and most people are. Though they eat three meals a day, have jobs, procreate children, drive cars, wear fine clothes, most people are as good as dead.

Do you know what it means to be sensitive? It means, surely, to have a tender feeling for things: to see an animal suffering and do something about it, to remove a stone from the path because so many bare feet walk there, to pick up a nail on the road because somebody's car might get a puncture. To be sensitive is to feel for people, for birds, for flowers, for trees – not because they are yours, but just because you are awake to the extraordinary beauty of things. And how is this sensitivity to be brought about?

The moment you are deeply sensitive you naturally do not pluck the flowers; there is a spontaneous desire not to destroy things, not to hurt people, which means having real respect, love. To love is the most important thing in life. But what do we mean by love? When you love someone because that person loves you in return, surely that is not love. To love is to have this extraordinary feeling of affection without asking anything in return. You may be very clever, you may pass all your examinations, get a doctorate and achieve a high position, but if you have not this sensitivity, this feeling of simple love, your heart will be empty and you will be miserable for the rest of your life.

So it is very important for the heart to be filled with this sense of affection, for then you won't destroy, you won't be ruthless, and there won't be wars any more. Then you will be happy human beings; and because you are happy you won't pray, you won't *seek* God, for that happiness itself is God.

Now, how is this love to come into being? Surely, love must begin with the educator, the teacher. If, besides giving you information about mathematics, geography, or history, the teacher has this feeling of love in his heart and talks about it; if he spontaneously removes the stone from the road and does not allow the servant to do all the dirty jobs; if in his conversation, in his work, in his play, when he eats, when he is with you or by himself, he feels this strange thing and points it out to you often, then you also will know what it is to love.

You may have a clear skin, a nice face, you may wear a lovely *sari* or be a great athlete, but without love in your heart you are an ugly human being, ugly beyond measure; and when you love, whether your face is homely or beautiful, it has a radiance. To love is the greatest thing in life; and it is very important to talk about love, to feel it, to nourish it, to treasure it, otherwise it is soon dissipated, for the world is very brutal. If while you are young you don't feel love, if you don't look with love at people, at animals, at flowers, when you grow up you will find that your life is empty; you will be very lonely, and the dark shadows of fear will follow you always. But the moment you have in your heart this extraordinary thing called love and feel the depth, the delight, the ecstasy of it, you will discover that for you the world is transformed.

XXII

ONE of our most difficult problems is what we call discipline, and it is really very complex. You see, society feels that it must control or discipline the citizen, shape his mind according to certain religious, social, moral and economic patterns.

Now, is discipline necessary at all? Please listen carefully, don't immediately say 'yes' or 'no'. Most of us feel, especially while we are young, that there should be no discipline, that we should be allowed to do whatever we like, and we think that is freedom. But merely to say that we should or should not have discipline, that we should be free, and so on, has very little meaning without understanding the whole problem of discipline.

The keen athlete is disciplining himself all the time, is he not? His joy in playing games and the very necessity to keep fit makes him go to bed early, refrain from smoking, eat the right food and generally observe the rules of good health. His discipline is not an imposition or a conflict, but a natural outcome of his enjoyment of athletics.

Now, does discipline increase or decrease human energy? Human beings throughout the world, in every religion, in every school of philosophy, impose discipline on the mind, which implies control, resistance, adjustment, suppression; and is all this necessary? If discipline brings about a greater output of human energy, then it is worth while, then it has meaning; but if it merely suppresses human energy, it is very harmful, destructive. All of us have energy, and the question is whether that energy through discipline can be made vital, rich and abundant, or whether discipline destroys whatever energy we have. I think this is the central issue.

Many human beings do not have a great deal of energy, and what little energy they have is soon smothered and destroyed by the controls, threats and taboos of their particular society with its so-called education; so they become imitative, lifeless citizens of that society. And does discipline give increased energy to the individual who has a little more to begin with? Does it make his life rich and full of vitality?

When you are very young, as you all are, you are full of energy, are you not? You want to play, to rush about, to talk; you can't sit still, you are full of life. Then what happens? As you grow up your teachers begin to curtail that energy by shaping it, directing it into various moulds; and when at last you become men and women the little energy you have left is soon smothered by society, which says that you must be proper citizens, you must behave in a certain way. Through so-called education and the compulsion of society this abounding energy you have when you are young is gradually destroyed.

Now, can the energy you have at present be made more vital through discipline? If you have only a little energy, can discipline increase it? If it can, then discipline has meaning; but if discipline really destroys one's energy, then discipline must obviously be put aside.

What is this energy which we all have? This energy is thinking, feeling; it is interest, enthusiasm, greed, passion, lust, ambition, hate. Painting pictures, inventing machines, building bridges, making roads, cultivating the fields, playing games, writing poems, singing, dancing, going to the temple, worshipping – these are all expressions of energy; and energy also creates illusion, mischief, misery. The very finest and most destructive qualities are equally the expressions of human energy. But, you see, the process of controlling or disciplining this energy, letting it out in one direction and restricting it in another, becomes merely a social convenience; the mind is shaped according to the pattern of a particular culture, and thereby its energy is gradually dissipated.

So, our problem is, can this energy, which in one degree or

another we all possess, be increased, given greater vitality – and if so, to do what? What is energy for? Is it the purpose of energy to make war? Is it to invent jet planes and innumerable other machines, to pursue some *guru*, to pass examinations, to have children, to worry endlessly over this problem and that? Or can energy be used in a different way so that all our activities have significance in relation to something which transcends them all? Surely, if the human mind, which is capable of such astonishing energy, is not seeking reality or God, then every expression of its energy becomes a means of destruction and misery. To seek reality requires immense energy; and, if man is not doing that, he dissipates his energy in ways which create mischief, and therefore society has to control him. Now, is it possible to liberate energy in seeking God or truth and, in the process of discovering what is true, to be a citizen who understands the fundamental issues of life and whom society cannot destroy? Are you following this, or is it a little bit too complex?

You see, man is energy, and if man does not seek truth, this energy becomes destructive; therefore society controls and shapes the individual, which smothers this energy. That is what has happened to the majority of grown-up people all over the world. And perhaps you have noticed another interesting and very simple fact: that the moment you really want to do something, you have the energy to do it. What happens when you are keen to play a game? You immediately have energy, have you not? And that very energy becomes the means of controlling itself, so you don't need outside discipline. In the search for reality, energy creates its own discipline. The man who is seeking reality spontaneously becomes the right kind of citizen, which is not according to the pattern of any particular society or government.

So, students as well as teachers must work together to bring about the release of this tremendous energy to find reality, God or truth. In your very seeking of truth there will be discipline, and then you will be a real human being, a complete individual, and not merely a Hindu or a Parsi limited by his particular society and culture. If, instead of curtailing his energy as it is doing now, the school can help the student to awaken his energy in the pursuit of truth, then you will find that discipline has quite a different meaning.

Why is it that in the home, in the classroom and in the hostel you are always being told what you must do and what you must not do? Surely, it is because your parents and teachers, like the rest of society, have not perceived that man exists for only one purpose, which is to find reality or God. If even a small group of educators were to understand and give their whole attention to that search, they would create a new kind of education and a different society altogether.

Don't you notice how little energy most of the people around you have, including your parents and teachers? They are slowly dying, even when their bodies are not yet old. Why? Because they have been beaten into submission by society. You see, without understanding its fundamental purpose which is to free the extraordinary thing called the mind, with its capacity to create atomic submarines and jet planes, which can write the most amazing poetry and prose, which can make the world so beautiful and also destroy the world – without understanding the fundamental purpose, which is to find truth or God, this energy becomes destructive; and then society says, 'We must shape and control the energy of the individual.'

So, it seems to me that the function of education is to bring about a release of energy in the pursuit of goodness, truth, or God, which in turn makes the individual a true human being and therefore the right kind of citizen. But mere discipline, without full comprehension of all this, has no meaning, it is a most destructive thing. Unless each one of you is so educated that, when you leave school and go out into the world, you are full of vitality and intelligence, full of abounding energy to find out what is true, you will merely be absorbed by society; you will be smothered, destroyed, miserably unhappy for the rest of your life. As a river creates the banks which hold it, so the energy which seeks truth creates its own discipline without any form of imposition; and as the river finds the sea, so that energy finds its own freedom.

XVIII

HAVE you ever wondered why it is that as people grow older they seem to lose all joy in life? At present most of you who are young are fairly happy; you have your little problems, there are examinations to worry about, but in spite of these troubles there is in your life a certain joy, is there not? There is a spontaneous, easy acceptance of life, a looking at things lightly and happily. And why it is that as we grow older we seem to lose that joyous intimation of something beyond, something of greater signficance? Why do so many of us, as we grow into so-called maturity, become dull, insensitive to joy, to beauty, to the open skies and the marvellous earth?

You know, when one asks oneself this question, many explanations spring up in the mind. We are so concerned with ourselves – that is one explanation. We struggle to become somebody, to achieve and maintain a certain position; we have children and other responsibilities, and we have to earn money. All these external things soon weigh us down, and thereby we lose the joy of living. Look at the older faces around you, see how sad most of them are, how careworn and rather ill, how withdrawn, aloof and sometimes neurotic, without a smile. Don't you ask yourself why? And even when we do ask why, most of us seem to be satisfied with mere explanations.

Yesterday evening I saw a boat going up the river at full sail, driven by the west wind. It was a large boat, heavily laden with firewood for the town. The sun was setting, and this boat against the sky was astonishingly beautiful. The boatman was just guiding it, there was no effort, for the wind was doing all the work. Similarly, if each one of us could understand the problem of struggle and conflict, then I think we would be able to live effortlessly, happily, with a smile on our face.

I think it is effort that destroys us, this struggling in which we spend almost every moment of our lives. If you watch the older people around you, you will see that for most of them life is a series of battles with themselves, with their wives or husbands, with their neighbours, with society; and this ceaseless strife dissipates energy. The man who is joyous, really happy, is not caught up in effort. To be without effort does not mean that you stagnate, that you are dull, stupid; on the contrary, it is only the wise, the extraordinarily intelligent who are really free of effort, of struggle.

But, you see, when we hear of effortlessness we want to be like that, we want to achieve a state in which we will have no strife, no conflict; so we make that our goal, our ideal, and strive after it; and the moment we do this, we have lost the joy of living. We are again caught up in effort, struggle. The object of struggle varies, but all struggle is essentially the same. One may struggle to bring about social reforms, or to find God, or to create a better relationship between oneself and one's wife or husband, or with one's neighbour; one may sit on the bank of the Ganges, worship at the feet of some *guru*, and so on. All this is effort, struggle. So what is important is not the object of struggle, but to understand struggle itself.

Now, is it possible for the mind to be not just casually aware that for the moment it is not struggling, but completely free of struggle all the time so that it discovers a state of joy in which there is no sense of the superior and the inferior?

Our difficulty is that the mind feels inferior, and that is why it struggles to be or become something, or to bridge over its various contradictory desires. But don't let us give explanations of why the mind is full of struggle. Every thinking man knows why there is struggle both within and without. Our envy, greed, ambition, our competitiveness leading to ruthless efficiency – these are obviously the factors which cause us to struggle, whether in this world or in the world to come. So we don't have to study psychological books to know why we struggle; and what is important, surely, is to find out if the mind can be totally free of struggle.

After all, when we struggle, the conflict is between what we are and what we *should* be or *want* to be. Now, without giving explanations, can one understand this whole process of struggle so that it comes to an end? Like that boat which was moving with the wind, can the mind be without struggle? Surely, this is the question, and not how to achieve a state in which there is no struggle. The very effort to achieve such a state is itself a process of struggle, therefore that state is never achieved. But if you observe from moment to moment how the mind gets caught in everlasting struggle – if you just observe the fact without trying to alter it, without trying to force upon the mind a certain state which you call peace – then you will find that the mind spontaneously ceases to struggle; and in that state it can learn enormously. Learning is then not merely the process of gathering information, but a discovery of the extraordinary riches that lie beyond the scope of the mind; and for the mind that makes this discovery there is joy.

Watch yourself and you will see how you struggle from morning till night, and how your energy is wasted in this struggle. If you merely explain why you struggle, you get lost in explanations and the struggle continues; whereas, if you observe your mind very quietly without giving explanations, if you just let the mind be aware of its own struggle, you will soon find that there comes a state in which there is no struggle at all, but an astonishing watchfulness. In that state of watchfulness there is no sense of the superior and the inferior, there is no big man or little man, there is no *guru*. All those absurdities are gone because the mind is fully awake; and the mind that is fully awake is joyous.

ONE of the many problems confronting all of us, and especially those who are now being educated and must soon go out and face the world, is this question of reform. Various groups of people – the socialists, the communists, and reformers of every kind – are concerned with trying to bring about certain changes in the world, changes which are obviously necessary. Although in some countries there is a fair degree of prosperity, throughout the world there is still hunger, starvation, and millions of human beings have insufficient clothing and no proper place to sleep. And how is a fundamental reformation to take place without creating more chaos, more misery and strife? That is the real problem, is it not? If one reads a little history and observes present-day political trends, it becomes obvious that what we call reformation, however desirable and necessary, always brings in its wake still other forms of confusion and conflict; and to counteract this further misery, more legislation, more checks and counterchecks become necessary. Reformation creates new disorders; in putting these right, still further disorders are produced, and so the vicious circle continues. This is what we are faced with, and it is a process which seems to have no end.

Now, how is one to break through this vicious circle? Mind you, it is obvious that reformation is necessary; but is reformation possible without bringing about still further confusion? This seems to me to be one of the fundamental issues with which any thoughtful person must be concerned. The question is not what kind of reformation is necessary, or at what level, but whether any reformation is possible at all without bringing with it other problems which again create the need of reform. And what is one to do in order to break up this endless process? Surely, it is the function of education, whether in the small school or in the large university, to tackle this problem, not abstractly, theoretically, not by merely philosophizing or writing books about it, but by actually facing it in order to find out how to solve it. Man is caught in this vicious circle of reformation which always needs further reform and, if it is not broken up, our problems can have no solution.

So, what kind of education, what kind of thinking is necessary to break up this vicious circle? What action will put an end to the increase of problems in all our activities? Is there any movement of thought, in any direction, that can free man from this manner of living, the reformation of which always needs further reform? In other words, is there an action which is not born of reaction?

I think there is a way of life in which there is not this process of reformation breeding further misery, and that way may be called religious. The truly religious person is not concerned with reform, he is not concerned with merely producing a change in the social order; on the contrary, he is seeking what is true, and that very search has a transforming effect on society. That is why education must be principally concerned with helping the student to seek out truth or God, and not merely preparing him to fit into the pattern of a given society.

I think it is very important to understand this while we are young; because, as we grow older and begin to set aside our little amusements and distractions, our sexual appetites and petty ambitions, we become more keenly aware of the immense problems confronting the world, and then we want to do something about them, we want to bring about some kind of amelioration. But unless we are deeply religious we shall only create more confusion, further misery; and religion has nothing to do with priests, churches, dogmas, or organized beliefs. These things are not religion at all, they are merely social conveniences to hold us within a particular pattern of thought and action; they are the means of exploiting our credulity, hope and fear. Religion is the seeking out of what is truth, what is God, and this search requires enormous energy, wide intelligence, subtle thinking. It is in this very seeking of the immeasurable that there is right social action, not in the so-called reformation of a particular society.

To find out what is truth there must be great love and a deep awareness of man's relationship to all things – which means that one is not concerned with one's own progress and achievements. The search for truth is true religion, and the man who is seeking truth is the only religious man. Such a man, because of his love, is outside of society, and his action upon society is therefore entirely different from that of the man who is in society and concerned with its reformation. The reformer can never create a new culture. What is necessary is the search of the truly religious man, for this very search brings about its own culture and it is our only hope. You see, the search for truth gives an explosive creativeness to the mind, which is true revolution, because in this search the mind is uncontaminated by the edicts and sanctions of society. Being free of all that, the religious man is able to find out what is true; and it is the discovery of what is true from moment to moment that creates a new culture.

That is why it is very important for you to have the right kind of education. For this the educator himself must be rightly educated so that he will not regard teaching merely as a means of earning a livelihood, but will be capable of helping the student to put aside all dogmas and not be held by any religion or belief. The people who come together on the basis of religious authority, or to practise certain ideals, are all concerned with social reform, which is merely the decorating of the prison walls. Only the truly religious man is truly revolutionary; and it is the function of education to help each one of us to be religious in the true sense of the word, for in that direction alone lies our salvation.

PART THREE

Questions and Answers

Questioner: We know sex as an inescapable physical and psychological necessity and it seems to be a root-cause of chaos in the personal life of our generation. How can we deal with this problem?

KRISHNAMURTI: Why is it that whatever we touch we turn into a problem? We have made God a problem, we have made love a problem, we have made relationship, living, a problem, and we have made sex a problem. Why? Why is everything we do a problem, a horror? Why are we suffering? Why has sex become a problem? Why do we submit to living with problems, why do we not put an end to them? Why do we not die to our problems instead of carrying them day after day, year after year? Sex is certainly a relevant question but there is the primary question, why do we make life into a problem? Working, sex, earning money, thinking, feeling, experiencing – you know, the whole business of living – why is it a problem? Is it not essentially because we always think from a particular point of view, from a fixed point of view? We are always thinking from a centre towards the periphery but the periphery is the centre for most of us and so anything we touch is superficial. But life is not superficial; it demands living completely and because we are living only superficially we know only superficial reaction. Whatever we do on the periphery must inevitably create a problem, and that is our life: we live in the superficial and we are content to live there with all the problems of the superficial. Problems exist so long as we live in the superficial, on the periphery, the periphery being the 'me' and its sensations, which can be externalized or made subjective, which can be identified with the universe, with the country or with some other thing made up by the mind.

So long as we live within the field of the mind there must be complications, there must be problems; that is all we know. Mind is sensation, mind is the result of accumulated sensations and reactions and anything it touches is bound to create misery, confusion, an endless problem. The mind is the real cause of our problems, the mind that is working mechanically night and day, consciously and unconsciously. The mind is a most superficial thing and we have spent generations, we spend our whole lives, cultivating the mind, making it more and more clever, more and more subtle, more and more cunning, more and more dishonest and crooked, all of which is apparent in every activity of our life. The very nature of our mind is to be dishonest, crooked, incapable of facing facts, and that is the thing which creates problems; that is the thing which is the problem itself.

What do we mean by the problem of sex? Is it the act, or is it a thought about the act? Surely it is not the act. The sexual act is no problem to you, any more than eating is a problem to you, but if you *think* about eating or anything else all day long because you have nothing else to think about, it becomes a problem to you. Is the sexual act the problem or is it the thought about the act? Why do you think about it? Why do you build it up, which you are obviously doing? The cinemas, the magazines, the stories, the way women dress, everything is building up your thought of sex. Why does the mind build it up, why does the mind think about sex at all? Why? Why has it become a central issue in your life? When there are so many things calling, demanding your attention, you give complete attention to the thought of sex. What happens, why are your minds so occupied with it? Because that is a way of ultimate escape, is it not? It is a way of complete self-forgetfulness. For the time being, at least for that moment, you can forget yourself – and there is no other way of forgetting yourself. Everything else you do in life gives emphasis to the 'me', to the self. Your business, your religion, your gods, your leaders, your political and economic actions, your escapes, your social activities, your joining one party and rejecting another – all that is emphasizing and giving strength to the 'me'. That is, there is only this one act in which there is no emphasis on the 'me', so it becomes a problem, does it not? When there is only one thing in your life which is an avenue to ultimate escape, to complete forgetfulness of yourself if only for a few seconds, you cling to it because that is the only moment in which you are happy. Every other issue you touch becomes a nightmare, a source of suffering and pain, so you cling to the one thing which gives complete self-forgetfulness, which you call happiness. But when you cling to it, it too becomes a nightmare, because then you want to be free from it, you do not want to be a slave to it. So you invent, again from the mind, the idea of chastity, of celibacy, and you try to be celibate, to be chaste, through suppression, all of which are operations of the mind to cut itself off from the gact. This again gives particular emphasis to the 'me' who is trying to become something, so again you are caught in travail, in trouble, in effort, in pain,

Sex becomes an extraordinarily difficult and complex problem so long as you do not understand the mind which thinks about the problem. The act itself can never be a problem but the thought about the act creates the problem. The act you safeguard; you live loosely, or indulge yourself in marriage, thereby making your wife into a prostitute which is all apparently very respectable, and you are satisfied to leave it at that. Surely the problem can be solved only when you understand the whole process and structure of the 'me' and the 'mine': my wife, my child, my property, my car, my achievement, my success; until you understand and resolve all that, sex as a problem will remain. So long as you are ambitious, politically, religiously or in any way, so long as you are emphasizing the self, the thinker, the experiencer, by feeding him on ambition whether in the name of yourself as an individual or in the name of the country, of the party or of an idea which you call religion – so long as there is this activity of self-expansion, you will have a sexual problem. You are creating, feeding, expanding yourself on the one hand, and on the other you are trying to forget yourself, to lose yourself if only for a moment.

How can the two exist together? Your life is a contradiction; emphasis on the 'me' and forgetting the 'me'. Sex is not a problem; the problem is this contradiction in your life; and the contradiction cannot be bridged over by the mind, because the mind itself is a contradiction. The contradiction can be understood only when you understand fully the whole process of your daily existence. Going to the cinemas and watching women on the screen, reading books which stimulate the thought, the magazines with their half-naked pictures, your way of looking at women, the surreptitious eyes that catch yours – all these things are encouraging the mind through devious ways to emphasize the self and at the same time you try to be kind, loving, tender. The two cannot go together. The man who is ambitious, spiritually or otherwise, can never be without a problem, because problems cease only when the self is forgotten, when the 'me' is non-existent, and that state of the non-existence of the self is not an act of will, it is not a mere reaction. Sex becomes a reaction; when the mind tries to solve the problem, it only makes the problem more confused, more troublesome, more painful. The act is not the problem but the mind is the problem, the mind which says it must be chaste. Chastity is not of the mind. The mind can only suppress its own activities and suppression is not chastity. Chastity is not a virtue, chastity cannot be cultivated. The man who is cultivating humility is surely not a humble man; he may call his pride humility, but he is a proud man, and that is why he seeks to become humble. Pride can never become humble and chastity is not a thing of the mind – you cannot become chaste. You will know chastity only when there is love, and love is not of the mind nor a thing of the mind.

Therefore the problem of sex which tortures so many people all over the world cannot be resolved till the mind is understood. We cannot put an end to thinking but thought comes to an end when the thinker ceases, and the thinker ceases only when there is an understanding of the whole process. Fear comes into being when there is division between the thinker and his thought; when there is no thinker, then only is there no conflict in thought. What is implicit needs no effort to understand. The thinker comes into being through thought; then the thinker exerts himself to shape, to control his thoughts or to put an end to them. The thinker is a fictitious entity, an illusion of the mind. When there is a realization of thought as a fact, then there is no need to think about the fact. If there is simple, choiceless awareness, then that which is implicit in the fact begins to reveal itself. Therefore thought as fact ends. Then you will see that the problems which are eating at our hearts and minds, the problems of our social structure, can be resolved. Then sex is no longer a problem, it has its proper place, it is neither an impure thing nor a pure thing. Sex has its place; but when the mind gives it the predominant place, then it becomes a problem. The mind gives sex a predominant place because it cannot live without some happiness and so sex becomes a problem; when the mind understands its whole process and so comes to an end, that is when thinking ceases, then there is creation and it is that creation which makes us happy. To be in that state of creation is bliss, because it is self-forgetfulness in which there is no reaction as from the self. This is not an abstract answer to the daily problem of sex – it is the only answer. The mind denies love and without love there is no chastity; it is because there is no love that you make sex into a problem.

Questioner: What do you mean by love?

KRISHNAMURTI: We are going to discover by understanding what love is not, because, as love is the unknown, we must come to it by discarding the known. The unknown cannot be discovered by a mind that is full of the known. What we are going to do is to find out the values of the known, look at the known, and when that is looked at purely, without condemnation, the mind becomes free from the known; then we shall know what love is. So, we must approach love negatively, not positively.

What is love with most of us? When we say we love somebody, what do we mean? We mean we possess that person. From that possession arises jealousy, because if I lose him or her what happens? I feel empty, lost; therefore I legalize possession; I hold him or her. From holding, possessing that person, there is jealousy, there is fear and all the innumerable conflicts that arise from possession. Surely such possession is not love, is it?

Obviously love is not sentiment. To be sentimental, to be emotional, is not love, because sentimentality and emotion are mere sensations. A religious person who weeps about Jesus or Krishna, about his *guru* or somebody else is merely sentimental, emotional. He is indulging in sensation, which is a process of thought, and thought is not love. Thought is the result of sensation, so the person who is sentimental, who is emotional, cannot possibly know love. Again, aren't we emotional and sentimental? Sentimentality, emotionalism, is merely a form of self-expansion. To be full of emotion is obviously not love, because a sentimental person can be cruel when his sentiments are not responded to, when his feelings have no outlet. An emotional person can be stirred to hatred, to war, to butchery. A man who is sentimental, full of tears for his religion, surely has no love.

Is forgiveness love? What is implied in forgiveness? You insult me and I resent it, remember it; then, either through compulsion or through repentance, I say, 'I forgive you'. First I retain and then I reject. Which means what? I am still the central figure; it is I who am forgiving somebody. As long as there is the attitude of forgiving it is I who am important, not the man who is supposed to have insulted me. So when I accumulate resentment and then deny that resentment, which you call forgiveness, it is not love. A man who loves, obviously has no enmity and to all these things he is indifferent. Sympathy, forgiveness, the relationship of possessiveness, jealousy and fear – all these things are not love. They are all of the mind, are they not? As long as the mind is the arbiter, there is no love, for the mind arbitrates only through possessiveness and its arbitration is merely possessiveness in different forms. The mind can only corrupt love, it cannot give birth to love, it cannot give beauty. You can write a poem about love but that is not love.

Obviously there is no love when there is no real respect, when you don't respect another, whether he is your servant or your friend. Have you not noticed that you are not respectful, kindly, generous, to your servants, to people who are so-called 'below' you? You have respect for those above, for your boss, for the millionaire, for the man with a large house and a title, for the man who can give you a better position, a better job, from whom you can get something. But you kick those below you, you have a special language for them. Therefore where there is no respect, there is no love; where there is no mercy, no pity, no forgiveness, there is no love. And as most of us are in this state we have no love. We are neither respectful nor merciful nor generous. We are possessive, full of sentiment and emotion which can be turned either way: to kill, to butcher or to unify over some foolish, ignorant intention. So how can there be love?

You can know love only when all these things have come to an end, only when you don't possess, when you are not merely emotional with devotion to an object. Such devotion is a supplication, seeking something in a different form. A man who prays does not know love. Since you are possessive, since you seek an end, a result, through devotion, through prayer, which makes you sentimental, emotional, naturally there is no love.

When the things of the mind don't fill your heart, then there is love; and love alone can transform the present madness and insanity in the world – not systems, not theories, either of the left or the right. You really love only when you do not possess, when you are not envious, not greedy, when you are respectful, when you have mercy and compassion, when you have consideration for your wife, your children, your neighbour, your unfortunate servants.

Love cannot be thought about, love cannot be cultivated, love cannot be practised. The practice of love, the practice of brotherhood, is still within the field of the mind, therefore it is not love. When all this has stopped, then love comes into being, then you will know what it is to love. Then love is not quantitative but qualitative. You do not say, 'I love the whole world', but when you know how to love one, you know how to love the whole. Because we do not know how to love one, our love of humanity is fictitious. When you love, there is neither one nor many: there is only love. It is only when there is love that all our problems can be solved and then we shall know its bliss and its happiness.

Questioner: How can we live happily?

KRISHNAMURTI: Do you know when you are living happily? You know when you are suffering, when you have physical pain. When somebody hits you or is angry with you, you know suffering. But do you know when you are happy? Are you conscious of your body when you are healthy? Surely, happiness is a state of which you are unconscious, of which you are not aware. The moment you are aware that you are happy, you cease to be happy, don't you? But most of you suffer; and being conscious of that, you want to escape from suffering into what you call happiness. You want to be consciously happy; and the moment you are consciously happy, happiness is gone. Can you ever say that you are joyous? It is only afterwards, a moment or a week later that you say, 'How happy I was, how joyous I have been'. In the actual moment you are unconscious of happiness, and that is the beauty of it.

Questioner: Is it practicable for a man to free himself from all sense of fear and at the same time to stay with society?

KRISHNAMURTI: What is society? A set of values, a set of rules, regulations and traditions, is it not? You see these conditions from outside and you say, 'Can I have a practical relationship with all that?' Why not? After all, if you merely fit into that framework of values, are you free? And what do you mean by 'practicable'? Do you mean earning a livelihood? There are many things you can do to earn a livelihood; and if you are free, can you not choose what you want to do? Is that not practicable? Or would you consider it practicable to forget your freedom and just fit into the framework, becoming a lawyer, a banker, a merchant, or a road sweeper? Surely, if you are free and have cultivated your intelligence, you will find out what is the best thing for you to do. You will brush aside all traditions and do something which you really love to do, regardless of whether your parents and society approve or disapprove. Because you are free, there is intelligence, and you will do something which is completely your own, you will act as an integrated human being.

Questioner: How can we make our minds free when we live in a society full of tradition?

KRISHNAMURTI: First you must have the urge, the demand to be free. It is like the longing of the bird to fly, or of the waters of the river to flow. Have you this urge to be free? If you have, then what will happen? Your parents and society try to force you into a mould. Can you resist them? You will find it difficult, because you are afraid. You are afraid of not getting a job, of not finding the right husband or the right wife; you are afraid you will starve, or that people will talk about you. Though you want to be free, you are afraid, so you are not going to resist. Your fear of what people may say, or of what your parents may do, blocks you, and so you are forced into the mould.

Now, can you say, 'I want to know, and I do not mind starving. Whatever happens, I am going to battle against the barriers of this rotten society, because I want to be free to find out.'? Can you say that? When you are frightened, can you withstand all these barriers, all these impositions?

So, it is very important from the tenderest age to help the child to see the implications of fear, and be free of it. The moment you are frightened, there is an end to freedom.

Questioner: What is real freedom, and how is one to acquire it?

KRISHNAMURTI: Real freedom is not something to be acquired, it is the outcome of intelligence. You cannot go out and buy freedom in the market You cannot get it by reading a book, or by listening to someone talking.

But what is intelligence? Can there be intelligence when there is fear, or when the mind is conditioned? When your mind is prejudiced, or when you think you are a marvellous human being, or when you are very ambitious and want to climb the ladder of success, worldly or spiritual, can there be intelligence? When you are concerned about yourself, when you follow or worship somebody, can there be intelligence? Surely, intelligence comes when you understand and break away from all this stupidity. So you have to set about it; and the first thing is to be aware that your mind is not free. You have to observe how your mind is bound by all these things, and then there is the beginning of intelligence, which brings freedom. You have to find the answer for yourself. What is the use of someone else being free when you are not, or of someone else having food when you are hungry?

To be creative, which is to have real initiative, there must be freedom; and for freedom there must be intelligence. So you have to inquire and find out what is preventing intelligence. You have to investigate life, you have to question social values, everything, and not accept anything because you are frightened.

Questioner: What is the real goal of life?

KRISHNAMURTI: It is, first of all, what you make of it. It is what you make of life.

Questioner: As far as reality is concerned, it must be something else. I am not particularly interested in having a personal goal, but I want to know what is the goal for everybody.

KRISHNAMURTI: How will you find out? Who will show you? Can you discover it by reading? If you read, one author may give you a particular method, while another author may offer quite a different method. If you go to a man who is suffering, he will say that the goal of life is to be happy. If you go to a man who is starving, who has not had sufficient food for years, his goal will be to have a full tummy. If you go to a politician, his goal will be to become one of the directors, one of the rulers of the world. If you ask a young woman, she will say, 'My goal is to have a baby'. If you go to a *sannyasi*, his goal is to find God. The goal, the under-lying desire of people is generally to find something grati-fying, comforting; they want some form of security, safety, so that they will have no doubts, no questions, no anxiety, no fear. Most of us want something permanent to which we can cling, do we not?

So, the general goal of life for man is some kind of hope, some kind of safety, some kind of permanency. Don't say, 'Is that all?' That is the immediate fact, and you must first be fully acquainted with that. You must question all that – which means, you must question yourself. The general goal of life for man is embedded in you, because you are part of the whole. You yourself want safety, permanency, happiness; you want something to which to cling.

Now, to find out if there is something else beyond, some truth which is not of the mind, all the illusions of the mind must be finished with; that is, you must understand them and put them aside. Only then can you discover the real thing, whether there is a goal or not. To stipulate that there must be a goal, or to believe that there is a goal, is merely another illusion. But if you can question all your conflicts, struggles, pains, vanities, ambitions, hopes, fears, and go through them, go beyond and above them, then you will find out.

Questioner: *Why is there sorrow and misery in the world?*

KRISHNAMURTI: I wonder if that boy knows what those

words mean. He has probably seen an over-loaded donkey with its legs almost breaking, or another boy crying, or a mother beating her child. Perhaps he has seen older people quarrelling with each other. And there is death, the body being carried away to be burnt; there is the beggar; there is poverty, disease, old age; there is sorrow, not only outside, but also inside us. So he asks, 'Why is there sorrow?' Don't you want to know too? Have you never wondered about the cause of your own sorrow? What is sorrow, and why does it exist? If I want something and cannot get it, I feel miserable; if I want more *saris*, more money, or if I want to be more beautiful, and cannot have what I want, I am unhappy. If I want to love a certain person and that person does not love me, again I am miserable. My father dies, and I am in sorrow. Why?

Why do we feel unhappy when we cannot have what we want? Why should we necessarily have what we want? We think it is our right, do we not? But do we ever ask ourselves why we should have what we want when millions have not got even what they *need*? And besides, why do we want it? There is our need of food, clothing and shelter; but we are not satisfied with that. We want much more. We want success, we want to be respected, loved, looked up to, we want to be powerful, we want to be famous poets, saints, orators, we want to be prime ministers, presidents. Why? Have you ever looked into it? Why do we want all this? Not that we must be satisfied with what we are. I do not mean that. That would be ugly, silly. But why this constant craving for more and more and more? This craving indicates that we are dissatisfied, discontented; but with what? With what we are? I am *this*, I do not like it, and I want to be *that*. I think I shall look much more beautiful in a new coat or a new *sari*, so I want it. This means I am dissatisfied with what I am, and I think I can escape from my discontent by acquiring more clothes, more power, and so on. But the dissatisfaction is still there, is it not? I have only covered it up with clothes, with power, with cars.

So, we have to find out how to understand what we are.

Merely to cover ourselves with possessions, with power and position, has no meaning, because we will still be unhappy. Seeing this, the unhappy person, the person who is in sorrow, does not run away to *gurus*, he does not hide in possessions, in power; on the contrary, he wants to know what lies behind his sorrow. If you go behind your own sorrow you will find that you are very small, empty, limited, and that you are struggling to achieve, to become. This very struggle to achieve, to become something is the cause of sorrow. But if you begin to understand what you actually are, go deeper into it, then you will find that something quite different takes place.

Questioner: If a man is starving and I feel that I can be helpful to him, is this ambition or love?

KRISHNAMURTI: He is starving and you help him with food. Is that love? Why do you want to help him? Have you no motive, no incentive other than the desire to help him? Do you not get any benefit out of it? Think this out, do not say 'yes' or 'no'. If you are looking for some benefit out of it, politically or otherwise, some inward or outward benefit, then you do not love him. If you feed him in order to become more popular, or in the hope that your friends will help you to get into Parliament, then that is not love, is it? But if you love him, you will feed him without any ulterior motive, without wanting anything in return. If you feed him and he is ungrateful, do you feel hurt? If so, you do not love him. If he tells you and others that you are a wonderful man, and you feel very flattered, it means you are thinking about yourself; and surely that is not love. So, one has to be very alert to find out if one is deriving any kind of benefit from one's helpfulness, and what the motive is that leads one to feed the hungry.

Questioner: What should we ask God to give us?

KRISHNAMURTI: You are very interested in God, are you not? Why? Because your mind is asking for something, wanting something. So it is constantly agitated. If I am asking or expecting something from you, my mind is agitated, is it not?

This boy wants to know what he should ask of God. He does not know what God is, or what it is he really wants. But there is a general feeling of apprehension, the feeling, 'I must ask, I must pray, I must be protected'. The mind is always seeking in every corner to get something; it is always wanting, grasping, watching, pushing, comparing, judging, and so it is never still. Observe your own mind and you will see what it is doing, how it tries to control itself, to dominate, to suppress, to find some form of satisfaction, how it is constantly asking, begging, struggling, comparing. We call such a mind very alert; but is it alert? Surely, an alert mind is a still mind, not one that, like a butterfly, is chasing all over the place. And it is only a still mind that can understand what God is. A still mind never asks anything of God. It is only the impoverished mind that begs, that asks. What it asks, it can never have, because what it really wants is security, comfort, certainty. If you ask anything of God, you will never find God.

Questioner: *What is real greatness and how can I be great?*

KRISHNAMURTI: You see, the unfortunate thing is that we want to be great. We all want to be great. We want to be a great leader or a prime minister, we want to be great inventors, great writers. Why? In education, in religion, in all the departments of our life, we have examples. The great poet, the great orator, the great statesman, the great saint, the great hero – such people are held up as examples, and we want to be like them.

Now, when you want to be like another, you have created a pattern of action, have you not? You have set a limitation on your thought, bound it within certain limits. So your thought has already become crystallized, narrow, limited, stifled. Why do you want to be great? Why do you not look at what you are and understand that? You see, the moment you want to be like another, there is misery, conflict, there is envy, sorrow. If you want to be like the Buddha, what happens? You struggle everlastingly to achieve that ideal. If you are stupid and crave to be clever, you constantly try to leave what you are and go beyond it. If you are ugly and want to be beautiful, you long to be beautiful till you die, or you deceive yourself into thinking you are beautiful. So, as long as you are trying to be something other than what you actually are, your mind merely wears itself out. But if you say, 'This is what I am, it is a fact, and I am going to investigate, understand it', then you can go beyond; for you will find that the understanding of what you are brings great peace and contentment, great insight, great love.

Questioner: Is not love based on attraction?

KRISHNAMURTI: Suppose you are attracted to a beautiful woman or a handsome man. What is wrong with that? When you are attracted to a woman, to a man, or to a child, what generally happens? You not only want to be with that person, but you want to possess, to call that person your own. Your body must be near that person's body. So what have you done? The fact is that when you are attracted, you want to possess, you do not want that person to look at anybody else; and when you consider another human being as yours, is there love? Obviously not. The moment your mind creates a hedge as the 'mine' around that person, there is no love.

The fact is that our minds are doing this all the time. That is why we are discussing these things – to see how the mind is working; and perhaps, being aware of its own movements, the mind will be quiet of its own accord.

Questioner: What is prayer? Has it any importance in daily life?

KRISHNAMURTI: Why do you pray? And what is prayer? Most prayer is merely a petitioning, an asking. You indulge in this kind of prayer when you suffer. When you feel all alone, when you are depressed and in sorrow, you ask God for help; so what you call prayer is a petition. The form of prayer may vary, but the intent behind it is generally the same. Prayer, with most people is a petition, a begging, an asking. Are you doing that? Why do you pray? I am not saying that you should or should not pray. But why do you pray? Is it for more knowledge, for more peace? Do you pray that the world may be free from sorrow? Is there any other kind of prayer? There is prayer which is really not a prayer, but the sending out of good will, the sending out of love, the sending out of ideas. What is it you are doing?

When you pray, generally you are asking God, or some saint, to fill your empty bowl, are you not? You are not satisfied with what happens, with what is given, but you want your bowl filled according to your wishes. So your prayer is merely a petition; it is a demand that you should be satisfied, therefore it is not prayer at all. You say to God, 'I am suffering, please gratify me; please give me back my brother, my son. Please make me rich'. You are perpetuating your own demands, and that is obviously not prayer.

The real thing is to understand yourself, to see why you are perpetually asking for something, why there is in you this demand, this urge to beg. The more you know yourself through awareness of what you are thinking, what you are feeling, the more you will discover the truth of what *is*; and it is this truth that will help you to be free.

Questioner: Why do we feel a sense of pride when we succeed?

KRISHNAMURTI: What is success? Have you ever considered what it is to be successful as a writer, as a poet, as a painter, as a business man or politician? To feel that you have inwardly achieved a certain control over yourself which others do not have, or that you have succeeded where others have failed; to feel that you are better than somebody else, that you have become a successful man, that you are respected, looked up to by others as an example – what does all this indicate? Naturally, when you have this feeling, there is pride: *I* have done something, *I* am important. The feeling of 'I' is in its very nature a sense of pride. So pride grows with success; one is proud of being very important compared with other people. This comparison of yourself with another exists also in your pursuit of the example, the ideal, and it gives you hope, it gives you strength, purpose, drive, which only strengthens the 'I', the pleasurable feeling that you are much more important than anybody else; and that feeling, that sense of pleasure, is the beginning of pride.

Pride brings a great deal of vanity, an egotistic inflation. You can observe this in the older people and in yourself. When you pass an examination and feel that you are a little cleverer than another, a sense of pleasure comes in. It is the same when you outdo somebody in an argument, or when you feel that you are physically much stronger or more beautiful – immediately there is a sense of your own import-ance. This feeling of the importance of the 'me' in-evitably brings conflict, struggle, pain, because you have to maintain your importance all the time.

Questioner: How can we be free of pride?

KRISHNAMURTI: If you had really listened to the answer to the previous question, you would have understood how to be free of pride, and you would be free of pride; but you were concerned with how to put the next question, were you not? So you were not listening. If you really listen to what is being said, you will find out for yourself the truth of it.

Suppose I am proud because I have achieved something. I have become the Principal; I have been to England or to America; I have done great things, my photograph has appeared in the newspapers, and so on and so on. Feeling very proud, I say to myself, 'How am I to be free of pride?'

Now, why do I want to be free of pride? That is the im-portant question, not *how* to be free. What is the motive, what is the reason, what is the incentive? Do I want to be free of pride because I find it harmful to me, painful, spiritually not good? If that is the motive, then to try to free myself from pride is another form of pride, is it not? I am still concerned with achievement. Finding that pride is very painful, spiritually ugly, I say that I must be free of it. The 'I must be free' contains the same motive as the 'I must be successful'. The 'I' is still important, it is the centre of my struggle to be free.

So, what matters is not how to be free of pride, but to understand the 'I'; and the 'I' is very subtle. It wants one thing this year and another thing next year; and when that turns out to be painful, it then wants something else. So, as long as this centre of the 'I' exists, whether one is proud or so-called humble is of very little significance. They are only different coats to put on. When a particular coat appeals to me, I put it on; and next year, according to my fancies, my desires, I put on another coat.

What you have to understand is how this 'I' comes into being. The 'I' comes into being through the sense of achievement in various forms. This does not mean that you must not act; but the feeling that *you* are acting, that *you* are achieving, that *you* must be without pride, has to be understood. You have to understand the structure of the 'I'. You have to be aware of your own thinking; you have to observe how you treat your servant, your mother and father, and your teacher; you have to be conscious of how you regard those who are above you and those who are below you, those whom you respect and those whom you despise. All this reveals the ways of the 'I'. Through understanding the ways of the 'I' there is freedom from the 'I'. *That* is what matters, not just how to be free of pride.

Questioner: Though there is progress in different directions, why is there no brotherhood?

KRISHNAMURTI: What do you mean by 'progress'? From the bullock cart to the jet plane – that is progress, is it not? The means of transport in ancient times was very slow, and now it is very rapid. Through sanitation, through proper nutrition and medical care, there has been a great improvement also in matters of physical health All this is scientific progress; and yet we are not developing or progressing equally in brotherhood.

Now, is brotherhood a matter of progress? We know what we mean by 'progress'. It is evolution, achieving something through time. The scientists say that we have evolved from the monkey; they say that, through millions of years, we have progressed from the lowest forms of life to the highest, which is man. But is brotherhood a matter of progress? Is it something which can be evolved through time? There is the unity of the family and the unity of a particular society or nation; from the nation the next step is internationalism, and then comes the idea of one world. The one-world concept is what we call brotherhood. But is brotherly feeling a matter of evolution? Is the feeling of brotherhood to be slowly cultivated through the stages of family, community, nationalism, internationalism and world unity? Brotherliness is love, is it not? And is love to be cultivated step by step? Is love a matter of time? Do you understand what I am talking about?

If I say there will be brotherhood in ten, or thirty, or a hundred years, what does that indicate? It indicates, surely, that I do not love, I do not feel brotherly. When I say, 'I will be brotherly, I will love', the actual fact is that I do *not* love, I am *not* brotherly. As long as I think in terms of 'I will be', I am not. Whereas, if I remove from my mind this concept of being brotherly in the future, then I can see what I actually am; I can see that I am *not* brotherly, and begin to find out why.

Which is important, to see what I am, or to speculate about what I *will* be? Surely, the important thing is to see what I am, because then I can deal with it. What I *will* be is in the future, and the future is unpredictable. The actual fact is that I have no brotherly feeling, I do not really love; and with that fact I can begin, I can immediately do something about it. But to say that one will be something in the future is mere idealism, and the idealist is an individual who is escaping from what *is*; he is running away from the fact, which can be altered only in the present.

Questioner: What is love in itself?

KRISHNAMURTI: What is intrinsic love? Is that what you mean? What is love without motive, without incentive? Listen carefully and you will find out. We are examining the question, we are not looking for the answer. In studying mathematics, or in putting a question, most of you are more concerned with finding the answer than with understanding the problem. If you study the problem, look into it, examine it, understand it, you will find that the answer is in the problem. So let us understand what the problem is, and not look for an answer, either in the *Bhagavad Gita*, in the *Koran*, in the Bible, or from some professor or lecturer. If we can really understand the problem, the answer will come out of it; because the answer is not separate from the problem.

The problem is: what is love without motive. Can there be love without any incentive, without wanting something for oneself out of love? Can there be love in which there is no sense of being wounded when love is not returned? If I offer you my friendship and you turn away, am I not hurt? Is that feeling of being hurt the outcome of friendship, of generosity, of sympathy? Surely, as long as I feel hurt, as long as there is fear, as long as I help you hoping that you may help me – which is called service – there is no love.

If you understand this, the answer is there.

Questioner: What is religion?

KRISHNAMURTI: Do you want an answer from me, or do you want to find out for yourself? Are you looking for an answer from somebody, however great or however stupid? Or are you really trying to find out the truth of what religion is?

To find out what true religion is, you have to push aside everything that stands in the way. If you have many coloured or dirty windows and you want to see the clear sunlight, you must clean or open the windows, or go outside. Similarly, to find out what true religion is, you must first see what it is *not*, and put that aside. Then you can find out, because then there is direct perception. So let us see what is not religion.

Doing *puja*, performing a ritual – is that religion? You repeat over and over again a certain ritual, a certain *mantram* in front of an altar or an idol. It may give you a sense of pleasure, a sense of satisfaction; but is that religion? Putting on the sacred thread, calling yourself a Hindu, a Buddhist, or a Christian, accepting certain traditions, dogmas, beliefs—has all this got anything to do with religion? Obviously not. So religion must be something which can be found only when the mind has understood and put all this aside.

Religion, in the true sense of the word, does not bring about separation, does it? But what happens when you are a Moslem and I am a Christian, or when I believe in something and you do not believe in it? Our beliefs separate us; therefore our beliefs have nothing to do with religion. Whether we believe in God or do not believe in God has very little significance; because what we believe or disbelieve is determined by our conditioning, is it not? The society around us, the culture in which we are brought up, imprints upon the mind certain beliefs, fears and superstitions which we call religion; but they have nothing to do with religion. The fact that you believe in one way and I in another, largely depends on where we happen to have been born, whether in England, in India, in Russia or America. So belief is not religion, it is only the result of our conditioning.

Then there is the pursuit of personal salvation. I want to be safe; I want to reach *Nirvana*, or heaven; I must find a place next to Jesus, next to Buddha, or on the right hand of a particular God. Your belief does not give me deep satisfaction, comfort, so I have my own belief which does. And is that religion? Surely, one's mind must be free of all these things to find out what true religion is.

And is religion merely a matter of doing good, of serving

or helping others? Or is it something more? Which does not mean that we must not be generous or kind. But is that all? Is not religion something much greater, much purer, vaster, more expansive than anything conceived by the mind?

So, to discover what is true religion, you must inquire deeply into all these things and be free of fear. It is like going out of a dark house into the sunshine. Then you will not ask what is true religion; you will know. There will be the direct experiencing of that which is true.

Questioner: If somebody is unhappy and wants to be happy, is that ambition?

KRISHNAMURTI: When you are suffering, you want to be free of suffering. That is not ambition, is it? That is the natural instinct of every person. It is the natural instinct of us all not to have fear, not to have physical or emotional pain. But our life is such that we are constantly experiencing pain. I eat something that gives me a tummy-ache. Somebody says something to me, and I feel hurt. I am prevented from doing something which I long to do, and I feel frustrated, miserable. I am unhappy because my father or my son is dead, and so on. Life is constantly acting upon me whether I like it or not, and I am always getting hurt, frustrated, having painful reactions. So what I have to do is to understand this whole process. But you see, most of us run away from it.

When you suffer inwardly, psychologically, what do you do? You look to somebody for consolation; you read a book, or turn on the radio, or go and do *puja*. These are all indications of your running away from suffering. If you run away from something, obviously you do not understand it. But if you look at your suffering, observe it from moment to moment, you begin to understand the problem involved in it, and this is not ambition. Ambition arises when you run away from your suffering, or when you cling to it, or when you fight it, or when around it you gradually build theories and hopes. The moment you run away from suffering, the thing to which you run becomes very important because you identify yourself with it. You identify yourself with your country, with your position, with your God, and this is a form of ambition.

Questioner: Is beauty subjective or objective?

KRISHNAMURTI: You see something beautiful, the river from the verandah; or you see a child in tatters, crying. If you are not sensitive, if you are not aware of everything around you, then you just pass by and that incident is of very little value. A woman comes along carrying a burden on her head. Her clothes are dirty; she is hungry and tired. Are you aware of the beauty of her walk, or sensitive to her physical state? Do you see the colour of her *sari*, however soiled it may be? There are these objective influences all about you; and if you have no sensitivity, you will never appreciate them, will you?

To be sensitive is to be aware not only of the things which are called beautiful, but also of that which is called ugly. The river, the green fields, the trees in the distance, the clouds of an evening – these things we call beautiful. The dirty, half-starved villagers, the people who live in squalor, or who have very little capacity for thought, very little feeling – all this we call ugly. Now, if you observe you will see what most of us do is to cling to the beautiful and shut out the ugly. But is it not important to be sensitive to what is called ugliness as well as to beauty? It is the lack of this sensitivity that causes us to divide life into the ugly and the beautiful. But if we are open, receptive, sensitive to the ugly as well as to the beautiful, then we shall see that they are both full of meaning, and this perception gives enrichment to life.

So, is beauty subjective or objective? If you were blind, if you were deaf and could not hear any music, would you be without beauty? Or is beauty something inward? You may not see with your eyes, you may not hear with your ears; but if there is the experiencing of this state of being really open, sensitive to everything, if you are deeply aware of all that is happening inside you, of every thought, of every feeling –

is there not beauty also in that? But you see, we think beauty is something outside of us. That is why we buy pictures and hang them on the wall. We want to possess beautiful *saris*, suits, turbans, we want to surround ourselves with beautiful things; for we are afraid that without an objective reminder we shall lose something inwardly. But can you divide life, the whole process of existence, into the subjective and the objective? Is it not a unitary process? Without the outer there is not the inner; without the inner there is not the outer.

Questioner: Why do the strong suppress the weak?

KRISHNAMURTI: Do you suppress the weak? Let us find out. In an argument, or in matters of physical strength, don't you push away your younger brother, the one smaller than yourself? Why? Because you want to assert yourself. You want to show your strength, you want to show how much better or more powerful you are, so you dominate, you push the little child away; you throw your weight around. It is the same with the older people. They are bigger than you are, they know a little more from reading books, they have position, money, authority, so they suppress, they push aside; and you accept being pushed aside; and then you in your turn suppress somebody below you. Each one wants to assert himself, to dominate, to show that he has power over others. Most of us do not want to be as nothing. We want to be somebodies; and the showing of power over others gives us that satisfaction, the feeling that we *are* somebodies.

Questioner: Is that why the bigger fish swallow the small fish?

KRISHNAMURTI: In the animal world it may perhaps be natural for the big fish to live on the small fish. It is something we cannot alter. But the big human being need not live on the little human being. If we know how to use our intelligence, we can stop living on each other, not only physically but also in the psychological sense. To see this problem and understand it, which is to have intelligence, is to stop living on another. But most of us *want* to live on another, so we take advantage of somebody who is weaker than ourselves. Freedom does not mean being free to do anything you like. There can be real freedom only when there is intelligence; and intelligence comes through the understanding of relationship – the relationship between you and me, and between each one of us and somebody else.

Questioner: What is death?

KRISHNAMURTI: You have seen dead bodies being carried to the river; you have seen dead leaves, dead trees; you know that fruits wither and decay. The birds that are so full of life in the morning, chattering away, calling to each other, by evening may be dead. The person who is alive today may be struck down by disaster tomorrow. We see all this going on. Death is common to us all. We will all end that way. You may live for thirty, fifty, or eighty years, enjoying, suffering, being fearful; and at the end of it you are no more.

What is it that we call living, and what is it that we call death? If we can find out, if we can understand what living is, then perhaps we shall understand what death is. When we lose someone whom we love, we feel bereft, lonely; therefore we say that death has nothing to do with living. We separate death from life. But is death separate from life? Is not living a process of dying?

Now, what is it that comes to an end in death? Is it life? What is life? Is life merely a process of breathing in air and expelling it? Eating, hating, loving, acquiring, possessing, comparing, being envious – this is what most of us know as life. For most of us life is suffering, a constant battle of pain and pleasure, hope and frustration. And can that not come to an end? Should we not die? In the autumn, with the coming of cold weather, the leaves fall from the trees, and reappear in the spring. Similarly. should we not die to everything of yesterday, to all our accumulations and hopes, to all the successes that we have gathered? Should we not die to all that and live again tomorrow, so that, like a new leaf, we are fresh, tender, sensitive? To a man who is constantly dying, there is no death. But the man who says, 'I am somebody and I must continue' – to him there is always death and the burning-ghat; and that man knows no love.

Questioner: Is truth relative or absolute?

KRISHNAMURTI: First of all, let us look through the words at the significance of the question. We want something absolute, don't we? The human craving is for something permanent, fixed, immovable, eternal, something that does not decay, that has no death – an idea, a feeling, a state that is everlasting, so that the mind can cling to it. We must understand this craving before we can understand the question and answer it rightly.

The human mind wants permanency in everything – in relationship, in property, in virtue. It wants something which cannot be destroyed. That is why we say God is permanent, or truth is absolute.

But what is truth? Is truth some extraordinary mystery, something far away, unimaginable, abstract? Or is truth something which you discover from moment to moment, from day to day? If it can be accumulated, gathered through experience, then it is not truth; for behind this gathering lies the same spirit of acquisitiveness. If it is something far away which can be found only through a system of meditation, or through the practice of denial and sacrifice, again it is not truth, for that also is a process of acquisitiveness.

Truth is to be discovered and understood in every action, in every thought, in every feeling, however trivial or transient; it is to be observed at each moment of every day; it is to be listened to in what the husband and the wife say, in what the gardener says, in what your friends say, and in the process of your own thinking. Your thinking may be false, it may be conditioned, limited; and to discover that your thinking is conditioned, limited, is truth. That very discovery sets your mind free from limitation. If you discover that you are greedy – if you *discover* it, and are not just told by somebody else – that discovery is truth, and that truth has its own action upon your greed.

Truth is not something which you can gather, accumulate, store up and then rely on as a guide. That is only another form of possession. And it is very difficult for the mind not to acquire, not to store up. When you realize the significance of this, you will find out what an extraordinary thing truth is. Truth is timeless, but the moment you capture it – as when you say, 'I have found truth, it is mine' – it is no longer truth.

So, whether truth is 'absolute' or timeless depends on the mind. When the mind says, 'I want the absolute, something which never decays, which knows no death', what it really wants is something permanent to cling to; so it creates the permanent. But a mind that is aware of everything that is happening outwardly and within itself, and sees the truth of it – such a mind is timeless; and only such a mind can know that which is beyond names, beyond the permanent and the impermanent.

Questioner: What is external awareness?

KRISHNAMURTI: Are you not aware that you are sitting in this hall? Are you not aware of the trees, of the sunshine? Are you not aware that the crow is cawing, the dog is barking? Do you not see the colour of the flowers, the movement of the leaves, the people walking by? That is external awareness. When you see the sunset, the stars at night, the moonlight on the water, all that is external awareness, is it not? And as you are externally aware, so also you can be inwardly aware of your thoughts and feelings, of your motives and urges, of your prejudices, envies, greed and pride. If you are really aware outwardly, the inward awareness also begins to awaken, and you become more and more conscious of your reaction to what people say, to what you read, and so on. The external reaction or response in your relationship with other people is the outcome of an inward state of wanting, of hope, of anxiety, fear. This outward and inward awareness is a unitary process which brings about a total integration of human understanding.

Questioner: What is real and eternal happiness?

KRISHNAMURTI: When you are completely healthy, you are not conscious of your body, are you? It is only when there is disease, discomfort, pain, that you become conscious of it. When you are free to think completely, without resistance, there is no consciousness of thinking. It is only when there is friction, a blockage, a limitation, that you begin to be conscious of a thinker. Similarly, is happiness something of which you are aware? In the moment of joy, are you aware that you are joyous? It is only when you are unhappy that you want happiness; and then this question arises, 'What is real and eternal happiness?'

You see how the mind plays tricks on itself. Because you are unhappy, miserable, in poor circumstances, and so on, you want something eternal, a permanent happiness. And is there such a thing? Instead of asking about permanent happiness, find out how to be free of the diseases which are gnawing at you and creating pain, both physical and psychological. When you are free, there is no problem, you don't ask whether there is eternal happiness or what that happiness is. It is a lazy, foolish man who, being in prison, wants to know what freedom is; and lazy, foolish people will tell him. To the man in prison, freedom is mere speculation. But if he gets out of that prison, he does not speculate about freedom: it is there.

So is it not important, instead of asking what happiness is, to find out why we are unhappy? Why is the mind crippled? Why is it that our thoughts are limited, small, petty? If we can understand the limitation of thought, see the truth of it, in that discovery of the truth there is liberation.

Questioner: Why do people want things?

KRISHNAMURTI: Don't you want food when you are

hungry? Don't you want clothes and a house to shelter you? These are normal wants, are they not? Healthy people naturally recognize that they need certain things. It is only the diseased or unbalanced man who says, 'I do not need food'. It is a perverted mind that must either have many houses, or no house at all to live in.

Your body gets hungry because you are using energy, so it wants more food; that is normal. But if you say, 'I must have the tastiest food, I must have only the food that my tongue takes pleasure in', then perversion begins. All of us – not only the rich, but everybody in the world – must have food, clothing and shelter; but if these physical necessities are limited, controlled and made available only to the few, then there is perversion; an unnatural process is set going. If you say, 'I must accumulate, I must have everything for myself', you are depriving others of that which is essential for their daily needs.

You see, the problem is not simple, because we want other things besides what is essential for our daily needs. I may be satisfied with a little food, a few clothes and a small room to live in; but I want something else. I want to be a well-known person, I want position, power, prestige, I want to be nearest to God, I want my friends to think well of me, and so on. These inward wants pervert the outward interests of every human being. The problem is a little difficult because the inward desire to be the richest or most powerful man, the urge to be somebody, is dependent for its fulfilment on the possession of things, including food, clothing and shelter. I lean on these things in order to become inwardly rich; but as long as I am in this state of dependence, it is impossible for me to be inwardly rich, which is to be utterly simple inwardly.

Questioner: Does intelligence build character?

KRISHNAMURTI: What do we mean by 'character'? And what do we mean by 'intelligence'? Every tub-thumper continually uses such words as 'character', 'ideal', 'intelligence', 'religion', 'God'. We listen to these words with rapt attention, because they seem very important. Most of us live on words; and the more elaborate, the more exquisite the words, the more satisfied we feel. So, let us find out what we mean by 'intelligence' and what we mean by 'character'. Don't say I am not answering you definitely. To seek definitions, conclusions, is one of the tricks of the mind, and it means that you don't want to investigate and understand, you just want to follow words.

What is intelligence? If a man is frightened, anxious, envious, greedy; if his mind is copying, imitating, filled with other people's experiences and knowledge; if his thinking is limited, shaped by society, by environment – is such a man intelligent? He is not, is he? And can a man who is frightened, unintelligent, have character – character being something original, not the mere repeating of traditional *do's* and *don'ts*? Is character respectability?

Do you understand what that word 'respectability' means? You are respectable when you are looked up to, respected by a majority of the people around you. And what do the majority of people respect – the people of the family, the people of the mass? They respect the things which they themselves want and which they have projected as a goal or an ideal; they respect that which they see to be in contrast with their own more lowly state. If you are rich and powerful, or have a big name politically, or have written successful books, you are respected by the majority. What you say may be utter nonsense, but when you talk, people listen because they regard you as a great man. And when you have thus won the respect of the many, the following of the multitude, it gives you a sense of respectability, a feeling of having arrived. But the so-called sinner is nearer to God than the respectable man, because the respectable man is clothed in hypocrisy.

Is character the outcome of imitation, of being controlled by the fear of what people will say or won't say? Is character the mere strengthening of one's own tendencies, prejudices? Is it an upholding of the tradition, whether of India, of

Europe or America? That is generally called having character – being a strong person who supports the local tradition and so is respected by the many. But when you are frightened, is there intelligence, is there character? Imitating, following, worshipping, having ideals – that way leads to respectability, but not to understanding. A man of ideals is respectable; but he will never be near God, he will never know what it is to love, because his ideals are a means of covering up his fear, his imitation, his loneliness.

So, without understanding yourself, without being aware of all that is operating in your own mind – how you think, whether you are copying, imitating, whether you are frightened, whether you are seeking power – there cannot be intelligence. And it is intelligence that creates character, not hero-worship or the pursuit of an ideal. The understanding of oneself, of one's own extraordinarily complicated self, is the beginning of intelligence, which reveals character.

Questioner: Can we not cultivate understanding? When we constantly try to understand, does it not mean that we are practising understanding?

KRISHNAMURTI: Is understanding cultivable? Is it something to be practised as you practise tennis, or the piano, or singing, or dancing? You can read a book over and over again till you are thoroughly familiar with it. Is understanding like that, something to be learned through constant repetition, which is really the cultivation of memory? Is not understanding from moment to moment, and therefore something that cannot be practised?

When do you understand? What is the state of your mind and heart when there is understanding? When you hear me say something very true about jealousy – that jealousy is destructive, that envy is a major factor in the deterioration of human relationship – how do you respond to it? Do you see the truth of it immediately? Or do you begin to think about jealousy, to talk about it, rationalize it, analyse it? Is understanding a process of either rationalization or slow analysis? Can understanding be cultivated as you cultivate your garden to produce fruits or flowers? Surely, to understand is to see the truth of something directly, without any barrier of words, prejudices or motives.

Questioner: Is the power of understanding the same in all persons?

KRISHNAMURTI: Suppose something true is presented to you and you see the truth of it very quickly; your understanding is immediate because you have no barriers. You are not full of your own importance, you are eager to find out, so you perceive immediately. But I have many barriers, many prejudices. I am jealous, torn by conflicts based upon envy, full of my own importance. I have accumulated many things in life, and I really do not *want* to see; therefore I do not see, I do not understand.

Questioner: Can't one remove the barriers slowly by constantly trying to understand?

KRISHNAMURTI: No. I can remove the barriers, not by trying to understand, but only when I really feel the importance of not having barriers – which means that I must be willing to *see* the barriers. Suppose you and I hear someone say that envy is destructive. You listen and understand the significance, the truth of it, and you are free of that feeling of envy, of jealousy. But I do not want to see the truth of it, because if I did it would destroy my whole structure of life.

Questioner: I feel the necessity of removing the barriers.

KRISHNAMURTI: Why do you feel that? Do you want to remove the barriers because of circumstances? Do you want to remove them because somebody has told you that you should? Surely, the barriers are removed only when you see for yourself that to have barriers of any kind creates a mind which is in a state of slow decay. And when do you see this? When you suffer? But does suffering necessarily awaken you to the importance of removing all barriers? Or does it, on the contrary, lead you to create more barriers?

You will find that all barriers drop away when you yourself are beginning to listen, to observe, to find out. There is no reason for removing the barriers; and the moment you bring in a reason, you are not removing them. The miracle, the greatest blessing, is to give your own inward perception an opportunity to remove the barriers. But when you say that the barriers must be removed and then practise removing them, that is the work of the mind; and the mind cannot remove the barriers. You must see that no attempt on your part can remove them. Then the mind becomes very quiet, very still; and in this stillness you discover that which is true.

Questioner: What is the purpose of creation?

KRISHNAMURTI: Are you really interested in that? What do you mean by 'creation'? What is the purpose of living? Why do you exist, read, study, pass examinations? What is the purpose of relationship – the relationship of parents and children, of husband and wife? What is life? Is that what you mean when you ask this question, 'What is the purpose of creation?' When do you ask such a question? When inwardly you do not see clearly, when you are confused, miserable, in the dark, when you do not perceive or feel the truth of the matter for yourself, then you want to know what is the purpose of life.

Now, there are many people who will tell you the purpose of life; they will tell you what the sacred books say. Clever people will go on inventing various purposes of life. The political group will have one purpose, the religious group will have another, and so on and on. And how are you to find out what is the purpose of life when you yourself are confused? Surely, as long as you are confused, you can only receive an answer which is also confused. If your mind is disturbed, if it is not really quiet, whatever answer you receive will be through this screen of confusion, anxiety, fear; therefore the answer will be perverted. So the important thing is not to ask what is the purpose of life, but to clear away the confusion that is within you. It is like a blind man asking, 'What is light?' If I try to tell him what light is, he will listen according to his blindness, according to his darkness; but from the moment he is able to see, he will never ask what is light. It is there.

Similarly, if you can clarify the confusion within yourself, then you will find out what the purpose of life is; you will not have to ask, you will not have to look for it. To be free of confusion you have to see and understand the causes which bring about confusion; and the causes of confusion are very clear. They are rooted in the 'me' that is constantly wanting to expand itself through possessing, through becoming, through success, through imitation; and the symptoms are jealousy, envy, greed, fear. As long as there is this inward confusion, you are always seeking outward answers; but when the inward confusion is cleared away, then you will know the significance of life.

Questioner: Is there an element of fear in respect?

KRISHNAMURTI: What do you say? When you show respect to your teacher, to your parents, to your *guru*, and disrespect to your servant; when you kick the people who are not important to you, and lick the boots of those who are above you, the officials, the politicians, the big ones – is there not an element of fear in this? From the big ones, from the teacher, the examiner, the professor, from your parents, from the politician or the bank manager, you hope to get something; therefore you are respectful. But what can the poor people give you? So the poor you disregard, you treat them with contempt, you do not even know they are there when they pass you in the street. You do not look at them, it does not concern you that they shiver in the cold, that they are dirty and hungry. But you will give to the great of the land, even when you have very little, in order to receive more of their favours. In this there is definitely an element of fear, is there not? There is no love. If you have love in your heart, you would show respect to those who have nothing and also to those who have everything: you would neither be afraid of those who have, nor disregard those who have not. Respect in the hope of reward is the outcome of fear. In love there is no fear.

Questioner: Why do we feel inferior before our superiors?

KRISHNAMURTI: Whom do you consider your superiors? Those who know? Those who have titles, degrees? Those from whom you want something, some kind of reward or position? The moment you regard somebody as superior, do you not regard somebody else as inferior?

Why do we have this division of the superior and the inferior? It exists only when we want something, does it not? I feel less intelligent than you are, I do not have as much money or capacity as you have. I am not as happy as you seem to be, or I want something from you; so I feel inferior to you. When I am envious of you, or when I am trying to imitate you, or when I want something from you, I immediately become your inferior, because I have put you on a pedestal, I have given you a superior value. So, psychologically, inwardly, I create both the superior and the inferior; I create this sense of inequality between those who have and those who have not.

Among human beings there is enormous inequality of capacity, is there not? There is the man who designs the jet plane, and the man who guides the plough. These vast differences in capacity – intellectual, verbal, physical – are inevitable. But you see, we give tremendous significance to certain functions. We consider the governor, the prime minister, the inventor, the scientist, as being enormously more important than the servant; so function assumes status. As long as we give status to particular functions, there is bound to be a sense of inequality, and the gap between those who are capable and those who are not becomes unbridgeable.

If we can keep function stripped of status, then there is a possibility of bringing about a real feeling of equality. But for this there must be love; because it is love that destroys the sense of the inferior and the superior.

The world is divided into those who have – the rich, the powerful, the capable, those who have everything – and those who have not. And is it possible to bring about a world in which this division between the 'haves' and the 'have-nots' does not exist? Actually, what is happening is this: seeing the breach, this gulf between the rich and the poor, between the man of great capacity and the man of little or no capacity, the politicians and economists are trying to solve the problem through ecomomic and social reform. That may be all right. But a real transformation can never take place as long as we do not understand the whole process of antagonism, envy, malice; for it is only when this process is understood and comes to an end that there can be love in our hearts.

Questioner: Is it possible to have peace in our lives when at every moment we are struggling against our environment?

KRISHNAMURTI: What is our environment? Our environment is society, the economic, religious, national and class environment of the country in which we grow up; and also the climate. Most of us are struggling to fit in, to adjust ourselves to our environment, because we hope to get a job from that environment, we hope to have the benefits of that particular society. But what is that society made up of? Have you ever thought about it? Have you ever looked closely at the society in which you are living and to which you are trying to adjust yourself? That society is based on a set of beliefs and traditions which is called religion, and on certain economic values, is it not? You are part of that society, and you are struggling to adjust yourself to it. But that society is the outcome of acquisitiveness, it is the outcome of envy, fear, greed, possessive pursuits, with occasional flashes of love. And if you want to be intelligent, fearless, non-acquisitive, can you adjust yourself to such a society? **Can you?**

Surely, you have to create a new society, which means that you as an individual have to be free of acquisitiveness, of envy, of greed; you have to be free of nationalism, of patriotism, and of all narrowing down of religious thought. Only then is there a possibility of creating something new, a totally new society. But as long as you thoughtlessly struggle to adjust yourself to the present society, you are merely following the old pattern of envy, of power and prestige, of beliefs which are corruptive.

So it is very important, while you are young, to begin to understand these problems and bring about real freedom within yourself, for then you will create a new world, a new society, a new relationship between man and man. And to help you do this is surely the true function of education.

Questioner: Why do we suffer? Why can we not be free of disease and death?

KRISHNAMURTI: Through sanitation, through proper living conditions and nutritious food, man is beginning to free himself from certain diseases. Through surgery and various forms of treatment, medical science is trying to find a cure for incurable diseases like cancer. A capable doctor does all he can to relieve and eliminate disease.

And is death conquerable? It is a most extraordinary thing that, at your age, you are so interested in death. Why are you so preoccupied with it? Is it because you see so much of death about you – the burning-ghats, the body being carried to the river? To you, death is a familiar sight, it is so constantly with you; and there is the fear of death.

If you do not reflect and understand for yourself the implications of death, you will go endlessly from one preacher to another, from one hope to another, from one belief to another, trying to find a solution to this problem of death. Do you understand? Don't keep on asking somebody else, but try to find out for yourself the truth of the matter. To ask innumerable questions without ever trying to find out or discover, is characteristic of a petty mind.

You see, we fear death only when we cling to life. The understanding of the whole process of living is also the understanding of the significance of dying. Death is merely the extinction of continuity, and we are afraid of not being able to continue; but what continues can never be creative. Think it out; discover for yourself what is true. It is truth that liberates you from the fear of death, and not your religious theories, nor your belief in reincarnation or in life hereafter.

Questioner: What is obedience? Should we obey an order even without understanding it?

KRISHNAMURTI: Is that not what most of us do? Parents, teachers, the older people say, 'Do this'. They say it politely, or with a stick, and because we are afraid, we obey. That is also what governments, what the military people do to us. We are trained from childhood to obey, not knowing what it is all about. The more authoritarian our parents and the more tyrannical the government, the more we are compelled, shaped from our earliest years; and without understanding why we should do what we are told to do, we obey. We are also told what to think. Our minds are purged of any thought which is not approved by the State, by the local authorities. We are never taught or helped to think, to find out, but are required to obey. The priest tells us what is so, the religious book tells us what is so, and our own inward fear compels us to obey; because if we do not obey we shall be confused, we shall feel lost.

So we obey because we are very thoughtless. We don't want to think because to think is disturbing; to think, we have to question, to inquire, we have to find out for ourselves. And the older people don't want us to inquire, they have not the patience to listen to our questions. They are too busy with their own quarrels, with their ambitions and prejudices, with their *do's* and *don'ts* of morality and respectability; and we who are young are afraid to go wrong, because we also want to be respectable. Don't we all want to wear the same kind of clothes, to look alike? We don't want to do anything different, we don't want to think independently, to stand apart, because that is very disturbing; so we join the gang.

Whatever our age, most of us obey, follow, copy, because we are inwardly frightened of being uncertain. We want to be certain, both financially and morally; we want to be approved of. We want to be in a safe position, to be enclosed and never to be confronted with trouble, pain, suffering. It is fear, conscious or unconscious, that makes us obey the master, the leader, the priest, the government. It is fear of being punished that prevents us from doing something harmful to others. So, behind all our actions, our greeds and pursuits, lurks this desire for certainty, this desire to be safe, assured. Without being free of fear, merely to obey has little significance. What has significance is to be aware of this fear from day to day, to observe how it shows itself in different ways. Only when there is freedom from fear can there be that inward quality of understanding, that aloneness in which there is no accumulation of knowledge or experience.

Questioner: Society is based upon our interdependence. The doctor has to depend on the farmer, and the farmer on the doctor. How then can a man be completely interdependent?

KRISHNAMURTI: Life is relationship. Even the *sannyasi* has relationship; he may renounce the world, but he is still related to the world. We cannot escape from relationship. For most of us, relationship is a source of conflict; in relationship there is fear, because we psychologically depend on another, either on the husband, on the wife, on the parent, or on a friend. Relationship exists not only between oneself and the parent, between oneself and the child, but also between oneself and the teacher, the cook, the servant, the governor, the commander, and the whole of society; and as long as we do not understand this relationship, there is no freedom from the psychological dependence which brings about fear and exploitation. Freedom comes only through intelligence. Without intelligence, merely to seek independence or freedom from relationship is to pursue an illusion.

So what is important is to understand our psychological dependence in relationship. It is in uncovering the hidden things of the heart and mind, in understanding our own loneliness, emptiness, that there is freedom, not from relationship, but from the psychological dependence which causes conflict, misery, pain, fear.

Questioner: Why is truth unpalatable?

KRISHNAMURTI: If I think I am very beautiful and you tell me I am not, which may be a fact, do I like it? If I think I am very intelligent, very clever, and you point out that I am actually a rather silly person, it is very unpalatable to me. And your pointing out my stupidity gives you a sense of pleasure, does it not? It flatters your vanity, it shows how clever *you* are. But you do not want to look at your own stupidity; you want to run away from what you are, you want to hide from yourself, you want to cover up your own emptiness, your own loneliness. So you seek out friends who never tell you what you are. You want to show others what they are; but when others show you what *you* are, you do not like it. You avoid that which exposes your own inner nature.

Questioner: Up to now our teachers have been very certain and have taught us in the usual way; but after listening to what has been said here and after taking part in the discussions, they have become very uncertain. An intelligent student will know how to conduct himself under these circumstances; but what will those do who are not intelligent?

KRISHNAMURTI: What are the teachers uncertain about? Not about what to teach, because they can carry on with mathematics, geography, the usual curriculum. That is not what they are uncertain about. They are uncertain about how to deal with the student, are they not? They are uncertain in their relationship with the student. Until recently they were never particularly concerned about their relationship with the student; they just came to the class, taught, and went out. But now they are concerned as to whether they are creating fear by exercising their authority to make the student obey. They are concerned as to whether they are repressing the student, or are encouraging his initiative and helping him to find his true vocation. Naturally all this has made them uncertain. But surely the teacher as well as the student has to be uncertain; he too has to inquire, to search. That is the whole process of life from the beginning to the end, is it not? – never to stop in a certain place and say, 'I know'.

An intelligent man is never static, he never says, 'I know'. He is always inquiring, always uncertain, always looking, searching, finding out. The moment he says, 'I know', he is already dead. And whether we are young or old, most of us – because of tradition, compulsion, fear, because of bureaucracy and the absurdities of our religion – are all but dead, without vitality, without vigour, without self-reliance. So the teacher has also to find out. He has to discover for himself his own bureaucratic tendencies and cease to deaden the minds of others and that is a very difficult process. It requires a great deal of patient understanding.

So the intelligent student has to help the teacher, and the teacher has to help the student; and both have to help the dull boy or girl who is not very intelligent. That is relationship. Surely, when the teacher himself is uncertain, inquiring, he is more tolerant, more hesitant, more patient and affectionate with the dull student, whose intelligence may thereby be awakened.

Questioner: I have everything to make me happy, while others have not. Why is this so?

KRISHNAMURTI: Why do you think it is like that? You may have good health, kind parents, a good brain, and therefore think you are happy; whereas, somebody who is ill, whose parents are unkind, and who has not too good a brain, feels that he is unhappy. Now, why is this so? Why are you happy while somebody else is unhappy? Does happiness consist in having riches, cars, good houses, clean food, kind parents? Is that what you call happiness? And is a person unhappy who has none of these things? So, what do you mean by happiness? This is important to find out, is it not? Does happiness consist in comparing? When you say, 'I am happy', is your happiness born of comparison?

Have you not heard your parents say, 'So-and-so is not as well off as we are'? Comparison makes us feel that we have something, it gives us a sense of satisfaction, does it not? If one is clever and compares oneself with somebody who is not so clever, one feels very happy. That is, we think we are happy through pride, comparison; but the man who feels happy by comparing himself with another who has a little less, is a most miserable human being, because there is always somebody above him who has more; and so it goes on. Surely, comparison is not happiness. Happiness is entirely different; it is not a thing to be sought after. Happiness comes when you are doing something because you really love to do it, and not because it gives you riches or makes you a prominent person.

Questioner: What is the way to get rid of the fear that we have?

KRISHNAMURTI: First you must know what you are afraid of, must you not? You may be afraid of your parents, of the teachers, of not passing an examination, of what your sister, your brother, or your neighbour might say; or you may be afraid of not being as good or as clever as your father, who has a big name. There are many kinds of fear, and one must know what one is afraid of.

Now, do you know what you are afraid of? If you do, then don't run away from that fear, but find out why you are afraid. If you want to know how to get rid of fear, you must not escape from it, you must face it; and the very facing of it helps you to be free of it. As long as we are running away from fear, we do not look at it; but the moment we stop and look at fear, it begins to dissolve. The very running away is the cause of fear.

Questioner: Is it not important to have ideals in life?

KRISHNAMURTI: This is a good question, because you all have ideals. You have the ideal of non-violence, the ideal of peace, or the ideal of a person, have you not? Which means what? You are not important, but the ideal is very important. All that you are concerned with is to copy either a person or an idea. An idealist is a hypocrite, because he is always trying to become what he is not, instead of being and understanding what he is.

You see, the problem of idealism is really a complex one, and you don't understand it because you have never been encouraged to think about it; no one has ever talked it over with you. All your books, all your teachers, all the newspapers and magazines say you must have ideals, you must be like this hero or that, which only makes the mind like a monkey who imitates, or like a gramophone record which repeats a lot of words. So you must not accept, but begin to question everything and find out; and you cannot question if you are inwardly afraid. To question everything means being in revolt, which is to create a new world. But you see, your teachers and parents do not want you to be in revolt, because they want to control you, they want to shape and mould you into their patterns; and so life continues to be an ugly thing.

Questioner: If we are small, how can we create a new world?

KRISHNAMURTI: You cannot create a new world if you are small. But you are not going to be small for the rest of your life, are you? You are small if you are afraid. You may have a big body, a big car, a high position, but if you are afraid inside you will never create a new world. That is why it is very important to grow with intelligence, without fear, to grow in freedom. But to grow in freedom does not mean disciplining oneself to be free.

Questioner: What should be the system of education to make the child fearless?

KRISHNAMURTI: A system or a method implies being told what to do and how to do it; and will that make you fearless? Can you be educated with intelligence, without fear, through any kind of system? When you are young, you should be free to grow; but there is no system to make you free. A system implies making the mind conform to a pattern, does it not? It means locking you up in a framework, not giving you freedom. The moment you rely on a system you dare not step out of it, and then the very thought of stepping out of it breeds fear. So, there is really no *system* of education. What is important is the teacher and the student, not the system. After all, if I want to help you to be free of fear, I myself must be free of fear. Then I must study you; I must take the trouble to explain everything to you and tell you what the world is like; and to do all this I must love you. As a teacher I must have the feeling that when you leave school or college you should be without fear. If I really have that feeling, I can help you to be free of fear.

Questioner: Is it possible to know the quality of gold without testing it in a special way? Similarly, can the capacity of each child be known without some sort of examination?

KRISHNAMURTI: Do you really know the capacity of the child through examination? One child may fail because he is nervous, fearful of the examination, while another may slip through because he is less affected by it. Whereas, if you watch each child week after week, if you observe his character, the way he plays games, the way he talks, the interests he shows, how he studies, the food he eats, then you will begin to know the child without requiring examinations to tell you what he is capable of.

Questions and Answers

Questioner: What is your idea of a new world?

KRISHNAMURTI: I have no idea about the new world. The 'new' world cannot be new if I have an idea about it. This is not just a clever statement, it is a fact. If I have an idea about it, the idea is born of my study and experience, is it not? It is born of what I have learnt, of what I have read, of what other people have said the new world should be. So, the 'new' world can never be new if it is a creation of the mind, because the mind is the old. You don't know what is going to happen tomorrow, do you? You may know that there will be no school tomorrow because it is Sunday, and that on Monday you will be going to school again; but what is going to happen outside the school, what kind of feelings you are going to have, what kind of things you are going to see – all that you don't know, do you? Because you don't know what is going to happen tomorrow, or the next morning, when it happens it will be new; and to be able to meet the new is what matters.

Questioner: How can we create anything new if we don't know what it is we want to create?

KRISHNAMURTI: It is a sad thing not to know what it means to create, is it not? When you have a feeling, you may put what you feel into words. If you see a beautiful tree, you may write a poem describing, not the tree, but what the tree has awakened in you. That feeling is the new, it is the creative thing; but you cannot bring it about, it must happen to you.

Questioner: In your book on education* you suggest that modern education is a complete failure. I would like you to explain this.

KRISHNAMURTI: Is it not a failure, sir? When you go out on the street you see the poor man and the rich man; and when you look around you, you see all the so-called educated people throughout the world wrangling, fighting, killing each

* *Education and the Significance of Life*, Gollancz.

other in wars. There is now scientific knowledge enough to enable us to provide food, clothing and shelter for all human beings, yet it is not done. The politicians and other leaders throughout the world are educated people, they have titles, degrees, caps and gowns, they are doctors and scientists; and yet they have not created a world in which man can live happily. So modern education has failed, has it not? And if you are satisfied to be educated in the same old way, you will make another howling mess of life.

Questioner: You say that modern education is a failure. But if the politicians had not been educated, do you think they could have created a better world?

KRISHNAMURTI: I am not at all sure that they couldn't have created a better world if they had never received this kind of education. What does it mean to govern the people? After all, that is what politicians are supposed to do – to govern the people. But they are ambitious, they want power, position, they want to be respected, they want to be the leaders, to have the first place; they are not thinking of the people, they are thinking of themselves or their parties, which are an extension of themselves. Human beings are human beings, whether they live in India, in Germany, in Russia, in America, or in China; but you see, by dividing human beings according to countries, more politicians can have big jobs, so they are not interested in thinking of the world as a whole. They are 'educated', they know how to read, how to argue, and they talk everlastingly about being good citizens – but they must have the first place. To divide up the world and create wars – is that what we call education? The politicians are not alone in doing this; we all do it. Some people want war because it gives them profit. So it is not only the politicians who must have the right kind of education.

Questioner: Then what is your idea of the right kind of education?

KRISHNAMURTI: I have just told you. Look, I will show

you again. After all, a religious person is not one who worships a god, an image made by the hand or by the mind, but one who is really inquiring into what truth is, what God is; and such a person is really educated. He may not go to a school, he may have no books, he may not even know how to read; but he is freeing himself from fear, from his egotism, from his selfishness, ambition. So education is not merely a process of learning how to read, how to calculate, how to build bridges, how to do scientific research in order to find new ways of utilizing atomic power, and all the rest of it. The function of education is primarily to help man to free himself from his own pettiness and from his stupid ambitions. All ambition is stupid, petty – there is no great ambition. And education also implies helping the student to grow in freedom without fear, does it not?

Questioner: How can every man be educated like that?

KRISHNAMURTI: Don't *you* want to be educated like that?

Questioner: But how?

KRISHNAMURTI: First, do you want to be educated like that? Don't ask how, but have the feeling that you want to be educated in that way. If you have this intense feeling, as you grow up you will help to create it in others, will you not? Sir, look: if you are very keen on playing a certain game, you soon find other people to play it with you. Similarly, if you are really keen to be educated in the way we have been discussing, then you will help to create a school with the right kind of teachers who will provide that kind of education. But most of us don't really want that kind of education, and so we ask, 'How can it be brought about?' We look to somebody else for the answer. But if all of you – every student who is listening, and I hope the teachers too – want that kind of education, then you will demand it and bring it into being.

Take a simple example like chewing gum. If you all want chewing gum, the manufacturer produces it, but if you don't want it the manufacturer goes broke. Similarly, on quite a different level, if you all say, 'We want the right kind of education, not this phoney education which only leads to organized murder' – if you say that and really mean it, you will bring into being the right kind of education. But you see, you are still too young, too frightened, and that is why it is important to create this thing.

Questioner: If I want the right kind of education, do I need teachers?

KRISHNAMURTI: Of course you do. You need teachers to help you, do you not? But what is help? You are not living in the world alone, are you? There are your fellow-students, your parents, your teachers, the postman, the man who brings the milk – everybody is needed, we all help each other to live in this world. But if you say, 'The teacher is sacred, he is at one level and I am at another', then that kind of help is no help at all. The teacher is helpful only if he is not using teaching to feed his vanity or as a means of his own security. If he is teaching, not because he is unable to do anything else, but because he really loves to teach, then he will help the student to grow without fear. This means no examinations, no grading, no marks. If you are to create the right kind of education, you need such teachers to help you to create it; so it is very important for the teachers themselves to be rightly educated.

Questioner: If all ambitions are stupid, then how can man progress?

KRISHNAMURTI: Do you know what progress is? Now, have patience and let us go into it slowly. What is progress? Have you ever thought about it? Is it progress when you can get to Europe in a few hours by airplane instead of taking a fortnight to get there by boat? The invention of faster means of transportation and communication, the development of bigger guns, bigger and better ways of destroying each other, wiping out thousands of people with a single atomic bomb instead of shooting them down one by one with arrows – this we call progress, do we not? So there has been progress in the technological sense; but have we progressed in any other direction? Have we stopped wars? Are people more kind, more loving, more generous, more thoughtful, less cruel? You don't have to say yes or no, but just look at the facts. Scientifically and physically we have made tremendous progress; but inwardly we are at a standstill, are we not? For most of us education has been like lengthening only one leg of a tripod, so we have no balance; and yet we talk about progress, all the newspapers are full of it!

Questioner: What is the definition of a student?

KRISHNAMURTI: It is very easy to find a definition, is it not? All you have to do is to open a dictionary at the right place and it will give you the answer. But that is not the kind of definition you want, is it? You want to talk about it, you want to find out what a true student is. Is he a true student who passes examinations, gets a job, and then closes all books? Being a student implies studying life, not just reading the few books required by your curriculum; it implies the capacity to observe everything throughout life, not just a few things at a particular period. A student, surely, is not only one who reads, but one who is capable of observing all the movements of life, outward and inward, without saying, 'This is right, that is wrong'. If you condemn something, you don't observe it, do you? To observe you have to study without condemning, without comparing. If I compare you with somebody else, I am not studying you, am I? If I compare you with your younger brother or your elder sister, it is the sister or the brother who is important; therefore I am not studying you.

But our whole education is to compare. You are everlastingly comparing yourself or another with somebody – with your *guru*, with your ideal, with your father who is so clever, a great politician, and so on. This process of comparison and condemnation prevents you from observing, studying. So a real student is one who observes everything in life, outwardly as well as inwardly, without comparing, approving or condemning. He is not only capable of research into scientific matters, but is also able to observe the workings of his own mind, his own feelings – which is much more difficult than observing a scientific fact. To understand the whole operation of one's own mind requires a great deal of insight, a great deal of inquiry without condemnation.

Questioner: You say that all idealists are hypocrites. Whom do you call an idealist?

KRISHNAMURTI: Don't you know what an idealist is? If I am violent, I may say that my ideal is to be non-violent; but the fact remains that I am violent. The ideal is what I hope to be eventually. It will take years for me to become non-violent, and meanwhile I am violent – that is the real thing. Being violent, I am trying all the time to be non-violent, which is unreal; and is that not hypocrisy? Instead of understanding and dissolving my violence, I am trying to be something else. The man who is trying to be something other than he is, is obviously a hypocrite. It is like my putting on a mask and saying I am different, but behind the mask I am just the same old man. Whereas, if I can go into the whole process of violence and understand it, then there is a possibility of being free from violence.

Questioner: If all of us were educated rightly, would we be free of fear?

KRISHNAMURTI: It is very important to be free of fear, is it not? And you cannot be free of fear except through intelligence. So let us first find out how to be intelligent, not how to get rid of fear. If we can experience what it is to be intelligent, then we shall know how to get rid of fear. Fear is always with regard to something, it does not exist by itself. There is the fear of death, the fear of illness, the fear of loss, the fear of one's parents, the fear of what people will say, and so on; and the question is, not how to get rid of fear, but how to awaken the intelligence with which to face and to understand and go beyond fear.

Now, how can education help us to be intelligent? What is intelligence? Is it a matter of passing examinations, of being clever? You may read many books, meet prominent people, have a lot of capacity, but does all that make you intelligent? Or is intelligence something which comes into being only as you become integrated? We are made up of many parts; sometimes we are resentful, jealous, violent, at other times we are humble, thoughtful, calm. At different moments we are different beings; we are never whole, never totally integrated, are we? When a human being has many wants, he is inwardly broken up into many beings.

One must approach the problem simply. The question is how to be intelligent so that you can be rid of fear. If from your earliest childhood whatever difficulty you may have had has been talked over with you so that your understanding of it is not just verbal, but enables you to see the whole of life, then such education can awaken intelligence and thereby free the mind of fear.

Questioner: You have said that to be ambitious is to be stupid and cruel. Is it then stupid and cruel to have the ambition to get the right kind of education?

KRISHNAMURTI: Are you ambitious? What is ambition? When you want to be better than another, to get higher marks than someone else – surely that is what we call ambition. A little politician is ambitious in wanting to become a big politician; but is it ambitious to want to have the right kind of education? Is it ambition when you do something because you love to do it? When you write or paint – not because you want prestige, but because you love to write or paint – that is not ambition, surely. Ambition comes in when you compare yourself with other writers or artists, when you want to get ahead.

So, it is not ambition when you do something because you really love to do it.

Questioner: When one wants to find truth or peace, one becomes a sannyasi. So a sannyasi has simplicity.

KRISHNAMURTI: Does one know simplicity when one wants peace? Is it by becoming a *sannyasi* or a monk that one is simple? Surely, peace is something which is not of the mind. If I want peace, and I try to remove from my mind all thoughts of violence, will that bring me peace? Or if I have many desires and I say that I must have no desire, will I be peaceful? The moment you want something you are in conflict, struggle, and what brings about simplicity is your own understanding of the whole process of wanting.

Questioner: If, as you say, everyone is afraid, then no one is a saint or a hero. Are there no great men then in this world?

KRISHNAMURTI: That is mere logical reasoning, is it not? Why should we bother about great men, saints, heroes? What matters is what *you* are. If you are afraid, you are going to create an ugly world. That is the question, not whether there are great men.

Questioner: You said explanation is a bad thing. We have come here for explanation. Is that bad?

KRISHNAMURTI: I did not say explanation is bad; I said don't be satisfied with explanations.

Questioner: What is your idea about the future of India?

KRISHNAMURTI: I have no idea, no idea at all. I don't think India as India matters very much. What matters is the world. Whether we live in China or Japan, in England, India or America, we will say, 'My country matters very much,' and nobody thinks of the world as a whole; history books are full of the constant repetition of wars. If we can begin to understand ourselves as human beings, then perhaps we shall stop killing each other and put an end to wars; but as long as we are nationalistic and think only of our own country, we shall go on creating a terrible world. If once we see that this is *our* earth where we can *all* live happily and at peace, then together we shall build anew; but if we go on thinking of ourselves as Indians, Germans, or Russians, and regard everybody else as foreigners, then there will be no peace and no new world can be created.

Questioner: You say there are very few people in this world who are great. Then what are you?

KRISHNAMURTI: It does not matter what I am. What matters is to find out the truth or the falseness of what is being said. If you think such-and-such a thing is important because so-and-so is saying it, then you are not really listening, you are not trying to find out for yourself what is true and what is false.

But you see, most of us are afraid to find out for ourselves what is true and what is false, and that is why we merely accept what somebody else says. The important thing is to question, to observe, never to accept. Unfortunately, most of us only listen to those whom we regard as great people, to an established authority. We never listen to the birds, to the sound of the sea, or to the beggar. So we miss what the beggar is saying – and there may be truth in what the beggar is saying, and none at all in what is said by the rich man or the man in authority.

Questioner: We read books out of inquisitiveness. When you were young were you not inquisitive?

KRISHNAMURTI: Do you think that merely by reading books you find out for yourself what is true? Do you discover anything by repeating what others have said? Or do you discover only by searching, doubting, never accepting? Many of us read lots of books about philosophy, and this reading shapes our minds – which makes it very difficult to find out for ourselves what is true and what is false. When the mind is already moulded, shaped, it can discover the truth only with the greatest difficulty.

Questioner: Should we not be concerned about the future?

KRISHNAMURTI: What do you mean by the future? Twenty or fifty years hence – is that what you mean by the future? The future that is many years away is very uncertain, is it not? You do not know what is going to happen, so what is the good of being troubled or disturbed about it? There may be a war, an epidemic; anything may happen, so the future is uncertain, it is unknown. What matters is how you are living now, what you are thinking, feeling now. The present, which is today, matters very much, not tomorrow or what is going to happen twenty years hence; and to understand the present requires a great deal of intelligence.

Questioner: When we are young we are very playful, and do not always know what is good for us. If a father advises his son for the good of the son, should not the son follow his father's advice?

KRISHNAMURTI: What do *you* think? If I am a parent, I must first find out what my son really wants to do in life, must I not? Does the parent know enough about the child to advise him? Has the parent studied the child? How can a parent who has very little time to observe his child offer him advice? It sounds nice to say that the father should guide his son; but if the father does not know his son, then what is to be done? A child has his own propensities and capacities which have to be studied, not just for a certain time or at a particular place, but throughout the period of his childhood.

Questioner: By aiming at the well-being of our own country, do we not also aim at the well-being of humanity? Is it within the reach of the common man to aim directly at the well-being of humanity?

KRISHNAMURTI: When we seek the well-being of one country at the expense of other countries, it leads to exploitation and imperialism. As long as we think exclusively of our own country, it is bound to create conflict and war.

When you ask whether it is within the reach of the common man to aim directly at the well-being of humanity, what do you mean by the common man? Are not you and I the common man? Are we different from the common man? What is there so uncommon about us? We are all ordinary human beings, are we not? Just because we possess clean clothes, wear shoes, or have a car, do you think we are different from others who have not these things? We are all ordinary – and if we really understand this, we can bring about a revolution. It is one of the faults of our present education that it makes us feel so exclusive, so much on a pedestal above the so-called man in the street.

Questioner: If all individuals were in revolt, don't you think there would be chaos in the world?

KRISHNAMURTI: Is the present society in such perfect order that chaos would result if everyone revolted against it? Is there not chaos *now*? Is everything beautiful, uncorrupted? Is everyone living happily, fully, richly? Is man not against man? Is there not ambition, ruthless competition? So the world is already in chaos, that is the first thing to realize. Don't take it for granted that this is an orderly society; don't mesmerize yourself with words. Whether in Asia, in Europe, in America or Russia, the world is in a process of decay. If you see the decay, you have a challenge: you are challenged to find a way of solving this urgent problem. And how you respond to the challenge is important, is it not? If you respond as a Hindu or a Buddhist, a Christian or a Communist, then your response is very limited – which is no response at all. You can respond fully, adequately, only if there is no fear in you, only if you don't think as a Hindu, a communist or a capitalist, but as a total human being who is trying to solve this problem; and you cannot solve it unless you yourself are in revolt against the whole thing, against the ambitious acquisitiveness on which society is based. When you yourself are not ambitious, not acquisitive, not clinging to your own security – only then can you respond to the challenge and create a new world.

Questioner: To revolt, to learn, to love – are these three separate processes, or are they simultaneous?

KRISHNAMURTI: Of course they are not three separate processes; it is a unitary process. You see, it is very important to find out what the question means. This question is based on theory, not on experience; it is merely verbal, intellectual, therefore it has no validity. A man who is fearless, who is really in revolt, struggling to find out what it means to learn, to love – such a man does not ask if it is one process or three. We are so clever with words, and we think that by offering explanations we have solved the problem.

Do you know what it means to learn? When you are really learning you are learning throughout your life and there is no one special teacher to learn from. Then everything teaches you – a dead leaf, a bird in flight, a smell, a tear, the rich and the poor, those who are crying, the smile of a woman, the haughtiness of a man. You learn from everything, therefore there is no guide, no philosopher, no *guru*. Life itself is your teacher, and you are in a state of constant learning.

Questioner: It is true that society is based on acquisitiveness and ambition; but if we had no ambition would we not decay?

KRISHNAMURTI: This is really a very important question, and it needs great attention.

Do you know what attention is? Let us find out. In a class

room, when you stare out of the window or pull somebody's hair, the teacher tells you to pay attention. Which means what? That you are not interested in what you are studying and so the teacher compels you to pay attention – which is not attention at all. Attention comes when you are deeply interested in something, for then you love to find out all about it; then your whole mind, your whole being is there. Similarly, the moment you see that this question – if we had no ambition, would we not decay? – is really very important, you are interested and want to find out the truth of the matter.

Now, is not the ambitious man destroying himself? That is the first thing to find out, not to ask whether ambition is right or wrong. Look around you, observe all the people who are ambitious. What happens when you are ambitious? You are thinking about yourself, are you not? You are cruel, you push other people aside because you are trying to fulfil your ambition, trying to become a big man, thereby creating in society the conflict between those who are succeeding and those who are falling behind. There is a constant battle between you and the others who are also after what you want; and is this conflict productive of creative living?

Are you ambitious when you love to do something for its own sake? When you are doing something with your whole being, not because you want to get somewhere, or have more profit, or greater results, but simply because you love to do it – in that there is no ambition, is there? In that there is no competition; you are not struggling with anyone for first place. And should not education help you to find out what you really love to do so that from the beginning to the end of your life you are working at something which you feel is worth while and which for you has deep significance? Otherwise, for the rest of your days, you will be miserable. Not knowing what you really want to do, your mind falls into a routine in which there is only boredom, decay and death. That is why it is very important to find out while you are young what it is you really *love* to do; and this is the only way to create a new society.

Questioner: What is intelligence?

KRISHNAMURTI: Let us go into the question very slowly, patiently, and find out. To find out is not to come to a conclusion. I don't know if you see the difference. The moment you come to a conclusion as to what intelligence is, you cease to be intelligent. That is what most of the older people have done: they have come to conclusions. Therefore they have ceased to be intelligent. So you have found out one thing right off: that an intelligent mind is one which is constantly learning, never concluding.

What is intelligence? Most people are satisfied with a definition of what intelligence is. Either they say, 'That is a good explanation', or they prefer their own explanation; and a mind that is satisfied with an explanation is very superficial, therefore it is not intelligent.

You have begun to see that an intelligent mind is a mind which is not satisfied with explanations, with conclusions; nor is it a mind that believes, because belief is again another form of conclusion. An intelligent mind is an inquiring mind, a mind that is watching, learning, studying. Which means what? That there is intelligence only when there is no fear, when you are willing to rebel, to go against the whole social structure in order to find out what God is, or to discover the truth of anything.

Intelligence is not knowledge. If you could read all the books in the world it would not give you intelligence. Intelligence is something very subtle; it has no anchorage. It comes into being only when you understand the total process of the mind – not the mind according to some philosopher or teacher, but your own mind. Your mind is the result of all humanity, and when you understand it you don't have to study a single book, because the mind contains the whole knowledge of the past. So intelligence comes into being with the understanding of yourself; and you can understand yourself only in relation to the world of people, things and ideas. Intelligence is not something that you can acquire, like learning; it arises with great revolt, that is, when there is no fear – which means, really, when there is a sense of love. For when there is no fear, there is love

If you are only interested in explanations, I am afraid you will feel that I have not answered your question. To ask what is intelligence is like asking what is life. Life is study, play, sex, work, quarrels, envy, ambition, love, beauty, truth – life is everything, is it not? But you see, most of us have not the patience earnestly and consistently to pursue this inquiry.

Questioner: What is society?

KRISHNAMURTI: What is society? And what is the family? Let us find out, step by step, how society is created, how it comes into being.

What is the family? When you say, 'This is my family', what do you mean? Your father, your mother, your brother and sister, the sense of closeness, the fact that you are living together in the same house, the feeling that your parents are going to protect you, the ownership of certain property, of jewels, clothes – all this is the basis of the family. There are other families like yours living in other houses, feeling exactly the same things you feel, having the sense of 'my wife', 'my husband', 'my children', 'my house', 'my clothes', 'my car'; there are many such families living on the same piece of earth, and they come to have the feeling that they must not be invaded by still other families. So they begin to make laws. The powerful families build themselves into high positions, they acquire big properties, they have more money, more clothes, more cars; they get together and frame the laws, they tell the rest of us what to do. So gradually there comes into being a society with laws, regulations, policemen, with an army and a navy. Ultimately the whole earth becomes populated by societies of various kinds. Then people get antagonistic ideas and want to overthrow those who are established in high positions, who have all the means of power. They break down that particular society and form another.

Society is the relationship between people – the relationship between one person and another, between one family and another, between one group and another, and between the individual and the group. Human relationship is society, the relationship between you and me. If I am very greedy, very cunning, if I have great power and authority, I am going to push you out; and you will try to do the same to me. So we make laws. But others come and break our laws, establishing another set of laws, and this goes on all the time. In society, which is human relationship, there is constant conflict. This is the simple basis of society, which becomes more and more complex as human beings themselves become more and more complex in their ideas, in their wants, in their institutions and their industries.

Questioner: Since we are always related to one another, is it not true that we can never be absolutely free?

KRISHNAMURTI: We don't understand what relationship is, right relationship. Suppose I depend on you for my gratification, for my comfort, for my sense of security; how can I ever be free? But if I do not depend in that way, I am still related to you, am I not? I depend on you for some kind of emotional, physical or intellectual comfort, therefore I am not free. I cling to my parents because I want some kind of safety, which means that my relationship to them is one of dependence and is based on fear. How then can I have any relationship which is free? There is freedom in relationship only when there is no fear. So, to have right relationship, I must set about freeing myself from this psychological dependency which breeds fear.

Questioner: How can we be free when our parents depend on us in their old age?

KRISHNAMURTI: Because they are old, they depend on you to support them. So what happens? They expect you to earn a livelihood that will enable you to clothe and feed them; and if what you want to do is to become a carpenter or an artist, even though you may earn no money at all, they will say that you must not do it because you have to support them. Just think about this. I am not saying it is good or bad. By saying it is good or bad we put an end to thinking. Your parents' demand that you should provide for them prevents you from living your own life, and living your own life is considered selfish; so you become the slave of your parents.

You may say that the State should look after old people through old-age pensions and various other means of security. But in a country where there is over-population, insufficiency of national income, lack of productivity and so on, the State cannot look after old people. So elderly parents depend on the young, and the young always fit into the groove of tradition and are destroyed. But this is not a problem to be discussed by me. You all have to think about it and work it out.

I naturally want to support my parents within reasonable limits. But suppose I also want to do something which pays very little. Suppose I want to become a religious person and give my life to finding out what God is, what truth is. That way of living may not bring me any money, and if I pursue it I may have to give up my family – which means they will probably starve, like millions of other people. What am I to do? As long as I am afraid of what people will say – that I am not a dutiful son, that I am an unworthy son – I shall never be a creative human being. To be a happy, creative human being, I must have a great deal of initiative.

Questioner: How can we be free of dependence as long as we are living in society?

KRISHNAMURTI: Do you know what society is? Society is the relationship between man and man, is it not? Don't complicate it, don't quote a lot of books; think very simply about it and you will see that society is the relationship between you and me and others. Human relationship makes society; and our present society is built upon a relationship of acquisitiveness, is it not? Most of us want money, power, property, authority; at one level or another we want position, prestige, and so we have built an acquisitive society. As long as we are acquisitive, as long as we want position, prestige, power and all the rest of it, we belong to this society and are therefore dependent on it. But if one does not want any of these things and remains simply what one is with great humility, then one is out of it; one revolts against it and breaks with this society.

Unfortunately, education at present is aimed at making you conform, fit into and adjust yourself to this acquisitive society. That is all your parents, your teachers and your books are concerned with. As long as you conform, as long as you are ambitious, acquisitive, corrupting and destroying others in the pursuit of position and power, you are considered a respectable citizen. You are educated to fit into society; but that is not education, it is merely a process which conditions you to conform to a pattern. The real function of education is not to turn you out to be a clerk, or a judge, or a prime minister, but to help you understand the whole structure of this rotten society and allow you to grow in freedom, so that you will break away and create a different society, a new world. There must be those who are in revolt, not partially but totally in revolt against the old, for it is only such people who can create a new world – a world not based on acquisitiveness, on power and prestige.

I can hear the older people saying, 'It can never be done. Human nature is what it is, and you are talking nonsense'. But we have never thought about unconditioning the adult mind, and not conditioning the child. Surely, education is both curative and preventive. You older students are already shaped, already conditioned, already ambitious; you want to be successful like your father, like the governor, or somebody else. So the real function of education is not only to help you uncondition yourself, but also to understand this whole process of living from day to day so that you can grow in freedom and create a new world – a world that must be totally different from the present one. Unfortunately, neither your parents, nor your teachers, nor the public in general are interested in this. That is why education must be a process of educating the educator as well as the student.

Questioner: What are the duties of a student?

KRISHNAMURTI: What does the word 'duty' mean? Duty to what? Duty to your country according to a politician? Duty to your father and mother according to their wishes? They will say it is your duty to do as they tell you; and what they tell you is conditioned by their background, their tradition, and so on. And what is a student? Is it a boy or a girl who goes to school and reads a few books in order to pass some examination? Or is only he a student who is learning all the time and for whom there is therefore no end to learning? Surely, the person who merely reads up on a subject, passes an examination, and then drops it, is not a student. The real student is studying, learning, inquiring, exploring, not just until he is twenty or twenty-five, but throughout life.

To be a student is to learn all the time; and as long as you are learning, there is no teacher, is there? The moment you are a student there is no one in particular to teach you, because you are learning from everything. The leaf that is blown by the wind, the murmur of the waters on the banks of a river, the flight of a bird high in the air, the poor man as he walks by with a heavy load, the people who think they know everything about life – you are learning from them all, therefore there is no teacher and you are not a follower.

So the duty of a student is just to learn. Goya, when he was a very old man, wrote under one of his paintings, 'I am still learning'. You can learn from books, but that does not take you very far. A book can give you only what the author has to tell. But the learning that comes through self-knowledge has no limit, because to learn through your own self-knowledge is to know how to listen, how to observe, and therefore you learn from everything, from music, from what people say and the way they say it, from anger, greed, ambition.

This earth is *ours*, it does not belong to the communists, the socialists, or the capitalists; it is yours and mine, to be lived on happily, richly, without conflict. But that richness of life, that happiness, that feeling, 'This earth is ours,' cannot be brought about by enforcement, by law. It must come from within because we love the earth and all the things thereof; and that is the state of learning.

Questioner: What is the difference between respect and love?

KRISHNAMURTI: You can look up 'respect' and 'love' in a dictionary and find the answer. Is that what you want to know? Do you want to know the superficial meaning of those words, or the significance behind them?

When a prominent man comes around, a minister or a governor, have you noticed how everybody salutes him? You call that respect, don't you? But such respect is phony, because behind it there is fear, greed. You want something out of the poor devil, so you put a garland around his neck. That is not respect, it is merely the coin with which you buy and sell in the market. You don't feel respect for your servant or the villager, but only for those from whom you hope to get something. That kind of respect is really fear; it is not respect at all, it has no meaning. But if you really have love in your heart, then to you the governor, the teacher, your servant and the villager are all the same; then you have respect, a feeling, for them all, because love does not ask anything in return.

Questioner: What is happiness in life?

KRISHNAMURTI: If you want to do something pleasurable you think you will be happy when you do it. You may want to marry the richest man, or the most beautiful girl, or pass some examination, or be praised by somebody, and you think that by getting what you want you will be happy. But is that happiness? Does it not soon fade away, like the flower that blossoms in the morning and withers in the evening? Yet that is our life, and that is all we want. We are satisfied with such superficialities: with having a car or a secure position, with feeling a little emotion over some futile thing, like a boy who is happy flying a kite in a strong wind and a few minutes later is in tears. That is our life, and with that we are satisfied. We never say, 'I will give my heart, my energy, my whole being to find out what happiness is.' We are not very serious, we don't feel very strongly about it, so we are gratified with little things.

Happiness comes uninvited; and the moment you are conscious that you are happy, you are no longer happy. I wonder if you have noticed this? When you are suddenly joyous about nothing in particular, there is just the freedom of smiling, of being happy; but, the moment you are conscious of it, you have lost it, have you not? Being self-consciously happy, or pursuing happiness, is the very ending of happiness. There is happiness only when the self and its demands are put aside.

You are taught a great deal about mathematics, you give your days to studying history, geography, science, physics, biology, and so on; but do you and your teachers spend any time at all thinking about these far more serious matters? Do you ever sit quietly, with your back very straight, without movement, and know the beauty of silence? Do you ever let your mind wander, not about petty things, but expansively, widely, deeply and thereby explore, discover?

And do you know what is happening in the world? What is happening in the world is a projection of what is happening inside each one of us; what we are, the world is. Most of us are in turmoil, we are acquisitive, possessive, we are jealous and condemn people; and that is exactly what is happening in the world, only more dramatically, ruthlessly. But neither you nor your teachers spend any time thinking about all this; and it is only when you spend some time every day earnesly thinking about these matters that there is a possibility of bringing about a total revolution and creating a new world. And I assure you, a new world has to be created, a world which will not be a continuation of the same rotten society in a different form. But you cannot create a new world if your mind is not alert, watchful, expansively aware; and that is why it is so important, while you are young, to spend some time reflecting over these very serious matters and not just pass your days in the study of a few subjects, which leads nowhere except to a job and death. So do consider seriously all these things, for out of that consideration there comes an extraordinary feeling of joy, of happiness.

Questioner: What is real life?

KRISHNAMURTI: 'What is real life?' A little boy has asked this question. Playing games, eating good food, running, jumping, pushing – that is real life for him. You see, we divide life into the real and the false. Real life is doing something which you love to do with your whole being so that there is no inner contradiction, no war between what you are doing and what you think you *should* do. Life is then a completely integrated process in which there is tremendous joy. But that can happen only when you are not psychologically depending on anybody, or on any society, when there is complete detachment inwardly, for only then is there a possibility of really loving what you do. If you are in a state of total revolution, it does not matter whether you garden, or become a prime minister, or do something else; you will love what you do, and out of that love there comes an extraordinary feeling of creativeness.

Questioner: Are you happy or not?

KRISHNAMURTI: I don't know. I have never thought about it. The moment you think you are happy, you cease to be happy, don't you? When you are playing and shouting with joy, what happens the moment you become conscious that you are joyous? You stop being joyous. Have you noticed it? So happiness is something which is not within the field of self-consciousness.

When you try to be good, are you good? Can goodness be practised? Or is goodness something that comes naturally because you see, observe, understand? Similarly, when you are conscious that you are happy, happiness goes out of the window. To seek happiness is absurd, because there is happiness only when you don't seek it.

Do you know what the word 'humility' means? And can you cultivate humility? If you repeat every morning, 'I am going to be humble,' is that humility? Or does humility arise of itself when you no longer have pride, vanity? In the same way, when the things that prevent happiness are gone, when anxiety, frustration, the search for one's own security have ceased, then happiness is there, you don't have to seek it.

Why are most of you so silent? Why don't you discuss with me? You know, it is important to express your thoughts and feelings, however badly, because it will mean a great deal to you, and I will tell you why. If you begin to express your thoughts and feelings now, however hesitantly, as you grow up you will not be smothered by your environment, by your parents, by society, tradition. But unfortunately your teachers don't encourage you to question, they don't ask you what you think.

Questioner: Does the soul survive after death?

KRISHNAMURTI: If you really want to know, how are you going to find out? By reading what Shankara, Buddha or Christ has said about it? By listening to your own particular leader or saint? They may all be totally wrong. Are you prepared to admit this – which means that your mind is in a position to inquire?

You must first find out, surely, whether there is a soul to survive. What is the soul? Do you know what it is? Or have you merely been told that there is a soul – told by your parents, by the priest, by a particular book, by your cultural environment – and accepted it?

The word 'soul' implies something beyond mere physical

existence, does it not? There is your physical body, and also your character, your tendencies, your virtues; and transcending all this you say there is the soul. If that state exists at all, it must be spiritual, something which has the quality of timelessness; and you are asking whether that spiritual something survives death. That is one part of the question.

The other part is: what is death? Do you know what death is? You want to know if there is survival after death; but, you see, that question is not important. The important question is: can you know death while you are living? What significance has it if someone tells you that there is or is not survival after death? You still do not know. But you can find out for yourself what death is, not after you are dead, but while you are living, healthy, vigorous, while you are thinking, feeling.

This is also part of education. To be educated is not only to be proficient in mathematics, history or geography, it is also to have the ability to understand this extraordinary thing called death – not when you are physically dying, but while you are living, while you are laughing, while you are climbing a tree, while you are sailing a boat or swimming. Death is the unknown, and what matters is to know of the unknown while you are living.

Questioner: How did you learn all that you are talking about, and how can we come to know it?

KRISHNAMURTI: That is a good question, is it not?

Now, if I may talk about myself a little, I have not read any books about these things, either the *Upanishads*, the *Bhagavad Gita*, nor any psychological books; but as I told you, if you watch your own mind, it is all there. So when once you set out on the journey of self-knowledge, books are not important. It is like entering a strange land where you begin to find out new things and make astonishing discoveries; but, you see, that is all destroyed if you give importance to yourself. The moment you say, 'I have discovered, I know, I am a great man because I have found out this and that,' you are lost. If you have to take a long journey, you must carry very little; if you want to climb to a great height, you must travel light.

So this question is really important, because discovery and understanding come through self-knowledge, through observing the ways of the mind. What you say of your neighbour, how you talk, how you walk, how you look at the skies, at the birds, how you treat people, how you cut a branch – all these things are important, because they act like mirrors that show you as you are and, if you are alert, you discover everything anew from moment to moment.

Questioner: Why do we want to have a companion?

KRISHNAMURTI: Can you live alone in this world without a husband or a wife, without children, without friends? Most people cannot live alone, therefore they need companions. It requires enormous intelligence to be alone; and you *must* be alone to find God, truth. It is nice to have a companion, a husband or a wife, and also to have babies; but you see, we get lost in all that, we get lost in the family, in the job, in the dull, monotonous routine of a decaying existence. We get used to it, and then the thought of living alone becomes dreadful, something to be afraid of. Most of us have put all our faith in one thing, all our eggs in one basket, and our lives have no richness apart from our companions, apart from our families and our jobs. But if there is a richness in one's life – not the richness of money or knowledge, which anyone can acquire, but that richness which is the movement of reality with no beginning and no ending – then companionship becomes a secondary matter.

But, you see, you are not educated to be alone. Do you ever go out for a walk by yourself? It is very important to go out alone, to sit under a tree – not with a book, not with a companion, but by yourself – and observe the falling of a leaf, hear the lapping of the water, the fisherman's song, watch the flight of a bird, and of your own thoughts as they chase each other across the space of your mind. If you are able to be alone and watch these things, then you will discover extraordinary riches which no government can tax, no human agency can corrupt, and which can never be destroyed.

Questioner: Is it your hobby to give lectures? Don't you get tired of talking? Why are you doing it?

KRISHNAMURTI: I am glad you asked that question. You know, if you love something, you never get tired of it – I mean love in which there is no seeking of a result, no wanting something out of it. When you love something, it is not self-fulfilment, therefore there is no disappointment, there is no end. Why am I doing this? You might as well ask why the rose blooms, why the jasmine gives its scent, or why the bird flies.

You see, I have tried *not* talking, to find out what happens if I don't talk. That is all right too. Do you understand? If you are talking because you are getting something out of it – money, a reward, a sense of your own importance – then there is weariness, then your talking is destructive, it has no meaning because it is only self-fulfilment; but if there is love in your heart, and your heart is not filled with the things of the mind, then it is like a fountain, like a spring that is timelessly giving fresh water.

Questioner: What is destiny?

KRISHNAMURTI: Do you really want to go into this problem? To ask a question is the easiest thing in the world, but your question has meaning only if it affects you directly so that you are very serious about it. Have you noticed how many people lose interest once they have asked their question? The other day a man put a question and then began to yawn, scratch his head and talk to his neighbour; he had completely lost interest. So I suggest that you don't ask a question unless you are really serious about it.

This problem of what is destiny is very difficult and complex. You see, if a cause is set going it must inevitably produce a result. If a vast number of people, whether Russians, Americans, or Hindus, prepare for war, their destiny is war; though they may say they want peace and are preparing only for their own defence, they have set in motion causes which bring about war. Similarly, when millions of people have for centuries taken part in the development of a certain civilization or culture, they have set going a movement in which individual human beings are caught up and swept along, whether they like it or not; and this whole process of being caught up in and swept along by a particular stream of culture or civilization may be called destiny.

After all, if you are born as the son of a lawyer who insists that you also become a lawyer, and if you comply with his wishes even though you would prefer to do something else, then your destiny is obviously to become a lawyer. But if you refuse to become a lawyer, if you insist upon doing that which you feel to be the true thing for you, which is what you really love to do – it may be writing, painting, or having no money and begging – then you have stepped out of the stream, you have broken away from the destiny which your father intended for you. It is the same with a culture or civilization.

That is why it is very important that we should be rightly educated – educated not to be smothered by tradition, not to fall into the destiny of a particular racial, cultural or family group, educated not to become mechanical beings moving towards a predetermined end. The man who understands this whole process, who breaks away from it and stands alone, creates his own momentum; and if his action is a breaking away from the false towards the truth, then that momentum itself becomes the truth. Such men are free of destiny.

Questioner: How can we know ourselves?

KRISHNAMURTI: You know your face because you have often looked at it reflected in the mirror. Now, there is a mirror in which you can see yourself entirely – not your face, but all that you think, all that you feel, your motives, your appetites, your urges and fears. That mirror is the mirror of relationship: the relationship between you and your parents, between you and your teachers, between you and the river, the trees, the earth, between you and your thoughts. Relationship is a mirror in which you can see yourself, not as you would wish to be, but as you are. I may wish, when looking in an ordinary mirror, that it would show me to be beautiful, but that does not happen because the mirror reflects my face exactly as it is and I cannot deceive myself. Similarly, I can see myself exactly as I am in the mirror of my relationship with others. I can observe how I talk to people: most politely to those who I think can give me something, and rudely or contemptuously to those who cannot. I am attentive to those I am afraid of. I get up when important people come in, but when the servant enters I pay no attention. So, by observing myself in relationship, I have found out how falsely I respect people, have I not? And I can also discover myself as I am in my relationship with the trees and the birds, with ideas and books.

You may have all the academic degrees in the world, but if you don't know yourself you are a most stupid person. To know oneself is the very purpose of all education. Without self-knowledge, merely to gather facts or take notes so that you can pass examinations is a stupid way of existence. You may be able to quote the *Bhagavad Gita,* the *Upanishads*, the *Koran* and the Bible, but unless you know yourself you are like a parrot repeating words. Whereas, the moment you begin to know yourself, however little, there is already set going an extraordinary process of creativeness. It is a discovery to suddenly see yourself as you actually are: greedy, quarrelsome, angry, envious, stupid. To see the fact without trying to alter it, just to see exactly what you are is an astonishing revelation. From there you can go deeper and deeper, infinitely, because there is no end to self-knowledge.

Through self-knowledge you begin to find out what is God, what is truth, what is that state which is timeless. Your teacher may pass on to you the knowledge which he received from *his* teacher, and you may do well in your examinations, get a degree and all the rest of it; but, without knowing yourself as you know your own face in the mirror, all other knowledge has very little meaning. Learned people who don't know themselves are really unintelligent; they don't know what thinking is, what life is. That is why it is important for the educator to be educated in the true sense of the word, which means that he must know the workings of his own mind and heart, see himself exactly as he is in the mirror of relationship. Self-knowledge is the beginning of wisdom. In self-knowledge is the whole universe; it embraces all the struggles of humanity.

Questioner: Can we know ourselves without an inspirer?

KRISHNAMURTI: To know yourself must you have an inspirer, somebody to urge, stimulate, push you on? Listen to the question very carefully and you will discover the true answer. You know, half the problem is solved if you study it, is it not? But you cannot study the problem fully if your mind is occupied too eagerly with finding an answer.

The question is: in order to have self-knowledge must there not be someone to inspire us?

Now, if you must have a *guru*, somebody to inspire you, to encourage you, to tell you that you are doing well, it means that you are relying on that person, and inevitably you are lost when he goes away some day. The moment you depend on a person or an idea for inspiration there is bound to be fear, therefore it is not true inspiration at all. Whereas, if you watch a dead body being carried away, or observe two people quarrelling, does it not make you think? When you see somebody being very ambitious, or notice how you all fall at the feet of your governor when he comes in, does it not make you reflect? So there is inspiration in everything, from the falling of a leaf or the death of a bird to man's own behaviour. If you watch all these things, you are learning all the time; but if you look to one person as your teacher, then you are lost and that person becomes your nightmare. That is why it is very important not to follow anybody, not to have one particular teacher, but to learn from the river, the flowers, the trees, from the woman who carries a burden, from the members of your family and from your own thoughts. This is an education which nobody can give you but yourself, and that is the beauty of it. It demands ceaseless watchfulness, a constantly inquiring mind. You have to learn by observing, by struggling, by being happy and tearful.

Questioner: With all the contradictions in oneself, how is it possible to be and to do simultaneously?

KRISHNAMURTI: Do you know what self-contradiction is? If I want to do a particular thing in life and at the same time I want to please my parents, who would like me to do something else, there is in me a conflict, a contradiction. Now, how am I to resolve it? If I cannot resolve this contradiction in myself, there can obviously be no integration of being and doing. So the first thing is to be free of self-contradiction.

Suppose you want to study painting because to paint is the joy of your life, and your father says that you must become a lawyer or a businessman, otherwise he will cut you off and not pay for your education, there is then a contradiction in you, is there not? Now, how are you to remove that inner contradiction, to be free of the struggle and the pain of it? As long as you are caught in self-contradiction you cannot think; so you must remove the contradiction, you must do one thing or the other. Which will it be? Will you yield to your father? If you do, it means that you have put away your joy, you have wed something which you do not love; and will that resolve the contradiction? Whereas, if you withstand your father, if you say, 'Sorry, I don't care if I have to beg, starve, I am going to paint'; then there is no contradiction; then being and doing are simultaneous, because you know what you want to do and you do it with your whole heart. But if you become a lawyer or a businessman while inside you are burning to be a painter, then for the rest of your life you will be a dull, weary human being living in torment, in frustration, in misery, being destroyed and destroying others.

This is a very important problem for you to think out, because as you grow up your parents are going to want you to do certain things, and if you are not very clear in yourself about what you really want to do you will be led like a sheep to the slaughter. But if you find out what it is you love to do and give your whole life to it, then there is no contradiction, and in that state your being is your doing.

Questioner: How can we put into practice what you are telling us?

KRISHNAMURTI: You hear something which you think is right and you want to carry it out in your everyday life; so there is a gap between what you think and what you do, is there not? You think one thing, and you are doing something else; you want to put into practice what you think, so there is this gap between action and thought; and then you ask how to bridge the gap, how to link your thinking to your action.

Now, when you want to do something very much, you do it, don't you? When you want to go and play cricket, or do some other thing in which you are really interested, you find ways and means of doing it; you never ask how to put it into practice. You do it because you are eager, because your whole being, your mind and heart are in it.

But in this other matter you have become very cunning, you think one thing and do another. You say, 'That is an excellent idea and intellectually I approve, but I don't know what to do about it, so please tell me how to put it into practice' – which means that you don't want to do it at all. What you really want is to postpone action, because you like to be a little bit envious, or whatever it is. You say, 'Everybody else is envious, so why not I?', and you just go on as before. But if you really don't want to be envious and you see the truth of envy as you see the truth of a cobra, then you cease to be envious and that is the end of it; you never ask how to be free of envy.

So what is important is to see the truth of something, and not ask how to carry it out – which really means that you don't see the truth of it. When you meet a cobra on the road you don't ask, 'What am I to do?' You understand very well the danger of a cobra and you stay away from it. But you have never really examined all the implications of envy; nobody has ever talked to you about it, gone into it very deeply with you. You have been told that you must not be envious, but you have never looked into the nature of envy; you have never observed how society and all the organized religions are built on it, on the desire to become something. The moment you go into envy and really see the truth of it, envy drops away.

To ask, 'How am I to do it?' is a thoughtless question, because when you are really interested in something which you don't know how to do, you go at it and soon begin to find out. If you sit back and say, 'Please tell me a practical way to get rid of greed', you will continue to be greedy. But if you inquire into greed with an alert mind, without any prejudice, and if you put your whole being into it, you will discover for yourself the truth of greed; and it is the truth that frees you, not your looking for a way to be free.

Questioner: What makes us fear death?

KRISHNAMURTI: Do you think a leaf that falls to the ground is afraid of death? Do you think a bird lives in fear of dying? It meets death when death comes; but it is not concerned about death, it is much too occupied with living, with catching insects, building a nest, singing a song, flying for the very joy of flying. Have you ever watched birds soaring high up in the air without a beat of their wings, being carried along by the wind? How endlessly they seem to enjoy themselves! They are not concerned about death. If death comes, it is all right, they are finished. There is no concern about what is going to happen; they are living from moment to moment, are they not? It is we human beings who are always concerned about death – because we are not living. That is the trouble: we are dying, we are not living. The old people are near the grave, and the young ones are not far behind.

You see, there is this preoccupation with death because we are afraid to lose the known, the things that we have gathered. We are afraid to lose a wife or husband, a child or a friend; we are afraid to lose what we have learnt, accumulated. If we could carry over all the things that we have gathered – our friends, our possessions, our virtues, our character – then we would not be afraid of death, would we? That is why we invent theories about death and the hereafter. But the fact is that death is an ending, and most of us are unwilling to face this fact. We don't want to leave the known; so it is our clinging to the known that creates fear in us, not the unknown. The unknown cannot be perceived by the known. But the mind, being made up of the known, says, 'I am going to end', and therefore it is frightened.

Now, if you can live from moment to moment and not be concerned about the future, if you can live without the thought of tomorrow – which does not mean the superficiality of merely being occupied with today; if, being aware of the whole process of the known, you can relinquish the known, let it go completely, then you will find that an astonishing thing takes place. Try it for a day – put aside everything you know, forget it, and just see what happens. Don't carry over your worries from day to day, from hour to hour, from moment to moment; let them all go, and you will see that out of this freedom there comes an extraordinary life that includes both living and dying. Death is only the ending of something, and in that very ending there is a renewing.

Questioner: What do you mean by a total change, and how can it be realized in one's own being?

KRISHNAMURTI: Do you think there can be a total change if you try to bring it about? Do you know what change is? Suppose you are ambitious and you have begun to see all that is involved in ambition: hope, satisfaction, frustration, cruelty, sorrow, inconsideration, greed, envy, an utter lack of love. Seeing all this, what are you to do? To make an effort to change or transform ambition is another form of ambition, is it not? It implies a desire to be something else. You may reject one desire, but in that very process you cultivate another desire which also brings sorrow.

Now, if you see that ambition brings sorrow, and that the desire to put an end to ambition also brings sorrow, if you see the truth of this very clearly for yourself and do not act, but allow the truth to act, then that truth brings about a fundamental change in the mind, a total revolution. But this requires a great deal of attention, penetration, insight.

When you are told, as you all are, that you should be good, that you should love, what generally happens? You say, 'I must practise being good, I must show love to my parents, to the servant, to the donkey, to everything'. That means you are making an effort to show love – and then love becomes very shoddy, very petty, as it does with those nationalistic people who are everlastingly practising brotherhood, which is silly, stupid. It is greed that causes these practices. But if you see the truth of nationalism, of greed, and let that truth work upon you, let that truth act, then you will be brotherly without making any effort. A mind that practises love cannot love. But if you love and do not interfere with it, then love will operate.

Questioner: You said one day that we should sit quietly and watch the activity of our own mind; but our thoughts disappear as soon as we begin consciously to observe them. How can we perceive our own mind when the mind is the perceiver as well as that which it perceives?

KRISHNAMURTI: This is a very complex question, and many things are involved in it.

Now, is there a perceiver, or only perception? Please follow this closely. Is there a thinker, or only thinking? Surely, the thinker does not exist first. First there is thinking, and then thinking creates the thinker – which means that a separation in thinking has taken place. It is when this separation takes place that there comes into being the watcher and the watched, the perceiver and the object of perception. As the questioner says, if you watch your mind, if you observe a thought, that thought disappears, it fades away; but there is actually only perception, not a perceiver. When you look at a flower, when you just see it, at that moment is there an entity who sees? Or is there only seeing? Seeing the flower makes you say, 'How nice it is, I want it'; so the 'I' comes into being through desire, fear, greed, ambition, which follow in the wake of seeing. It is these that create the 'I', and the 'I' is non-existent without them.

If you go deeper into this whole question you will discover that when the mind is very quiet, completely still, when there is not a movement of thought and therefore no experiencer, no observer, then that very stillness has its own creative understanding. In that stillness the mind is transformed into something else. But the mind cannot find that stillness through any means, through any discipline, through any practice; it does not come about through sitting in a corner and trying to concentrate. That stillness comes when you understand the ways of the mind. It is the mind that has created the stone image which people worship; it is the mind that has created the *Gita*, the organized religions, the innumerable beliefs; and, to find out what is real, you must go beyond the creations of the mind.

Questioner: Is man only mind and brain, or something more than this?

KRISHNAMURTI: How are you going to find out? If you merely believe, speculate, or accept what Shankara, Buddha, or somebody else has said, you are not investigating, you are not trying to find out what is true.

You have only one instrument, which is the mind; and the mind is the brain also. Therefore, to find out the truth of this matter, you must understand the ways of the mind, must you not? If the mind is crooked you will never see straight; if the mind is very limited you cannot perceive the illimitable. The mind is the instrument of perception and, to perceive truly, the mind must be made straight, it must be cleansed of all conditioning, of all fear. The mind must also be free of knowledge, because knowledge diverts the mind and makes things twisted. The enormous capacity of the mind to invent, to imagine, to speculate, to think – must not this capacity be put aside so that the mind is very clear and very simple? Because it is only the innocent mind, the mind that has experienced vastly and yet is free of knowledge and experience – it is only such a mind that can discover that which is more than brain and mind. Otherwise what you discover will be coloured by what you have already experienced, and your experience is the result of your conditioning.

Questioner: Why are we fundamentally selfish? We may try our best to be unselfish in our behaviour, but when our own interests are involved we become self-absorbed and indifferent to the interests of others.

KRISHNAMURTI: I think it is very important not to call oneself either selfish or unselfish, because words have an extraordinary influence on the mind. Call a man selfish, and he is doomed; call him a professor, and something happens in your approach to him; call him a Mahatma, and immediately there is a halo around him. Watch your own responses and you will see that words like 'lawyer', 'businessman', 'governor', 'servant', 'love', 'God', have a strange effect on your nerves as well as on your mind. The word which denotes a particular function evokes the feeling of status; so the first thing is to be free of this unconscious habit of associating certain feelings with certain words, is it not? Your mind has been conditioned to think that the term 'selfish' represents something very wrong, unspiritual, and the moment you apply that term to anything your mind condemns it. So when you ask this question, 'Why are we fundamentally selfish?' it has already a condemnatory significance.

It is very important to be aware that certain words cause in you a nervous, emotional, or intellectual response of approval or condemnation. When you call yourself a jealous person, for example, immediately you have blocked further inquiry, you have stopped penetrating into the whole problem of jealousy. Similarly, there are many people who say they are working for brotherhood, yet everything they do is against brotherhood; but they don't see this fact because the word 'brotherhood' means something to them and they are already persuaded by it; they don't inquire any further and so they never find out what are the facts irrespective of the neurological or emotional response which that word evokes.

So this is the first thing: to experiment and find out if you can look at facts without the condemnatory or laudatory implications associated with certain words. If you can look at the facts without feelings of condemnation or approval, you will find that in the very process of looking there is a dissolution of all the barriers which the mind has erected between itself and the facts.

Just observe how you approach a person whom people call a great man. The words 'great man' have influenced you; the newspapers, the books, the followers all say he is a great man, and your mind has accepted it. Or else you take the opposite view and say, 'How stupid, he is *not* a great man'. Whereas, if you can dissociate your mind from all influence and simply look at the facts, then you will find your approach is entirely different. In the same way, the word 'villager', with its associations of poverty, dirt, squalor, or whatever it is, influences your thinking. But when the mind is free of influence, when it neither condemns nor approves but merely looks, observes, then it is not self-absorbed and there is no longer the problem of selfishness trying to be unselfish.

Questioner: I want to do social work, but I don't know how to start.

KRISHNAMURTI: Why do you want to do social work? Is it because you see misery in the world – starvation, disease, exploitation, the brutal indifference of great wealth side by side with appalling poverty, the enmity between man and man? Is that the reason? Do you want to do social work because in your heart there is love and therefore you are not concerned with your own fulfilment? Or is social work a means of escape from yourself? Do you understand? You see, for example, all the ugliness involved in orthodox marriage, so you say, 'I shall never get married', and you throw yourself into social work instead; or perhaps your parents have urged you into it, or you have an ideal. If it is a means of escape, or if you are merely pursuing an ideal established by society, by a leader or a priest, or by yourself, then any social work you may do will only create further misery. But if you have love in your heart, if you are seeking truth and are therefore a truly religious person, if you are no longer ambitious, no longer pursuing success, and your virtue is not leading to respectability – then your very life will help to bring about a total transformation of society.

I think it is very important to understand this. When we are young, as most of you are, we want to do something, and social work is in the air; books tell about it, the newspapers do propaganda for it, there are schools to train social workers, and so on. But you see, without self-knowledge, without understanding yourself and your relationships, any social work you do will turn to ashes in your mouth.

It is the happy man, not the idealist or the miserable escapee, who is revolutionary; and the happy man is not he who has many possessions. The happy man is the truly religious man, and his very living is social work. But if you become merely one of the innumerable social workers, your heart will be empty. You may give away your money, or persuade other people to contribute theirs, and you may bring about marvellous reforms; but as long as your heart is empty and your mind full of theories, your life will be dull, weary, without joy. So, first understand yourself, and out of that self-knowledge will come action of the right kind.

Questioner: Can one refrain from doing whatever one likes and still find the way to freedom?

KRISHNAMURTI: You know, it is one of the most difficult things to find out what we want to do, not only while we are adolescent, but throughout life. And unless you find out for yourself what you really want to do with your whole being, you will end by doing something which holds no vital interest for you, and then your life will be miserable; and, being miserable, you will seek distraction in cinemas, in drink, in reading innumerable books, in some kind of social reform and all the rest of it.

So, can the educator help you to find out what it is you want to do right through life, irrespective of what your parents and society may want you to do? That is the real question, is it not? Because, if once you discover what you love to do with your whole being, then you are a free man; then you have capacity, confidence, initiative. But if, without knowing what you really love to do, you become a lawyer, a politician, this or that, then there will be no happiness for you, because that very profession will become the means of destroying yourself and others.

You must find out for yourself what it is you love to do. Don't think in terms of choosing a vocation in order to fit into society, because in that way you will never discover what you love to do. When you love to do something, there is no problem of choice. When you love, and let love do what it will, there is right action, because love never seeks success, it is never caught up in imitation; but if you give your life to something which you don't love, you will never be free.

But merely doing whatever you like is not doing what you love to do. To find out what you really love to do requires a great deal of penetration, insight. Don't begin by thinking in terms of earning a livelihood; but if you discover what it is you love to do, then you will have a means of livelihood.

Questioner: Why is it that, from birth to death, the individual always wants to be loved, and that if he doesn't get this love he is not as composed and full of confidence as his fellow beings?

KRISHNAMURTI: Do you think that his fellow beings are full of confidence? They may strut about, they may put on airs, but you will find that behind the show of confidence most people are empty, dull, mediocre, they have no real confidence at all. And why do we want to be loved? Don't you want to be loved by your parents, by your teachers, by your friends? And, if you are a grown-up, you want to be loved by your wife, by your husband, by your children – or by your *guru*. Why is there this everlasting craving to be loved? Listen carefully. You want to be loved because you do not love; but the moment you love, it is finished, you are no longer inquiring whether or not somebody loves you. As long as you demand to be loved, there is no love in you; and if you feel no love, you are ugly, brutish, so why should you be loved? Without love you are a dead thing; and when the dead thing asks for love, it is still dead. Whereas, if your heart is full of love, then you never ask to be loved, you never put out your begging bowl for someone to fill. It is only the empty who ask to be filled, and an empty heart can never be filled by running after *gurus* or seeking love in a hundred other ways.

Questioner: How does age stand in the way of realizing God?

KRISHNAMURTI: What is age? Is it the number of years you have lived? That is part of age; you were born in such and such a year, and now you are fifteen, forty or sixty years old. Your body grows old – and so does your mind when it is burdened with all the experiences, miseries and weariness of life; and such a mind can never discover what is truth. The mind can discover only when it is young, fresh, innocent; but innocence is not a matter of age. It is not only the child who is innocent – he may not be – but the mind that is capable of experiencing without accumulating the residue of experience. The mind must experience, that is inevitable. It must respond to everything – to the river, to the diseased animal, to the dead body being carried away to be burnt, to the poor villagers carrying their burdens along the road, to the tortures and miseries of life – otherwise it is already dead; but it must be capable of responding without being held by the experience. It is tradition, the accumulation of experience, the ashes of memory, that make the mind old. The mind that dies every day to the memories of yesterday, to all the joys and sorrows of the past – such a mind is fresh, innocent, it has no age; and without that innocence, whether you are ten or sixty, you will not find God.

MORE ABOUT PENGUINS, PELICANS
AND PUFFINS

For further information about books available from Penguins please write to Dept E P, Penguin Books Ltd, Harmondsworth, Middlesex UB7 0DA.

In the U.S.A.: For a complete list of books available from Penguins in the United States write to Dept DG, Penguin Books, 299 Murray Hill Parkway, East Rutherford, New Jersey 07073.

In Canada: For a complete list of books available from Penguins in Canada write to Penguin Books Canada Ltd, 2801 John Street, Markham, Ontario L3R 1B4.

In Australia: For a complete list of books available from Penguins in Australia write to the Marketing Department, Penguin Books Australia Ltd, P.O. Box 257, Ringwood, Victoria 3134.

In New Zealand: For a complete list of books available from Penguins in New Zealand write to the Marketing Department, Penguin Books (N.Z.) Ltd, P.O. Box 4019, Auckland 10.

In India: For a complete list of books available from Penguins in India write to Penguin Overseas Ltd, 706 Eros Apartments, 56 Nehru Place, New Delhi 110019.

MAHARISHI MAHESH YOGI
ON THE BHAGAVAD-GITA

A new translation and commentary by the Eastern Guru who introduced the West to transcendental meditation.

The first six chapters of the *Bhagavad-Gita* with the original Sanskrit text, an introduction, and a commentary designed to restore the fundamental truths of the teachings delivered by the Lord Krishna to Arjuna on the battlefield.